Policy Planning and Local Government

Robin Hambleton was trained in town and regional planning at Sheffield University and has wide experience of policy making in local government. He is currently team leader of the Gateshead Comprehensive Community Programme, which is a nationally funded project aimed at redirecting the major policies and programmes of local and central government to those most in need. In 1976 he held the first Sidney Perry Fellowship from the Centre for Environmental Studies, London. This sabbatical provided the opportunity to research policy making in America as well as British local government. From 1974 to 1975 he was a corporate planner working for a Chief Executive in the Metropolitan Borough of Stockport and from 1971 to 1973 he worked on housing and social services policy for the City of Salford.

Policy Planning
and Local Government

Robin Hambleton

LandMark Studies

ALLANHELD, OSMUN Montclair
UNIVERSE BOOKS New York

ALLANHELD, OSMUN & CO. PUBLISHERS, INC.
Montclair, New Jersey

Published in the United States of America in 1979
by Allanheld, Osmun & Co., 19 Brunswick Road, Montclair, N.J. 07042
and by Universe Books, 381 Park Avenue South, New York 10016
Distribution: Universe Books

Library of Congress Cataloging in Publication Data

Hambleton, Robin.
  Policy planning and local government.

  "Landmark studies."
  Bibliography: p.
  Includes index.
  1. Local government – Great Britain.   2. Local
government – United States.   3. Political participation
– Great Britain.   4. Political participation – United
States.   5. Policy sciences.   I. Title.
JS3095 1978. H35 1978   352′.008′0941   78–73593
ISBN 0–87663–842–6

Printed in Great Britain

For Pam

Contents

Preface

In Britain we are witnessing significant changes in the nature of policy making and management in local government. Essentially, these changes represent a move away from the relatively passive performance of duties imposed by Parliament towards a more purposeful approach in which local authorities attempt to *learn* about the nature and causes of local problems and to *respond* accordingly. This book is intended to deepen understanding of these changes which may yet herald the development of a 'learning local government' and a revitalization of local politics.

In the current British circumstances this may seem an unreasonably optimistic way to introduce a book on local government. Most of those directly involved – whether as professionals, politicians or members of the public – are more concerned to maintain satisfactory levels of service in the face of declining resources. They may feel that a more significant change in recent years has been the shift from an era of expansion in local government services to one of retrenchment and that it is this shift which will have more far-reaching consequences than the development of local government as a learning system. This is understandable: the pressures are immediate and intense and there can be no denying the amount of fundamental re-thinking needed to shed the deeply-ingrained assumption of continuous annual growth in public services.

But, in practice, these two major developments cannot be viewed in isolation. How they influence each other is largely a question of personal attitudes. On the one hand, it has to be admitted that it is always more difficult to introduce innovation when expenditure is being held steady or reduced. Horizons tend to narrow, attention turns to the defence of particular budgets and balanced consideration of local needs, resources and priorities can founder. This view implies abandonment of the development of learning approaches during an era of restraint. On the other hand, the times when resources are severely limited are precisely the times when radical thinking about alternative approaches is most needed. It is at times of crisis when we simply cannot afford to put up the shutters to change for this merely allows ineffective policies and programmes to continue at the expense of effective ones and deprives government of the stimulus provided by political and management innovation. This view, and I share it, argues that, whilst it will inevitably be difficult in an era of restraint, it is nevertheless essential to continue, indeed accelerate, the development of more responsive policy making by local (and central) government.

This book attempts to link theory and practice but the starting point is practice. The ideas took root whilst I was working as a corporate planner in local government during the period immediately before and after local government reorganization in 1974. These were difficult, if challenging, times. However, this first-hand experience of being involved in an attempt to build a responsive local authority should help to keep discussion fairly firmly on the ground. At the same time there is no need to remain stuck in the mud and it is hoped that at least some of what follows will present a challenge to the *status quo* and a stimulus to innovation – not only in practice but also in the development of improved theories of public learning to inform and guide that practice.

Public learning

The idea of public learning is the major underlying theme of this book. It is an idea which is broad and persuasive – perhaps too persuasive – for it puts doubters under suspicion of being in favour of ignorance. It is important, therefore, to sharpen the concept a little at the outset by drawing on the work of Donald Schon who has identified two facets of public learning.[1*]

In the first government undertakes a continuing, directed inquiry into the nature, causes and resolutions of our problems. This requires a second for, if government is to learn to solve new public problems, it must also learn to create the systems for doing so and to discard the structure and mechanisms grown up around old problems. The first is concerned with the ability of government to perceive and understand the true complexity of problems in the community – the way they inter-relate and often reinforce one another and the way they change over time. For simplicity we can refer to this kind of public learning as *problem recognition*. The second is concerned

* Superior figures refer to the Notes on pages 317–59.

with the ability of government to respond to these differing and changing problems at the appropriate organizational level in a timely and effective manner. This requires the development of institutions which are capable of bringing about their own continuing transformation. We can refer to this kind of public learning as the development of *adaptive capacity*.

These two kinds of public learning are inextricably linked and form the central theme of this book. The particular perspective brought to bear on this theme is that, whilst opportunities for learning occur at all levels of government, the most fertile location is *at the point of contact between policy making and the community*. It is at the neighbourhood or sub-local authority level that most policies have their impact on people's lives and it is here, at the periphery of the governmental structure as opposed to the distant centre, where the scope for public learning is greatest. This is not only because policy can be evaluated and revised in the light of the reality of local life experienced 'in the round', but also because reservoirs of untapped human resources of knowledge, creativity and commitment – in area staff, in ward councillors, in local people – can be released. This relates to a further strongly held view that it is at the neighbourhood level that most progress is likely to be made in reducing the Us-and-Them split between citizen and local authority.

But, before the advocates of total neighbourhood control begin to nod their heads in approval, let me stress *emphatically* that area approaches must *not* be viewed in isolation from other ways of achieving understanding and guiding action and that attempts to localize control will do little to improve local government effectiveness or strengthen political accountability *unless* they are linked to and can influence decision-taking at higher levels of government. In arguing strongly for much greater attention to be given to problem recognition and adaptive capacity at the neighbourhood level I am not arguing for these initiatives to be pursued as the exclusive panacea – only that they have been sorely neglected and should be the focus of much wider experiment.

The layout of the book

The book is divided into four parts. Part One stresses the importance of the inter-relationships between the different levels of government as part of a broader discussion of moves towards learning. Chapter 1 focusses on the balance of control between central and local government since the degree to which local government is or is not constrained by central is critical to public learning. Chapter 2 turns to local government itself and outlines the origins and development of corporate planning and management and considers some of those features of this approach which have worked against learning. Chapter 3 moves down to a third level of government and presents a discussion of the complex motivations which seem to underlie various area approaches including neighbourhood decentralization.

Part Two looks more closely at the various area approaches which have mushroomed in Britain and America since the 1960s. Chapter 4 provides a context by comparing the local government systems of the two countries. Chapter 5 reviews British neighbourhood policies and Chapter 6 provides an over-view of American approaches to neighbourhoods. Chapter 7 summarizes the broad conclusions to be drawn from this comparison and develops an analytical framework which can be used to classify area approaches.

Part Three brings together the findings of a comparative study of area management in five cities which have pioneered this approach. Chapter 8 presents the detailed material on Stockport and Liverpool in England and on Boston, New York City and Dayton in the United States. Chapter 9 draws the main conclusions from this first-hand research which was executed during 1976.

Part Four homes in on the theme of public learning. In Chapter 10 four theoretical perspectives – planning and policy sciences, organization theory, cybernetics, and democratic theory – are reviewed and an attempt is made to highlight converging themes. The hope is that this review may prove useful to those concerned to develop improved theories of public learning.

Reading the book

A severe limitation of any book is that the relationship between writer and reader is not reciprocal. We simply cannot have a dialogue. This is frustrating for we cannot build a common ground between us or engage in mutual learning. Short of not writing a book at all the least that I can do is present the contents in a flexible way which provides the reader with real choices of assimilation.

A very brief synopsis of contents precedes each of the four parts of the book. Each part should be intelligible if read in isolation and the reader is invited to choose the sequence he or she prefers.

Individual chapters can also be read separately. Each has a short introduction and conclusion which should help the reader decide whether or not closer study of the chapter would be fruitful. For those with the time and the inclination the book is designed to be read straight through and I hope that those who do so will feel that the benefit derived from the whole is greater than that derived from the sum of its parts.

Three final points about presentation. First, the scholarly practice of inserting the bracketed names of cited authors into the text has been avoided for I personally find these distracting. However, numbered references divided by Chapter are provided at the end of the book so that the book should provide a spring-board into the literature of this subject area. Second, the text is complemented by an array of illustrations and tables. These are important not only for the information they convey but for the different way in which they communicate. Third, some care has been taken to provide a thorough index so that the book can be easily dipped into.

The book is fairly thick with suggestions on how to develop responsive policy making. But, to borrow from David Cooper,[2] I would never write a book that attempts to *spell* out solutions – it is difficult enough to hint at a *grammar* which the reader can revise and develop in the light of his or her own experience. This is the spirit in which this book is published.

Acknowledgements

This book was researched and put together during fifteen months full-time study in 1976–77. My first and greatest debt therefore is to the Sidney Perry Foundation who, by funding the Sidney Perry Fellowship from the Centre for Environmental Studies, London, provided me with the opportunity to take this sabbatical from local government practice. I thank warmly the Foundation and the Centre for their generous support and encouragement.

For the duration of the Fellowship I was attached to the School for Advanced Urban Studies, Bristol University, and I express my sincere thanks to that lively institution which provided the ideal base for my work. In particular I want to thank Professor Tony Eddison, the Director, for his support and encouragement and Professor Murray Stewart, the Deputy Director, for his continuous sound counsel and advice.

The nature of the research involved making contact with literally hundreds of people involved in various aspects of local government in Britain and America – whether as officers, politicians, researchers, teachers or activists. It really is impossible for me to thank them all adequately and the omissions in what follows are considerable.

First, I want to thank the hard-pressed officers of my five case study cities – Boston, New York City, Dayton, Stockport and Liverpool – who spared time to discuss their work, supplied me with internal documents and stimulated many of the practical suggestions advanced in the following pages. To these practitioners must be added a large number of officers working for other local authorities and for various central government departments who also shared information and ideas with me during the course of the fellowship.

My debt to the academic world is also embarrassingly large. Apart from the continuous dialogue with staff at the School for Advanced Urban Studies – notably Murray Stewart but also Colin Fudge and others – I was fortunate to receive help from several other academic institutions. Researchers at the Centre for Environmental Studies – notably Brian McLoughlin, Cynthia Cockburn and Jenny Thornley – provided valuable comment on my early ideas. I was particularly fortunate to benefit from the presence of Professor John Friedmann who was at the Centre on a sabbatical from the University of California during 1976. His ideas on learning approaches to policy making influenced me considerably. The Institute of Local Government Studies at Birmingham University was also most helpful. Professor John Stewart, the Director, provided invaluable advice at a critical stage during the Fellowship. Raul Espejo of the International Institute for Applied Systems Analysis shared ideas on how cybernetic insights might enlighten thinking about local government organization and this aspect of Chapter 10 owes much to his personal encouragement.

A range of American researchers also spared time to discuss my work and I would like to thank Allen Barton (Bureau of Applied Social Research, Columbia University), Robert Yin (Rand Corporation), Dr Douglas Yates (Yale University), Professor Aaron Wildavsky (Graduate School of Public Policy, Berkeley) and Professor Melvin Webber (Department of City and Regional Planning, Berkeley). Many people in Washington DC advised me on American developments but I would like to give special thanks to Milton Kotler (National Association of Neighborhoods) and Howard Hallman (Center for Governmental Studies). A valuable state government view was provided by Charles Kirchner of Illinois.

My wider intellectual debt to the many writers on local government and policy making is catalogued in the references at the end of the book. I have found the writings of Donald Schon, Edgar Dunn, Stafford Beer and John Stewart particularly stimulating.

Before closing I would like to thank the many people it is too easy to take for granted – the librarians who are so helpful in the search through literature, the administrators who quietly support the work of researchers, the telephone operators, the photocopiers and, of course, the typists. A number of remarkably good typists assisted with my manuscript and I have pleasure in giving special thanks to Carole Hunter, Doris Cook, and Geraldine Chalk.

Finally, I acknowledge that any weaknesses and shortcomings of this book are my own.

Robin Hambleton
Bollington, April 1977

Part One
Moves towards learning

Approaches to policy making and management in local government have changed significantly since the mid-1960s. Essentially, these changes represent a move away from the passive performance of duties imposed by Parliament towards a more purposeful approach in which local authorities attempt to learn about the nature and causes of local problems and to respond accordingly. Part One sets out a context for the remainder of the book by providing a critical review of these moves towards learning at three levels.

In Chapter 1 we start at the top – with the relationships between central and local government since the degree to which local government is or is not constrained by central is critical. Following a review of the methods of central supervision, a case is made out for less control and a range of other suggestions for improving central–local relationships is put forward.

Chapter 2 moves down to the level of the local authority and outlines the origins and development of corporate planning and management. The strengths and weaknesses of the corporate approach, as applied in practice, are considered and an attempt is made to point towards ways of recasting corporate planning practice.

Chapter 3 moves down to the sub-local authority level and presents a discussion of the complex motivations which underlie various area approaches. This is less a historical review and more an attempt to penetrate the confusion which clouds discussion of ideas like area management and neighbourhood decentralization. A checklist is presented which is used in later chapters of the book to give direction to the assessment of various area approaches.

1 Central government and local autonomy

The way to have good and safe government, is not to trust it all to one but to divide it among the many, distributing to every one exactly the functions he is competent to.

Thomas Jefferson writing to Joseph C. Cabell in 1816.

Introduction

The relationships between central government and local authorities leave much to be desired. This opening chapter will attempt to show why. The emphasis will be on highlighting promising changes that are afoot and pointing to possible developments which could improve the situation. A number of books are available which describe the institutions of central and local government in Britain[1] and no attempt is made to repeat these descriptions here. Instead, there is a brief outline of the evolution of local government which concentrates on trends and the challenges of a no-growth situation. This sets the scene for a critical discussion of how central government supervises local government. The debate about central–local relationships is then considered and ways of improving these relationships are discussed in relation to certain key issues. Throughout the under-lying aim is to provide a basic context for later chapters and to emphasize the importance of improving working relationships between central and local government.

The evolution of local government services

The origins of modern British local government are revealing for they throw light on the problem of separatism between services *and* help to explain the traditional emphasis on local government as the administrative agent of central government. As we shall see, both these assumptions are increasingly being called into question but their roots are very deep. The history of local government goes back for centuries but, as W. E. Jackson recounts, the most significant changes occurred in response to the ills of the industrial revolution:

An epidemic of cholera in 1831 led to the creation of local temporary boards of health, with a Central Board of Health to guide and supervise them. In 1834 the poor law organisation was taken in hand. Parishes were amalgamated into Unions for the purpose of granting poor relief; each Union had its elected Board of Guardians. Over all, central control was exercised by a body of Poor Law Commissioners. As the industrial revolution proceeded and towns developed, there came new needs – improved highways, street paving, and lighting, more efficient police, better public health, and, eventually, public education.[2]

The familiar approach was for central government to take the initiative in dealing with various social 'evils' by setting up a separate authority with powers relating to one function of government in a specific locality. The pattern of authorities became very confusing and towards the end of the nineteenth century the structure of local government was considerably simplified. In 1871 the Local Government Board was created, as the central department of state with general supervision over local government matters. The last two decades of the century saw the establishment of local government in its modern form although there were a number of modifications in the period up to 1939, e.g. the abolition of former school boards and the transfer of public education responsibilities to the new local government authorities in 1902.[3]

However, since the Second World War a number of important functions have been taken away from local government and transferred to various *ad hoc* bodies.[4] In the name of large-scale efficiency, and at the expense of local accountability, local authorities have been deprived of their responsibility for the following services since 1945: hospital service,[5] trunk roads,[6] the supply of gas,[7] and electricity,[8] and the direct influence of local authorities over water supply was drastically reduced by the introduction of district water boards in many areas.[9] With the more recent reorganization of 1974 water and sewage services have been entrusted not to local government but to the new regional water authorities[10] and what was left of the local government personal health service was transferred to the new area health authorities.[11] Taken together, these transfers, whatever their merits on grounds of efficiency (and these in themselves are open to question), have removed control of a number of key services from bodies which were at least in theory receptive to democratic pressure to bodies that are only remotely accountable to the local population.

At the same time local government continues to be responsible for a wide and impressive range of public services. The Layfield Committee emphasized the scope of local government services in the following way:

Some of these services affect the lives of everyone in the country. Police and fire services, for example, are of universal importance. Other services are of value to the majority of those who live here, such as the provision of roads, bridges and much of our public transport. Many services are of special value to people of different ages or interests, such as public libraries, parks and other open spaces, museums and art galleries. Numerous important services provide for the needs of particular sections of society, such as education, housing and personal social services. The list is too long and varied to set out in full here, but the scope of the services is so comprehensive that no-one can be indifferent to their provision or to the cost of their supply.[12]

Thus, we have an apparent paradox. Some functions were taken away from local government immediately after the war and yet the activities of local government have come to have an increasing impact on society. This is mainly because local government assumed a greater responsibility for services providing for the needs of particular sections of society, notably education and housing. Comprehensive new legislation such as the Education Act of 1944 and the Town and Country Planning Act of 1947 stimulated this growth. And, more recently, the personal social services have enjoyed rapid expansion following the passing of the Local Authority Social Services Act 1970. In 1973/74 the total revenue expenditure[13] on services by local authorities was £10 400 million. Figure 1 shows how education, housing and health and personal social services accounted for 60 per cent of this figure. Figure 2 shows that the total (i.e. revenue and capital) expenditure of local authorities rose from £1300 million to £14 800 million in the years 1949/50 to 1973/74. Over the same twenty-five-year period local government expenditure on goods and services has taken an increasing share of the gross domestic product, rising from 8·6 per cent in 1949 to 12·4 per cent in 1974. From 1890 up until 1974 there was, in fact, an almost continuous growth in local government expenditure both in absolute terms and in the share of gross domestic product which it has taken.

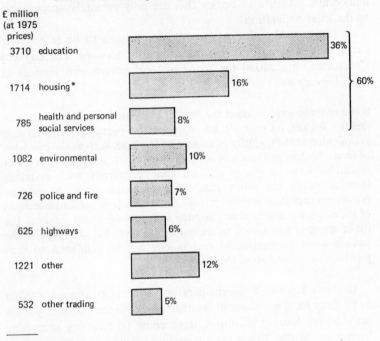

Figure 1 Revenue expenditure on different services by local authorities in Great Britain during 1973/74

£ million
(at 1975 prices)

3710	education	36%
1714	housing*	16%
785	health and personal social services	8%
1082	environmental	10%
726	police and fire	7%
625	highways	6%
1221	other	12%
532	other trading	5%

(education and housing bracketed: 60%)

10395   total

*Housing Revenue Account and Rate Fund Account combined.

Note This figure excludes superannuation and special funds which amounted to £338 million in 1973/74.

Source: Layfield Committee, *Report on Local Government Finance*, May 1976, p. 382.

How times have changed! It is now abundantly clear that the financial year 1974/75 marked the end of a remarkable era of growth in local government services. Figure 3 shows how the mid-1970s are at the fulcrum of a major shift in resource trends with the spirited ascents in expenditure of the previous decade levelling out abruptly. The extent of the need for fundamental re-thinking resulting from this dramatic change is only just beginning to be appreciated for the change requires a great deal more than the trimming of proposed expansions. It requires an overhaul of the whole way the local authority goes about its business. The central problem confronting such a transformation is that the assumption

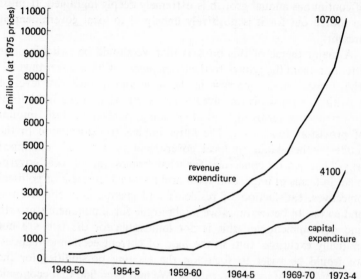

Figure 2 Growth in expenditure by local authorities in Great Britain, 1949/50–1973/74

Note Revenue expenditure includes expenditure on local government superannuation and special funds.
Source: Layfield Committee, *Report on Local Government Finance*, May 1976, p. 380.

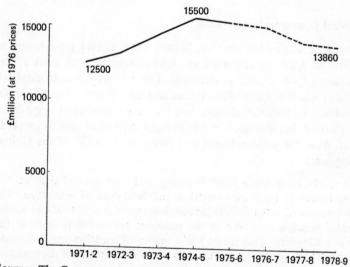

Figure 3 Actual and projected total level of expenditure by local authorities in Great Britain

Source: *The Government's expenditure plans*, Cmnd 6721, Part 1, January 1977, p. 18.

of continuous annual growth is extremely deeply ingrained. It must be rooted out for it is positively unhelpful to local government at present.

A major theme of this book is that we should be switching our attention from the *growth* to the *development* of local government.[14] The former implies increase in the scale and quantitative level of activities and usually involves a focus on what 'goes into' local government in terms of level of spending, number of staff, amount of provision and so on. The latter implies transformation in the modes of behaviour of local government in new and unmapped ways. The central concern is for what 'comes out' of local government in terms of impact on local problems, achievement of political objectives, satisfaction of residents and clients, cost effectiveness and so on. In better times we might argue for simultaneous growth and development and this is not impossible for the two are not mutually exclusive. But, in the light of current economic realities, we would be wiser to focus on the exciting possibilities for the 'development' of local government. We may even find that economic stringency is a positive advantage, at least in the short term, for it helps to turn attention away from the marginal, annual increments in expenditure towards the massive on-going public expenditures which may no longer be in tune with local needs. It can also help to shift attention to a wider consideration of *all* investment planning – public and private.

Central government supervision

At risk of stating the obvious, Britain has a unitary government in which all local governments are subordinate to, and exist at the pleasure of, the central government. The current moves to establish directly elected assemblies in Scotland and Wales, do, of course, involve constitutional change. But they are not without opposition and, even if implemented, it is important to be clear that the government does not see devolution as a threat to the unity of the United Kingdom:

The government agree wholeheartedly with the Commission on the Constitution in rejecting separatism and federalism as a solution. The Government, like the Royal Commission, regard it as a vital and fundamental principle to maintain the economic and political unity of the United Kingdom. This is not just a matter of tradition and sentiment, important though they are. The unity of the country and of the economy is essential both to the strength of our international position and to the growth of our industry and national wealth. . . . It is crucial for the central management of the economy and so to the redistribution of resources in favour of all the less prosperous areas of the United Kingdom.[15]

Leaving aside devolution and the modifications that this may bring about in Scotland and Wales, how does central government control and influence the activities of local government? There are four main ways: (1) legislation; (2) circulars and guidance; (3) planning processes; and (4) finance. These inter-relate but, for convenience, are now considered in turn.

1 Legislation

By imposing specific duties and powers on local authorities central government controls the broad scope of local government activity. The principle of *ultra vires* is strictly applied so that local authorities can only undertake those activities specifically approved by Parliament. This has led some authorities to work for local acts to give them special powers. For example, the authorities of Buckinghamshire, Manchester and the Shetlands, have used local acts to give them the power to form companies or acquire shares in existing ones.[16] Within the framework of legislation there is, however, considerable variation in the amount of discretion left with local government. In some cases there is no room for manoeuvre as, for example, with electoral registration, rent and rate rebates, registration of births, deaths and marriages, and mandatory awards to students. In other cases local government legislation is more concerned with the provision of powers than with the imposition of duties. Thus, for example, much of recreation policy is at the discretion of the local authority including parks, recreation grounds, swimming baths, museums and art galleries.

Many local government services fall between these two extremes: they are broadly within the mandatory category but the statutes lay down duties only in very broad terms. A good example is the Education Act 1944 which requires local authorities to secure 'that efficient education shall be made available to meet the needs of the population in the area'. Another is 'to make provision for fire-fighting purposes'. Thus, and contrary to widespread belief, legislation does, on the whole, leave fairly wide scope for local interpretation. Indeed, at least one recent law lords' ruling enlarged the area for local discretion. This concerned the local authority of Tameside and its refusal in 1976 to introduce a comprehensive system of secondary education in line with national policy. The law lords' ruling effectively nullified the long accepted power of the Education Secretary to intervene (under section 68 of the Education Act 1944) when a local authority is, in educational terms, acting 'unreasonably'. The government can, of course, introduce new legislation to fill this gap but the conflict over Tameside emphasizes the limitations and fragility of some aspects of central government's *legal* control over local government.

2   Circulars and guidance

Interpretation of the legislation and fuller exposition of central government intentions are provided by a constant flow of circulars, by the inspectorates of central departments, by ministerial speeches, by communication with the local authority associations, and by a wide range of informal contacts between departmental and local government officers. The major method of communication is the circular which may instruct or may be merely advisory or explanatory. The inadequacies of these modes of communication between central and local government have, with the exception of one important study,[17] only recently begun to receive the attention they deserve. A very brief summary of some of the defects follows.

First, the balance between coercion and advice varies erratically with the result that the status and purpose of many communications is uncertain. This works in two directions. On the one hand, important guidance may be ignored and, on the other, casual pointers for consideration may harden into firm and rigid targets and so blunt thinking about local needs and priorities.[18] Second, the process of communication has tended to be one-way – from central to local government. There are some signs that this may be changing. For example, the local authority associations (the Association of Metropolitan Authorities, the Association of County Councils, the Association of District Councils and the London Boroughs Association) are increasingly consulted at an early stage in the preparation of central government initiatives and they all sit on the Consultative Council on Local Government Finance. Also, green papers and openly consultative documents seem to be gaining in popularity with central government.[19] Third, many communications sent by central government to local authorities seem to place too much emphasis on uniform national policies. Given the social, economic, geographical and cultural differences between local authority areas uniformity virtually guarantees a misapplication of resources. Fourth, central government needlessly involves itself in the minutiae of local government administration. This example is drawn from J. A. G. Griffith: 'The letter from an inspector who had visited two homes in one local authority's area drew attention to the fact that, contrary to regulations, one of the record books was not up to date.'[20] Even staunch centralists would find difficulty in justifying Whitehall's need for observations of this degree of detail! Fifth, and most seriously, central government guidelines focus attention on the *provision* of services when what really matters is the achievement of *results* by that provision. They indicate quantity of service, not impact or effectiveness, so that it is mere conjecture as to whether an authority with higher levels of provision is any 'better' than one with lower levels. Sixth, central government guidance tends to treat services separately and has often failed to grasp the inter-relationships between different policies and between resources and aspirations. Some attempts have been made by the central departments to issue joint circulars[21] but these are exceptional. It is certainly true that central government still has great difficulty in relating to a local authority 'in the round'.

The implication of the points made so far is that central government is largely to blame for the inadequacy of central–local communication. But local government has also contributed to the confusion for, whilst protesting about too much guidance in some fields, the local authorities have actively sought guidance in others. This was most clearly demonstrated in 1974 when the local authority associations pressed the Secretary of State for the Environment for detailed guidance on how to curtail spending.[22] This was a sad time for those who believe in greater autonomy for local government but, in the more recent rounds of the rate support grant negotiations, local government has regained its composure and has argued against detailed central guidance. Table 1 gives quotations from five circulars (all influenced by local authority association pressure) to illustrate this fascinating shift in the perception of local government's ability to deal with difficult decisions.

3 *Planning processes*
Central government sets down a number of planning processes which control and influence the work of local authorities. Six should

Table 1 *The changing emphasis of central government guidance on how to curtail local authority expenditure*

Date	Guidance	Source
December 1974	'It is necessary that the Government should offer detailed guidance to local authorities on the way in which limitations in services might be made.'	*Rate fund expenditure and rate calls in 1975/76.* DoE Circular 171/74, para 5.
September 1975	'The Government will need to give detailed advice, service by service, on the type of action that should be taken.'	*Local authority expenditure in 1976/77 – forward planning.* DoE Circular 88/75, para 5.
December 1975	'The local authority representatives on the Consultative Council on Local Government Finance have recognised the importance of guidance from the Government but at the same time have been concerned that such guidance should not prevent local authorities from exercising their own responsibility for deciding on priorities for expenditure in their own areas.'	*Rate Support Grant Settlement 1976/77.* DoE Circular 129/75, para 28.
August 1976	'Local authorities will know of the advice given in previous circulars on how to deal with reductions but should themselves decide how the reductions in expenditure . . . should be allocated as between their services in the light of local circumstances and their own priorities.'	*Local authority expenditure 1976/78.* DoE Circular 84/76, para 10.
December 1976	'What (this circular) means for particular services will be for (individual) authorities to determine in the light of their own circumstances and priorities.'	*Rate Support Grant Settlement 1977/78.* DoE Circular 120/76, para 29.

be mentioned: (a) statutory land use planning; (b) community land programming; (c) transport policies and programmes; (d) housing investment plans; (e) ten-year social service plans, and (f) comprehensive community programmes. There are others which have an important but less direct impact on local authorities, notably health service planning and joint care planning but these need not concern us here.

a)   *Structure and local plans* prepared under the Town and Country Planning Act 1971 must be drawn up according to the immensely detailed Town and Country Planning (Structure and Local Plans Regulations) 1974. Essentially the plans are supposed to state and justify the authority's proposals for the development and other use of land. The statutory process of structure and local planning is coming under fire for a range of reasons. Some local authorities have managed to negotiate the procedural requirements whilst still producing useful guidance to local elected members. But a growing number of practitioners now feel that the statutory planning system is too slow, too unwieldy, ineffective, weakly related to resource questions, imperfectly related to other aspects of local government activity and generally of declining relevance to major urban problems. Arguably its saving grace is the protection it affords to the individual (or community) against arbitrary local action.

The planning system in Scotland has developed differently and has certain significant advantages. Section 173 of the Local Government (Scotland) Act 1973 directed regional authorities (the upper tier of local government) to prepare regional reports which, in essence, are rolling five-year physical development plans but with a strong corporate emphasis. The style is brisk and to the point with the first round of reports being prepared and submitted within a matter of months. Scotland is also developing a more flexible system of financial planning involving the issue to each local authority of a series of block allocations for capital expenditure. The precise relationship of the new financial plans to the new regional reports needs further clarification but, if the two can be successfully welded together, the Scottish system will have begun to meet many of the criticisms levelled at statutory planning in England and Wales.[23]

(b)   *The Community Land Act 1975*, as originally envisaged, was to involve local authorities in the preparation of ongoing rolling programmes for the acquisition, holding and disposal of land and in the maintenance of closely specified community land accounts. These accounts were to be kept in a form designed to illustrate not merely the extent to which deficit or surplus was generated, but also a variety of aspects of management including the profit and loss on transactions, the financial effects of holding, and the capital value of leases. The chief weakness of this process, which has been delayed in implementation by cuts in public expenditure, would seem to be the overemphasis on detailed accounting procedures. Some remain hopeful that annual land programmes can inject at least some firm investment proposals into structure and local plan policies but the need to plan swiftly and positively at site level may increase pressure on the creaking statutory planning system. It has been suggested, for example, that current local plans may need to be replaced by land implementation programmes (detailing specific sites and giving priorities for acquisition, holding and disposal over the next five years) set within the framework of an annually updated land policy statement.[24]

(c) *Transport policies and programmes* (*TPPs*) In 1973 the Department of the Environment announced proposals for a new system of grants for local transportation purposes which was designed to bring about a corporate approach by county councils to the formulation and execution of transport policy. This system, known as the TPP approach, is a considerable advance on the previous system of specific grants. It aims to reduce central government intervention in the details of local transport policies by introducing block grants for transport expenditure. The TPP is an annual process focussing attention on policy objectives and requiring costed five-year programmes set within budget constraints together with clear statements of priorities.[25] The approach has much to commend it, so much so that its application to other policy areas has been encouraged with, for example, housing investment plans for housing. A key difficulty, however, surrounds the relationship of the TPP to structure planning and local planning. Clearly there is much common ground between these policy instruments but there is not a great deal of evidence suggesting effective policy integration between them. With the creation, in September 1976, of a Department of Transport separate from the Department of the Environment it may become more difficult to forge links between transport and land use planning.

(d) *Housing investment plans (HIPs)* Block grants and allocations to local housing authorities on the basis of relative needs have been suggested for some time, with TPPs providing a model. In June 1977 the Department of the Environment finally issued a circular on Housing Investment Programmes.[26] The new system is to be introduced from 1978/79 and is designed to enable local authorities to present co-ordinated analyses of housing conditions in their area and to formulate coherent policies and programmes of capital spending on public housing.

In May of each year local authorities are to be invited to submit proposals covering the next four years for their spending on housing under seven specified, but broad, expenditure heads. In November of each year local authorities will receive financial allocations formed, into three spending blocks which cover, basically, council housing, private sector and housing association spending. This block grant approach should increase local discretion and improve forward planning on housing. There is a danger, however, that the HIP and, for that matter the TPP, will become dislocated from the other planning budgetary processes operated by the local authority. This is because submissions have to be finalized early in the financial year and this may work against a corporate approach.

(e) *Ten-year social service plans* In 1972 the Department of Health and Social Security asked local authorities to submit ten-year plans for the development of their personal social services.[27] The plans represented an important attempt by at least some social service departments to take a comprehensive look at the needs they should be trying to meet.[28] But the process left a lot to be desired and it is unlikely to be repeated in the same way. A striking drawback was the narrow sectional approach. First the process was initiated by the DHSS without reference to other departments, and local authorities were not expected to consider the relationships of the plan with other services. Second, even within the plan, the emphasis was on the preparation of a series of ten-year projections for separate services. Local authorities were not required to develop any views about priorities. Perhaps social services (and education) planning will, in future, follow the rolling programme approach developed for TPPs and HIPs. If so this will involve central government spelling out more planning processes for local government.

(f) *Comprehensive community programmes* (CCPs) differ from the relatively narrow planning processes so far discussed. The CCP is less a new process than an attempt to add a new dimension – the dimension of urban deprivation – to all existing planning processes of local and central government as they relate to a given local authority area. The CCP is intended to bring together a range of central government departments, the two tiers of local government and other executive bodies, in the development of a joint strategy to tackle urban deprivation. The approach is being pioneered in the Metropolitan Borough of Gateshead.

4   Finance

The fourth way in which central government exerts control over local government is through finance – a channel of influence which takes on increased importance during an era of no growth. The main methods of financial control are discussed under the following three headings: (a) government grants; (b) external audit, and (c) loan sanction.

(a)   *Government grants*   Local authority income is derived from three main sources: rates, grants from central government and charges for services rendered. As a proportion the last category, which is comprised mainly of rents for council housing, has held fairly steady since the early 1960s at around 27 to 29 per cent of total income. Turning to the remaining 70 per cent or so, hard-pressed ratepayers may be surprised to learn that government grants have provided more income than rates since the early 1950s. Further, since 1965, the proportion of government grants has crept slowly upwards. Figure 4 shows how in 1975/76 government grants provided twice as much income as rates. It is argued that, when central government is providing an increasing proportion of funds, it inevitably exercises greater control. Noel Hepworth has challenged this view suggesting that, in the absence of specific controls, it creates only an 'atmosphere of dependence'.[29] But he also points out that as a condition of the 1975/76 rate support grant settlement the central government insisted upon additional information being made available about staff numbers. This is a significant development in central scrutiny but the fact remains that the vast bulk of government grant support to local government is difficult to monitor. The rate support grant[30] provides over 80 per cent of government support to local authorities and is a block grant paid in respect of rate fund expenditure as a whole and not earmarked for particular purposes. Thus, whilst the government can control the *general*

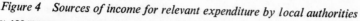

Figure 4   Sources of income for relevant expenditure by local authorities

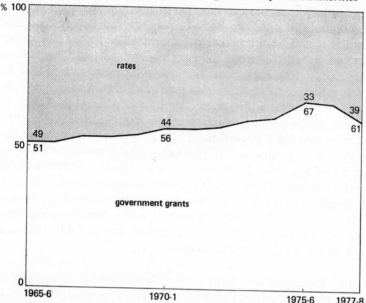

Note Relevant expenditure is that expenditure financed solely by means of rates and the aggregate Exchequer grant – it ignores income such as rent, fees, charges etc.
Source: Layfield Committee on Local Government Finance, May 1976, p. 385 and D O E Circular 120/76.

level of expenditure by reducing the total rate support grant, as it did in the 1977/78 settlement by lowering the level of grant to 61 per cent of relevant expenditure (see Figure 4), it cannot direct how this grant should be spent. As discussed earlier it may offer guidance (see Table 1) and urge restraint but, as a detailed control on expenditure, the grant system is perhaps not as restrictive as many have supposed.

(b) *External audit* The accounts of all local authorities are subject to annual external audit. In England and Wales the auditors are either civil servants ('district auditors') appointed by the Secretary of State for the Environment or auditors ('approved auditors') appointed by the local authority, subject to approval by the Secretary of State, from professional practice. Apart from normal auditing duties, such as ensuring that proper accounting practices have been observed, the auditor has to satisfy himself that there is legal authority for all the expenditure. In practice, the auditors often concentrate in a narrow book-keeping way on finding such legal authority and, once legality has been established, they may neglect to consider whether expenditure has been well-advised. The auditor's Code of Practice does specify that one of his concerns is to look for 'loss arising from waste, extravagance, inefficient financial adminis-tration, poor value for money, mistake or other cause' but the service is ill-equipped to interpret this item widely. The Layfield Report calls for a strengthening of the audit service so that it can play a more positive role in promoting local government efficiency and ensuring value for money by, for example, initiating major reviews of trends in the use of manpower in local authority services.[31] It would be wrong, however, to understate the controlling power of the external audit – at the very least it ensures that a local authority only spends money in a way permitted by law and this remains a crucial check on local government activity.

(c)   *Loan sanction*   Most local authority capital expenditure is financed by borrowing. Before a local authority can borrow money it must receive permission to do so from central government in the form of a loan sanction which may be specific to a particular project or may cover a group of projects. The original purpose of the loan sanction system was to keep the debt of individual local authorities down to manageable proportions but now the system is used mainly to regulate local authority capital spending to keep it in line with national economic plans, and in particular with plans outlined in the annual public expenditure survey. In 1970 central government streamlined the loan sanction procedures by dividing local authority capital expenditure into two main categories: 'key sector schemes' and 'locally determined schemes'.[32] *Key sector schemes* are those for which ministers have special responsibilities in determining standards or co-ordinating development on a national basis. They are closely scrutinized by Whitehall and include: acquisition of development land, housing, education, personal social services, police, derelict land reclamation, docks and harbours, and transportation projects costing more than £0·5 million. *Locally determined schemes* are funded by a block allocation made annually to each authority and include projects which generally have less political significance such as swimming pools, parks, libraries, offices, school furniture and equipment, vehicles and transportation projects below £0·5 million.

We can see, therefore, that a wide range of local government capital spending is more or less directly controlled by Whitehall by means of the power to prevent the borrowing of money. In addition there are cost controls over capital expenditure, such as the housing cost yardstick, which also limit expenditure. These controls on capital expenditure deprive councillors of control over many fundamental aspects of local government services. The problem is compounded by the inability of central government to co-ordinate the issue of loan sanctions by different departments. The result is that local authority corporate plans, seeking to attach clear priorities to various capital projects and to co-ordinate their execution, have often been frustrated. Local authorities, seeing the system as a form of roulette, have, in the past, boosted their loan sanction applications with additional schemes in the hope that some will 'come up'. For this reason and in entire contradiction to its purpose, the loan sanction system may have acted as a hidden incentive to spend – and probably on non-priority projects! In some ways the current, severe curtailment of capital programmes may be seen as a blessing in disguise – it at least provides the breathing space which could be used to create an improved approach to the programming of capital expenditure.

The central–local debate

Central government always *says* it wants to see a vigorous and powerful local government. Both the major parties have made this quite clear. Thus the Labour Government 1970 White Paper, *Reform of Local Government in England* stated:

. . . only if such change occurs, and local government is organised in strong units with power to make major decisions, will present trends towards centralisation be reversed, and local democracy resume its place as a major part of our democratic system.[33]

And the Conservative White Paper in the following year said:

A vigorous local democracy means that authorities must be given real functions – with powers of decision and the ability to take action without being subjected to excessive regulation by central government through financial or other controls.[34]

But in practice our review of the way central government supervises local government suggests that these aims are far from being realized. As the Layfield Committee rightly observed:

What has been clearly visible over recent years is a growing propensity for the government to determine, in increasing detail, the pace and direction in which local services should be developed, the resources which should be devoted to them and the priorities between them.[35]

A linked problem, also revealed in the discussion of central government supervision, is that the complex division of responsibilities and the equally complex forms of governmental intervention in local authority functions frustrate accountability for they conceal from the public the true responsibility for the decisions that are taken. This, of course, is the central message of the Layfield Report:

Our report finds a lack of clear accountability for local government expenditure which results from the present confusion of responsibilities between the government and local authorities. We are unanimous that measures are needed which will not merely be adjustments to the present arrangements but will establish a financial system based on a clear identification of responsibility for expenditure and for the taxation to finance it.[36]

The Report goes on to suggest proposals which are centred around two groups of possibilities – one based on mainly central and one on mainly local accountability. In the first alternative central government would assume the main responsibility for local spending and would determine the expenditure of each authority. The second, and preferred, alternative would increase local authority responsibility over, for example, education, social services, transport and housing where government influence is at present strongest. To ensure local accountability local government would need local taxing powers in addition to rates in order to finance a larger share of local government expenditure than it does at present and the Committee argue that a local income tax would be the only practicable additional source.

It should be stressed that the choice posed by the Committee is *not* between complete central control and total local autonomy. It is, instead, a choice between two broad approaches for determining the general character of the relationships between the two levels of government. The Committee believe that to choose the middle ground would not remove the present muddle. A third alternative was proposed in a note of reservation to the Report. This involved the central government financing the full cost of meeting defined minimum standards leaving local discretion to finance higher standards out of local sources of revenue. The main report rejects this alternative because, first, it is not possible at present to define objective costed minimum standards and, second, that even if it were a consequence would be increased central control to ensure compliance with them. The Layfield Report raised the whole level of debate about central–local relationships and those interested are urged to read the report itself rather than rely solely on the many commentaries.[37]

The government's response to the Layfield Report

The government's response to the Layfield Report was published as a Green Paper in May 1977.[38] The government prefers not to choose between the centralist and the localist approaches and seeks a middle way. This would not, however, follow the alternative put forward in the note of reservation to the Report for this is felt to be impractical. Instead 'the Government see the duties and responsibilities involved in the provision of local public services as being shared on a partnership basis between central and local government. Within this framework the balance of responsibilities will vary over time as circumstances change'.[39] Few would disagree with these broad sentiments. The danger, however, is that they do little to stem the trend towards centralization.

The Green Paper rejects the case for local income tax but does accept some of the Layfield Report's suggestions for improving the rating system. In particular, the government wants to see a switch in the basis of domestic property valuation from annual rental value to capital value. In relation to capital expenditure the government accept that the project-by-project controls exercised under the present system are unnecessarily detailed. There are to be discussions with the local authority associations regarding a new system of capital expenditure approvals under which individual local authorities would be given approval for expenditure on programmes (e.g. education, personal social services) rather than on projects. This represents a development of the Transport Policies and Programmes (TPP) and Housing Investment Plan (HIP) approaches discussed earlier.

Improving central–local relationships

There will always be tensions and disagreements between central and local government and this is no bad thing. Both have an important role to play in tackling urban and rural problems and each will naturally bring different perspectives to the task. The aim should not be to submerge differences of view but to improve mutual understanding between the two tiers. An important step is to clarify the issues which should be considered by those seeking to improve central–local relationships. Five are briefly set out below, not as a prescription but as a series of points for discussion: (1) national economic planning; (2) responsibility for services; (3) autonomy and equity; (4) local democracy; and (5) learning and action.

1   National economic planning

The government is responsible for the overall management of the economy and, as local government accounts for about a third of total public expenditure, it has considerable economic significance. This can, of course, result in a conflict of interest for national economic policy may require a curtailment of public expenditure at a time when local interests point to the need for expansion. In practice local authority spending *is* increasingly subject to control for national economic reasons but so too are other aspects of the public and private sector. Given that controls are not excessive for their purpose and that they are not employed in an arbitrary 'stop-go' fashion, there can be little doubt about the legitimacy of a central government role in local government expenditure planning purely from the economic management point of view.

2   Responsibility for services

In relation to policies for services there will always be a potential conflict between ministers and local authorities for they both claim responsibility for the services provided by local government and they both have election results to back up their claim. There would seem to be considerable scope for closer consultation to avoid unnecessary conflict. For example, it is not impossible to achieve overall national goals for a particular service in a way which is also sensitive to the differing needs of different areas. Such an approach would require a little more thought and imagination than the application of a uniform policy to all local authorities but it would clearly result in a better use of resources from every point of view. There are some welcome signs that central and local government are beginning to get together in more productive ways than hitherto.

The Consultative Council on Local Government Finance set up in 1975 is a step towards regular consultation and co-operation between central and local government on major issues of common concern. Educational institutions such as the School for Advanced Urban Studies at Bristol and the Institute of Local Government Studies at Birmingham, are increasingly running courses which bring together officers from central and local government. These developments could be taken further with, for example, transfer or secondment of staff between central and local government – a practice virtually unheard of at present.

However, there remains a very real problem and this stems from the current close association of ministerial with departmental performance. Pushing forward the interests of his department has been one of the prime ways in which the reputation and career of a minister is built. Thus, through no personal fault of the individuals, we have developed a system which positively encourages departmentalism. This tends to work against the development of a corporate approach to policy making in Whitehall although there have been one or two promising developments in recent years.[40] Perhaps we need to reconsider the terms of reference given to ministers in order to leave them with a broader political focus. Ministers for client groups are not unknown – we have one for the disabled and one for children has been advocated[41] – and there are a number of other important policy problems cutting across departmental jurisdictions which might benefit from a direct ministerial interest. Less ambitiously there would seem to be a strong case for central departments to review their existing arrangements for supervising local government with a view to identifying how far these frustrate the development of more corporate approaches by local authorities.

3 Autonomy and equity

Questions of autonomy and equity lead us into the age-long tension between liberty and equality. We can caricature the conflicting arguments by raising two questions. To what extent should local authorities be *free* to carry out local services as they think fit? Conversely, to what extent should central government intervene to ensure *fairness* both between individuals and between areas? The founding fathers of the American constitution wrestled with this problem 200 years ago and their words continue to strike at the heart of the problem. Thomas Jefferson believed that the principal political danger was 'the tyranny of arbitrary centralized autocracy'. His main opponent, James Madison, felt that the major concern was 'the tyranny of arbitrary local majorities'. The outcome of that particular debate was the concept of federalism and we shall develop the comparison between local government in Britain and America in Chapter 4. In the British context there is a body of evidence which, by pointing to the variations in service provision between local authority areas, suggests that local government already has sufficient freedom of discretion.[42] But our review of central government supervision has shown that the current balance of power unmistakably favours centralization at the expense of local autonomy. We have seen that certain central controls involve too much red tape (e.g. procedures for town and country planning) and that some may be counter-productive or, at least, work against the best use of resources (e.g. procedures for loan sanction). There would seem, therefore, to be room for a significant increase in the liberty of local government *without* seriously impairing central government's legitimate interest in seeking redistribution of resources in favour of deprived areas and minorities.

4   Local democracy

There is widespread support for the concept of local democracy and we have seen that both the major parties want to see a vigorous and powerful local government. Because local authorities are the only elected political bodies outside Parliament and they are the means by which people can take part in decisions affecting their area, they have a value in promoting democracy. Local government spreads political power. It provides opportunities for people of different political persuasion and different backgrounds to engage in the political process. It can also be claimed that local government strengthens accountability by retaining responsibility at a local level and promotes innovation by experimenting with new approaches to community problems. The existing relationships between central and local government tend to suppress rather than release these energies. This was a central theme of the Redcliffe-Maud *Report on Local Government in England* which argued that a strengthened local government would attract greater public interest and a higher calibre of councillor and officer. The wider goals of local democracy were expressed thus: 'The whole Commission is unanimous in its conviction that if the present local government system is drastically reformed, its scope extended to include functions now in the hands of nominated bodies, and the grip of central government relaxed, England can become a more efficient, democratic and humane society.'[43] The Commission's bold proposals were not implemented but their desire for a fully responsible local government lives on.

5 *Learning and action*

A great danger in the discussion of central–local relationships is that attention is focussed inwards – on responsibilities, procedures, controls, planning processes, consultation arrangements and the like – so that we lose sight of the problems and issues 'out there' in the community. It has already been argued that a serious drawback of existing central government guidelines is that they focus attention on the provision of services when what really matters is the achievement of results by that provision. Central government is well equipped to measure inputs (for instance the number of teachers employed) but finds it more difficult to assess outputs (for instance the amount of educational benefit acquired by pupils).

Local government, too, has yet to make significant progress in the development of easily captured output measures, but it does have important advantages over central government when it comes to learning about the impact of policy. First, it is closer to the problems on the ground and can analyse the detailed effects of policies. This is very important for there can be great geographical variations in the nature of a policy problem and the required response. Examples are housing and urban deprivation which are seen as critical national issues but which also have important local dimensions. Thus actions prescribed for their solution will differ greatly, say, between inner London and Salford in Greater Manchester. A second and related advantage is that local government is extremely well placed to understand the *combined* impact on an area or client group of a whole range of policies. And, in the end, it is only the combined impact which really matters. At the same time it is also true that some of the problems learned about at local authority level will require action by central government if significant progress is to be made in their resolution.

The requirements of learning and action imply both a need to recognize the value of more local government discretion in setting priorities and a need to develop closer joint-working by central and local government on policy analysis. These ends could be furthered by giving local government greater powers of virement between major government programmes and by enlarging allocations for joint financial support to facilitate co-operative priority-setting between local government and the local branches of central government, as has already started in a modest way in relation to the health service.[44] There is also a key role for the regional branches of central government which, if departments were able to collaborate more closely, could play a particularly important part in the development of a learning *central* government. The rejection of arguments in favour of devolution to the regions within England[45] must not be allowed to prevent the development of more integrated approaches to regional management by central government. Such developments are one way of injecting some ongoing relevance into the strategic work of the Regional Economic Planning Councils whose plans have often been treated as discussion documents of marginal importance because arrangements for implementation have been neglected.

For some time central government has played a valuable role in taking up good ideas developed by particular authorities and securing their application elsewhere. In addition, central government encourages a good deal of research on local government problems. But how many good ideas don't get promoted? And just how relevant is much of the research conducted in the name of improving local government effectiveness? Is it altogether unfair to suggest that our great centres of 'learning' – our universities, polytechnics and research institutions – have been less than successful when it comes to helping local and central government learn? There is surely enormous scope for more joint research involving central government, local government and further education institutions. This is true at the level of the local authority, the region and nationally. At a time of no growth the case for greater collaboration is particularly strong. On the one hand the country can ill afford not to make better use of the talent residing in academic institutions and, conversely, the problems of government present an increasingly provocative intellectual, as well as political, challenge.

Conclusion

It has been argued that we should be switching our attention from the *growth* to the *development* of local government and that this is likely to involve transformation in the modes of behaviour of local government in new and unmapped ways. The focus of attention should be on results – on ways of improving the effectiveness of local government in terms of impact on local problems, achievement of political objectives, satisfaction of residents and clients, and value for money. This means building a creative and inventive local authority capable of establishing effective working relationships with other agencies in its area and of developing new approaches, testing them out and, above all, *learning for itself*. The current relationships between central and local government are, on the whole, not designed to foster developments of this kind. They are more concerned with regulation than with spurring new initiatives. It has been suggested that central controls could be relaxed considerably without endangering legitimate central government interests in local government planning and management. Further there is considerable scope for improving the relationships between central and local government for mutual understanding between the two sides is low. At the same time a number of promising moves designed to correct this have been touched on. It is to be hoped that these initiatives, particularly those which involve a joint approach to policy making, will spread and develop. In the next chapter we look more closely at this idea of a joint or corporate approach with particular emphasis on the way it has so far been applied in local government practice.

2 The purposeful local authority

Introduction

There is nothing more difficult to carry out, nor more doubtful of success, nor more dangerous to conduct than to initiate a new order of things. For the reformer has enemies in all who profit by the old order, and only luke-warm defenders in all those who profit by the new order.

Machiavelli in *The Prince* (1513

Since the late 1960s both local and central government have been struggling to develop more coherent and purposeful approaches to the process of public policy making. These efforts have manifested themselves in, for example, the development of corporate planning and management in local government and in the PESC (Public Expenditure Survey Committee) and PAR (Programme Analysis and Review) processes in central government. In this chapter the main focus is on policy making and management at the level of the local authority. First, the main features of a purposeful as opposed to passive approach are outlined. The origins and evolution of corporate planning and management are then considered with the aim of providing insights on the current 'state of the art'. This review is followed by a critical appraisal of the corporate approach as applied in practice. An underlying theme is to show how corporate working has been a major force in the development of a learning local government but that, particularly in the more recent years of 'no growth', its potential as an innovative force seems to have been stunted. The jargon which permeates much discussion of corporate planning can be off-putting and every effort has, therefore, been made to keep the terminology as simple as possible.

The purposeful approach

Corporate planning in local government takes many forms so that definitions cannot be categorical. Generally speaking, however, we can say that a corporate approach means taking an overall view of a local authority's activities and the way they relate to the changing needs and problems of its area. More specifically it involves the local authority developing management *and* political processes and structures which will enable it to plan, control and review its activities as a whole to satisfy the needs of the people in its area to the maximum extent consistent with available resources. Thus, the two words 'corporate planning' communicate two fundamental ideas – that the local authority should consider its resources and activities as a *corporate* whole and that it should *plan* and review them in relation to the needs and problems of its environment. To appreciate these ideas it is necessary to contrast them with the traditional view of management in local government.[1] As the historical outline at the beginning of Chapter 1 implied, this tradition sees the central task of the authority as the provision of separate services directed at essentially separate problems. Further, it views the local authority as the passive administrative agent of central government – an agent which is incapable of mapping out its own future. Corporate planning presents a firm challenge to both of these traditions. To explore the nature of this challenge is to outline the two main characteristics of corporate planning.[2]

1 Inter-relationships

Corporate planning argues that the work of government is seriously hampered by the relatively arbitrary fragmentation of effort between departments, professions, committees, units of government and agencies. These compartments restrict the ability of government to perceive and react to problems in society. Examples are: vandalism, unemployment, the elderly, homelessness, the under-fives. Corporate planning tries to bridge organizational gaps both within the local authority, and, more recently, between the local authority and other government agencies serving the same area. This latter activity has been dubbed inter-corporate planning.[3]

It is important to distinguish two sets of inter-relationships: between substantive problems (e.g. between traffic and environment; between educational deprivation and poverty) and between forms of response (e.g. rearranging departmental responsibilities; pooling resources for more flexible use; developing new ways of linking hitherto separate policy processes). Responses are, of course, often stimulated by substantive problems. For example, social service departments were established in 1971 because it was felt that personal social problems could not be treated effectively as a series of isolated maladies – they required a response at the level of the family and this was the main reason why the existing children and welfare departments were unified and strengthened. But we can also see that the two sets of interactions have sometimes lost touch with each other, with alarming consequences. For example, in the 1960s there was a sudden American-led growth in academic research on the city as an urban system. This work made important strides forward in developing our understanding of the complex inter-relationships of activities in the city.[4] But planning theory[5] and structure planning practice have slanted their efforts too heavily towards generalized substantive questions, often involving the construction of elaborate mathematical models of urban and regional systems, and have failed to pay sufficient attention to how the plans could be implemented.[6] The result has been a great deal of disillusion and frustration.

The opposite mistake of allowing the procedural response to become out of step with the substantive problems in the environment has also occurred. Examples can be quoted from those authorities where hosts of inter-departmental 'working' groups of officers have proliferated in a way which is poorly related to the inter-connected problems actually facing the authority. Many important substantive problems *do* require a corporate response but there remain many where functionally organized management should be capable of doing the job. If our key criterion of government action is relevance then perhaps the crucial inter-relationship is between problem and response. This leads us to the second important characteristic of corporate planning.

2   *Planning*

The traditional focus of departmental activity is the *administration* of a service. The pressures of coping with the day-to-day problems of running a service can loom so large that there may be little or no consideration of whether the service is still required in its present form. In this way the provision of a service or the execution of an activity can become an end in itself. This tendency can be reinforced by management changes which seek to improve *efficiency* whilst neglecting effectiveness. High standards of efficiency and administration are important in local government but it is easy to forget that efficient administration of the wrong policy is likely to accelerate the speed at which matters get worse. The administrative machines set up during the 1950s in the large cities to clear slum housing are a case in point. Whilst the problems remained the same their performance was generally acclaimed. But, when it was realized during the 1960s that the problems were different, that wholesale clearance was no longer an effective policy, it took nearly a decade to bring about a significant re-direction of effort. The resistance to change within bureaucracies is, as Donald Schon has observed, more than a question of passive inertia. It is more nearly a form of 'dynamic conservatism' – that is a tendency to fight to remain the same.[7]

The idea of corporate *planning* with its emphasis on the need for continuous review of the *effectiveness* of activities in terms of their impact on substantive problems, is posed against these traditional forces. It stresses the importance of learning about what is happening in the environment and adapting to what is learnt. It seeks to identify and anticipate changing needs and problems and to assess the known and likely impact of local authority activities upon these problems. The focus of study is *policy* – its content and the processes by which it is formulated, implemented and evaluated.

There are many models of the policy making (or planning) process and we shall discuss these further in Chapter 10 in relation to theories of public learning. At this point, Figure 5 is presented to provide a picture of a basic policy making process, not because this is the only nor necessarily the best approach to public policy making, but because it illustrates the rational approach which corporate planning has often stood for. There is little need to enlarge on the diagram only to emphasize that the process is continuous and iterative. However, it is important to draw attention to the absence of abstract goals. The starting point in the process is *not* abstract – it is down to earth. It is likely to be an issue which excites current political interest such as an important resource question, or a policy problem arousing community opposition, or a predicted shift in the age groups of the local population. There was an interesting academic debate at the beginning of the 1970s about whether there was a difference between goal-seeking and problem-solving approaches to planning.[8] The debate concluded that there was only a difference of degree. The formulation 'Problem = Goal + Impediment to the Goal' resolved the issue neatly.[9] Whilst advancing no intellectual quarrel with this conclusion, I would argue that practical realities should

Figure 5   A model of the policy making process

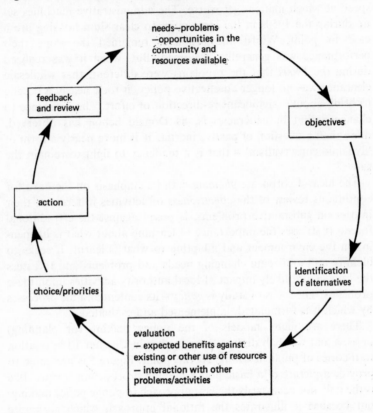

lead us away from a goal oriented approach. The nature of local politics, the kinds of issue which actually excite and motivate people and the changing resource situation are some of the reasons why the starting point of the process should have more immediate relevance. Notice that rejection of a goal oriented approach is in no way a rejection of a purposeful approach to policy making. On the contrary, it is the necessary looseness and vagueness of goals[10] which diminishes *their* relevance to purposeful planning. This has been a major fault with structure planning but corporate planning has also sometimes fallen into this trap.

Corporate planning: American origins and PPBS

Corporate planning was first used in practice by private companies in the United States during the late 1950s.[11] Its origins can be traced back to the strategic war studies of the 1940s which stimulated a growth in various approaches designed to assist in the management of complex systems. These approaches were developed in a number of American business schools but a key role was played by the Rand Corporation which carried out analytical work in the systematic comparison of weapons for the Air Force – and still does. It is not surprising to learn, therefore, that the first public service to experiment with the developing approach to planning and programming was the US Defense Department. Beginning in 1961, Secretary Robert McNamara restructured the whole work of his department to focus all planning and procurement around missions or objectives that cut across the boundaries of the three services and extended beyond the confines of annual budgets. President Johnson was very impressed with this approach and, in 1965, he directed that PPBS (planning-programming-budgeting system) be introduced into all departments of the federal government. In the same year the extremely influential book[12] by David Novick of the Rand Corporation appeared and the approach soon spread into American local government. In Chapter 8 we shall see, for example, that Boston, Dayton and New York all have planning budgetary systems which derive from the PPBS approach.

There is an ample literature on PPBS and its relevance to British local government.[13] In essence, PPBS is an approach which seeks to improve decision making by providing information on the allocation of resources between meaningful sets of existing and proposed activities. It centres on the objectives met by an activity rather than on the department responsible for the activity, on the output from an activity as well as on the resources required by that activity, on the longer term implications of expenditure rather than on a limited time-span, on both revenue and capital expenditure together, and on alternative ways of achieving results. It usually involves the creation of a programme structure which is a budgetary framework within which existing and proposed activities are classified according to their objectives. This structure takes the form of a hierarchy of choices usually of three or four tiers. At each level – programme, sub-programme, activities, elements – it sets out the significant choices for the decision maker. Figure 6 provides a

Figure 6   A simplified programme structure

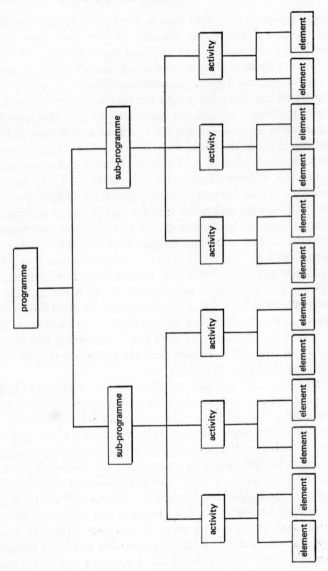

Figure 7 Example of part of a programme structure

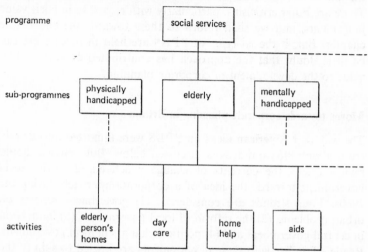

Source: Metropolitan Borough of Stockport, Social Services Position Statement 1973.

simplified illustration of such a hierarchy and Figure 7 provides an example by illustrating part of a programme structure used by the Metropolitan Borough of Stockport. The PPBS approach represented a major step forward from traditional budgeting for it changed the role of the budget. Conventional vote accounting saw the budget simply as a tool for financial control and therefore focussed attention on the authorization of expenditure. PPBS saw the budget as a key decision aid and focusses attention on the results expenditure is designed to achieve.

PPBS has met with considerable criticism.[14] It has been accused of being a mechanistic technique which, even as it struggles to free thinking from departmental blinkers, succeeds in imposing another form of straitjacket on public policy making. Sometimes those involved in implementing PPBS *have* failed to take the longer and larger view with the result that they have become regular budget officers whose main task is putting out fires on a day-to-day basis. It is also true that the high expectations of PPBS have not been fulfilled. Consider this view expressed in 1967: 'The new techniques of PPBS are beginning to be recognised as the greatest advance in the art of government since the introduction nearly a hundred years ago of a civil service based upon competence.'[15] But should PPBS carry the blame for poor implementation or over-extravagant claims? There are other criticisms, particularly with regard to implicit value judgements, and we shall return to these towards the end of the chapter. But, if the *concepts* of PPBS are held in focus there can be little doubt that the approach has contributed a great deal of value to the development of corporate planning.

Moves towards corporate planning in Britain

The way that American ideas on PPBS were imported into Britain from about 1968 onwards is discussed below. But first we should review briefly the currents of change which edged British local government towards the idea of a corporate approach during the 1960s. Four strands are considered: (1) government reports on urban problems, (2) the reform of local government, (3) innovation in central government and (4) political changes in local government. Readers familiar with these developments are invited to skip to the next section.

1   Urban problems

First there was a wave of government publications which began to map some of the inter-relationships between urban problems and to hint at more integrated approaches. In 1963 the Buchanan Report exposed the trade-offs which have to be made between vehicular access, environment and resources.[16] In 1965 the report of the Planning Advisory Group advanced proposals, later implemented by the Town and Country Planning Act 1968, to strengthen the policy content of land use planning.[17] The Denington Report, published in 1966, argued that house improvement should be combined with environmental improvement.[18] The Plowden Report of the following year concluded that the problem of educational deprivation could not be treated separately from the many other problems in the children's social and physical environment.[19] Finally, the Seebohm Report of 1968 stressed that personal social problems could not be viewed in isolation from other urban problems.[20] All of these reports were, of course, relatively restricted by their terms of reference but they each helped to pave the way for more comprehensive approaches.

2 Local government reform

A second movement for change was concerned with the reform of local government beginning in 1957 with the establishment of the Herbert Commission to consider the reorganization of local government in London.[21] This resulted in the London Government Act 1963 which created the Greater London Council and the thirty-two London boroughs. In 1964 the Ministry of Housing and Local Government established two committees – the Maud Committee on management in local government[22] and the Mallaby Committee on staffing.[23] Their reports, published in 1967, were broadly consistent. A striking feature was the way they stressed the need to break down departmental and professional boundaries. The Maud Report outlined many of the features of management structure which were to be popularized five years later by the Bains Committee.[24] For example, it called for a streamlining of committees, management boards of chief officers and a strong head of the officer structure. It even talked of objectives and the preparation of plans to attain them. But these new ideas were curiously neglected, partly because they were not adequately described but partly because, as John Stewart has pointed out, the report stood between two movements – the movement towards administrative efficiency and the movement towards corporate planning.[25] It expressed something of the ideas underlying each but, because it was a turning point, the older ideas were recognized and the newer ideas were ignored.

Meanwhile, once London government had been reorganized, there was pressure to reform the rest of local government. The Redcliffe-Maud Commission[26] was established in 1966 to consider the structure of local government in England and their report, published in 1969, called for the establishment of unitary authorities across the whole country. Part of their reasoning was that services which should be in the hands of one authority were split up among several. In 1970 the Conservative party ousted the Labour government and rejected the Redcliffe-Maud proposals. However, the work of the Commission did stimulate a great deal of fresh thinking about local government and, in particular, the need for it to relate more positively to patterns of living in the community. The Local Government Act 1972 created the more-or-less uniform two-tier system of counties and districts in England which started work on 1 April 1974.[27] In the six main conurbations outside London the relationship between the two tiers is different from the shire counties as the metropolitan districts exercise the majority of local government powers. This division partly explains the relatively high level of corporate planning activity in metropolitan districts and the London boroughs. These authorities are faced with particularly complex urban problems and wield a relatively wide range of local government powers – on both counts the case for a corporate approach is more pressing.

3   Innovation in central government

In the late 1950s there was a growing feeling in central government that expenditure planning was 'constipated' by the annual estimates approach and that it was too closely tied to the yearly cycle of Parliamentary business. In 1959 the Conservative government set up an internal Committee on the Control of Public Expenditure chaired by Lord Plowden.[28] This reported in 1961 and recommended that a committee of officials (the present Public Expenditure Survey Committee) should make regular surveys of public expenditure as a whole over a five-year period, and in relation to prospective resources. From 1961 onwards annual surveys of public expenditure were prepared for ministers along these lines but there were several limitations. For example, initially they only dealt with the first and fifth years, the White Papers were occasional rather than regular and Parliament's own consideration of expenditure continued to be related to the supply estimates for the forthcoming year. In 1968 the Labour government, in the wake of devaluation, took a serious look at controlling the size of public sector spending.[29] This resulted in a major change establishing the current, comprehensive and powerful PESC system which manifests itself to the public in the annual public expenditure White Paper published each winter.[30]

In 1970 the incoming Conservative government brought in two further important innovations. First, it established a small multi-disciplinary central policy review staff (CPRS) in the Cabinet Office.[31] This was to review the government's overall strategy in applying its programme and to undertake specific study projects in almost any area to evaluate the government's policy and possible options available. Some of the CPRS work has been directly concerned with the development of a corporate approach, for example, the proposals for a joint framework for social policies.[32] A second innovation was the introduction of Programme Analysis and Review (PAR). PARs were in-depth studies of departmental programmes designed to assess how effective they were in attaining their objectives.[33] To some extent we have jumped ahead, for PESC, CPRS and PAR all owe a great deal to the concepts of PPBS. But it is also true that the Plowden Committee was pointing the way some time before the influx of American ideas on programme planning.

4 Political change in local government

A fourth strand in the changing climate of ideas was political change in the composition of local councils during the period 1966 to 1972. Large numbers of new members were elected and in some councils party control changed for the first time since the war.

These changes brought onto the councils, or into positions of power, councillors who were less attached to traditional systems of management and more inclined to challenge them. They had not been socialised into the system. The challenge of the councillor to the existing system was part of the driving force to corporate planning.[34]

It is, of course, notoriously difficult to generalize about local politics but a familiar pattern is for local elections to swing against the party in office at Westminster. Thus, the Conservatives did very well in the 1968 local government elections (during the Wilson administration) and in 1972 the swing favoured Labour (during the Heath administration). In both these years, and in those in between, the influx of large numbers of young, enthusiastic councillors did much to unsettle established attitudes and to prepare a political climate where change was more acceptable.

Corporate planning takes off (1967–74)

In the mid-1960s the various moves towards a more purposeful approach to local government policy making lacked an intellectual focus. The gap was filled by the Institute of Local Government Studies (Inlogov) at Birmingham University which has been enormously influential in the development of corporate planning. Since 1967 some 7000 senior local government officers and members have attended various management courses at the Institute. In the early days teaching emphasized the PPBS approach and drew heavily on the latest American ideas. Management consultants provided a second important channel for the dissemination of these new ideas. The studies of McKinsey and Co. Inc. for Liverpool and

Hull and those of Booz-Allen and Hamilton for Islington and Stockport are examples of reports which were widely read and emulated.

Perhaps 1971 marks a turning point from PPBS styles to more emphasis on corporate planning:

There were those who thought PPBS, some having sampled it, had little to offer local government, those who disagreed, and a growing body who felt that some of the principles of PPBS could usefully be developed without necessarily embracing PPBS as a 'total package'. The greater flexibility of approach gave the terms 'corporate planning' and 'corporate management' a common currency in the local government service.[35]

By 1971 the office of chief executive was no longer a rarity and policy committees were not uncommon. Some idea of the growing practical interest in corporate planning is provided by a series of nine articles, published in autumn 1971 by *Municipal Journal*, in which eight chief executives discuss their approaches.[36]

It was in this climate of considerable optimism that the Bains Committee[37] was set up to produce advice for the new local authorities on management structures at both member and officer level. Its report, published in August 1972, was consulted widely by the 'shadow' councils and joint officer groups during 1973. It drew on the 'best' practice of the pioneering authorities and stressed the view that local government is not limited to the narrow provision of a series of services, important as these may be. Rather it has within its purview the overall economic, cultural and physical well-being of the community. The committee argued that, because of this overall responsibility and because of the inter-relationships of problems in the environment, the ingrained departmental approach of traditional local government should give way to a wider-ranging corporate outlook. The Bains recommendations on structures had an astonishing impact. In 1974 every new county council had a Policy Committee, a Principal Officer and a Management Team and almost all district councils followed the same pattern. In more than a few authorities the Bains Report was accepted as a blueprint. This is disturbing for it implies a mechanistic approach paying insufficient attention to local needs, problems and political realities.

Two other management reports paralleled the Bains Report – the 'grey book' on management in the reorganized health service[38] and the Ogden Report on management structures for the new regional water authorities.[39] The McKinsey management consultants assisted in the preparation of the 'grey book' and the report includes recommendations on a coherent management structure and a planning cycle. The Ogden Report believed that the case for corporate management has even greater force in relation to water services than it does for local government[40] and recommended a 'multi-functional multi-disciplinary approach' with chief executives and management teams.

The Bains Report, 'grey book' and Ogden Report were all stronger on structure than on process. It was left to the Paterson Report[41] of 1973 on management of the new local authorities in Scotland to place official emphasis on the corporate planning process, which it saw as the 'whole core' of the authority's activity. The process outlined by Paterson is very similar to that presented in Figure 5. The policy process was also stressed in another government publication of the same year based on research in Sunderland.[42] This outlined a problem-oriented community review process and discussed various approaches to policy analysis. The enforced upheaval of local government reorganization in 1974 created unprecedented opportunities for the introduction of new approaches and the overwhelming majority of the new authorities accepted the need for some form of corporate planning.

Corporate planning in the mid-1970s

Two factors make generalization about recent developments precarious. First, there is a growing diversity of approaches in different authorities and, second, ideas are undergoing radical modifications in response to the changing resource situation. There is a further, and greater danger, and this is to concentrate on documents, techniques, organizational structures and the like whilst neglecting the less tangible, but much more important, areas of attitudes, interpersonal relationships and commitments to new ways of thinking and working. Necessarily, therefore, what follows only provides a brief indication of some of the major trends in recent corporate planning practice.

Position statements

As a first step many authorities have prepared position statements. These vary a great deal but the general idea is to provide an explicit statement of current activities, policies and commitments at a given point in time.[43] As a rule they have been used to describe the current position of programmes and have usually been prepared on a committee by committee basis. However, there are other ways of viewing the world. For example, Stockport has prepared position statements for particular geographical areas within the borough (known as area digests) and these are discussed further in Chapter 8. There are, perhaps, two main reasons for preparing position statements. First, as straightforward information they have a valuable role in clarifying: what the authority is doing, what it is trying to achieve, for whom, by when and where, with what success and at what cost. In many authorities members and officers still don't know the current position. Second, the process of preparing the statements can be more important than the statements themselves. If it is handled in the right way the work of uncovering and assembling the information can educate officers and members alike. Perhaps the main danger is that position statements may be prepared for their own sake with little thought to the way they will be used.

Policy analysis

A second fairly popular way of introducing and/or developing corporate planning is by policy analysis (sometimes referred to as issue analysis). Policy analysis, in the sense used here,[44] might be described as a systematic investigation of a particular policy area probably executed by a small inter-departmental team of officers. The process might, but need not necessarily, follow the pattern shown in Figure 5. It could be a speedy and robust appraisal drawing on readily available information or it could be a deeper study involving more rigorous research over a longer time period. Elected members should determine the issues to be investigated but this has often not been the case in practice. In my experience the selection of the issue is at least as important as the selection of the course of action following completion of the analysis. This is because selection involves choosing all those areas which will *not* be investigated and is, thus, a more significant demonstration of *corporate* priorities than selection of options resulting from a report with particular terms of reference. In a few authorities members have joined with the team of officers carrying out the analysis. There can be serious time-constraints for members involved in work of this kind but it does seem to be an excellent way of involving councillors in the formative stages of policy making. Too often we hear of members complaining in committee meetings that they have been faced with a *fait accompli* prepared by the officers. Indeed, the Bains Report itself has been described as an 'officers' charter' – that it advocates a system which gives more control to the officer and less to the member. Joint discussions on the preparation of policy analysis reports are one way of establishing communication before ideas harden.[45] We shall return to the role of the member later.

Performance review

Elected members have often played a more active role in performance review possibly because the Bains Committee recommended the establishment of a Performance Review Sub-Committee to act as 'a watchdog body . . . with the standing and formal authority to make detailed investigation into any project, department or area of activity'.[46] At the same time it is also true that the Performance Review Sub-Committee is one of the few recommendations of the Bains Report to meet with widespread resistance – 60 per cent of local authorities rejected the idea.[47] Many of those authorities which did establish a sub-committee left it 'in abeyance' for a year or so – to give the new authority time to settle. Even so the precise role(s) of performance review still seemed to provoke a good deal of confusion in many authorities during 1975 and 1976. Most of the work at this time was focussed on efficiency rather than effectiveness. Examples are control of council contracts, use of fuel and light, car allowances etc. However, there have been wider-ranging studies investigating, for example, the multiple use of all local authority premises. With the increasing pressure on resources there would seem to be considerable scope for wider use of the performance review approach. Perhaps the main weakness in work carried out so far is that performance review reports have not been sufficiently penetrating and critical, and this tends to reflect the subservient role of the sub-committees. In a continued 'no-growth' situation the political rewards for improving performance might be expected to increase and we may see the development of more powerful Performance Review Committees.

Annual planning budgetary cycles

In the traditional method of local authority budgeting the time-scale tended to be very short and somewhat 'hit and miss'. Service committees would prepare estimates in the autumn or winter for submission to the rate fixing meeting of council in February or March. By developing more refined annual time-tables some authorities have been able to extend the period for budgetary choice very considerably. One example of an annual planning budgetary cycle, drawn from Stockport, is shown as Figure 25 in Chapter 8.

In this case the corporate plan was for a five-year period and this was rolled forward annually taking into account the various inputs shown – policy analysis reports, performance review reports, community views, forecasts of population, forecasts of resources (finance, manpower, land), the rate support grant settlement and so on. A planning budgetary cycle can act as the linchpin for all planning processes involving expenditure by the authority. Developments of this kind have, however, not been running smoothly. As mentioned in Chapter 1, central government has created a number of difficulties – the level of rate support grant has varied unpredictably, has been announced for a one-year period only and is generally settled too late in the financial year; the loan sanction system has thwarted corporate planning of capital programmes; several types of plan covering different policy areas have been required and some of these, notably land use plans, are weighed down with red tape and so on. But local authorities themselves could be more bold in their efforts to develop an overall policy process. This would seem to be a central task for the Chief Executive and his management team. It could be used as one lever to lift the level of debate in Policy Committees – a title which is in danger of becoming a misnomer in many authorities.

No growth

It's as long ago as December 1974 that the words 'no growth' were used in a government circular discussing local authority expenditure[48] and, in successive years, the pressure to curtail spending has increased. Corporate planning was introduced into British local government at a time of (albeit declining rate of) growth and attention was nearly always focussed on the additional, annual increments of expenditure. The ongoing 'base' of expenditure was rarely challenged. The onset of 'no growth' has had a double-edged effect on corporate planning. On the one hand horizons have tended to narrow, attention has turned to the defence of particular budgets and balanced consideration of local needs, resources and priorities has tended to founder.[49] On the other hand, the case for corporate planning has been strengthened for the times when resources are severely limited are *precisely* the times when rigorous consideration of corporate priorities is most needed. It is easy to be too sweeping, and it is almost certainly true that the next few years will see substantial improvements, but the experience up to 1977 suggests that corporate planning practice is having difficulty in meeting the challenge. Thus, a large amount of top-level time has often been spent on relatively minor aspects of policy. For example, many authorities developed highly centralized control systems for the filling of vacancies with Chief Executives, Council Leaders and Personnel Committee Chairman scrutinizing every post. There *have* to be better ways of operating a manpower policy. Besides, there are many much more fundamental aspects of policy which require re-thinking if the response to no growth is to permit the continued, creative development of local government. In particular there is considerable scope for transfer of resources (finance, manpower, buildings) from marginal to high priority uses.

A critique of corporate planning in practice

We have now scanned the origins and evolution of corporate planning in British local government. Its main strengths and some of its shortcomings have been touched on. The intention now is to offer a series of specific criticisms of corporate planning in practice. As the quotation from Machiavelli at the beginning of this chapter implies, it is not difficult to attack a new set of ideas particularly if they have had relatively little time to find their feet. Rather than pick and complain, the commentary which follows, whilst it hinges on weaknesses, tries to hint at avenues which could be explored with a view to improving corporate planning.

Mechanistic emphasis

Much of corporate planning practice has been mechanistic. There has been too much emphasis on structural change and the introduction of new procedures all of which may create the impression but not necessarily the *reality* of corporate planning. It is, perhaps, unfair to single out one document to illustrate this point but the PA Management Consultants report[50] on introducing corporate planning into local government was widely acclaimed when it appeared in 1975 and, presumably, reflects aspirations of that time fairly well. This report was virtually an instruction manual spelling out the 'correct' steps to be taken, such as, 'The first step is a position statement' and actually set down 'rules' for policy planning. The Bains Report, through no fault of its own, has also sometimes been used almost word for word as a recipe book for corporate planning. This, of course, is the very reversal of the learning approach which corporate planning stands for.

Perhaps there are three sets of questions which an authority can consider as a means of moving away from or avoiding a mechanistic emphasis. First, how well does their approach stand up to uncertainty? Do changes in the environment, such as a reduced rate support grant settlement, send corporate planning principles to the wall or is there sufficient commitment and elasticity to cope with changes of this kind? Second, how far does their approach ensure implementation and follow-through of corporate policy? Is implementation a mysterious process of sales and persuasion or is there (also!) an *effective* monitoring system which discloses and explains deviations from policy? Third, just what is the *content* of council policy? How far is corporate planning actually forming and developing what actually gets done by the council?

Centralization

Much of corporate planning activity 'has been built *at* the centre of the authority *by* the centre. But there is much that cannot be learnt at the centre of the organization. The centre finds it easier to handle the hard data of statistics than the softer data of opinion.'[51] In formal terms we might conceive of the 'centre' as the Policy and Resources Committee, the Chief Officer's Management Team and, perhaps, parts of the Chief Executive's, Finance and Administration Departments. But the centre of the authority is more complicated than this and may be more informally described as those who feel themselves to be 'in the know'[52] – those who are abreast of the subtleties of the developing ideas and scheme of things. Those members and officers at the 'centre' are likely to approve of the changes taking place but what about the others – the back bench members and the great majority of officers? Those on the 'periphery' may not be hostile but there is every chance that they will be unenthusiastic and lack commitment to the new ideas. This is often *not* the fault of the ideas but the way they have been introduced and put into practice as an exclusively central initiative.

There is a genuine dilemma here. Having worked as a 'corporate planner' in a Chief Executive's Department for two years I can safely say that such a job description is a serious misnomer. It helps to create the illusion that corporate planning is, somehow, carried out by appointed individuals working somewhere in the centre of the authority. The establishment of large corporate or programme planning units in some authorities has done nothing to dispel this illusion. But it is too easy to criticize corporate planners in this vein. Despite the drawbacks I feel that there may well be a role for a *small* unit in many authorities. It should not be asked to dictate the central line but should be used as a lever to help release the creative potential which rests within every department. The accent would be less on central co-ordination and more on helping to build new networks and linkages to create new opportunities for learning and action. This approach, to borrow terms from community work, would seek to *enable* not to impose. The need for new networks of communication cutting across lines of formal responsibility is growing so that the case for individuals – contacts, fixers, reticulists,[53] call them what you like – who work to promote the development of such networks gathers force.

Redirecting the efforts of 'corporate planners' is one way of reducing the centre–periphery split but much more than this is needed. Corporate working needs to be built at a number of different levels within the authority in a way reflecting the problems facing the authority. Mention has been made of policy analysis and the way that members (why not back benchers?) could be involved from the outset. The next chapter discusses area approaches and the idea of involving ward members and local area-based officers in new forms of area management. Some authorities have had most success in developing joint working in relation to particular projects.[54] The opportunities are legion and the surface has only just been scratched.

Collaboration

Developments in inter-corporate planning between public authorities – between counties, districts, area health authorities, regional water authorities, regional branches of central government – have moved at a pedestrian pace. There have, of course, been some formal linkages and there has been some day-to-day contact in relation to particular cases or issues. For example, there are joint committees which bring together local authorities and area health authorities

serving the same area, and there is often a good, working relationship between health service personnel and social service departments.
But, given the interdependence between the problems public
authorities set out to tackle, the lack of progress on collaborative or
'community' planning (i.e. joint planning of all government services)
is surprising. [55] At a very basic level it is, for example, still not difficult
to find situations where local authority and health authority staff are
busily preparing population projections for the same area in total
ignorance of each other's efforts.

Some authorities have been a little more adventurous than others
in developing inter-corporate planning and perhaps Stockport is
one of these. For example, in 1974 the authority established a
project group of officers, including representatives of the area health
authority and voluntary service, to investigate the needs of the
elderly in Stockport and to develop policies accordingly. The group
shared information about services and resources, and conceived and
executed a comprehensive research project to survey local needs.
The strategy for the elderly published in March 1976[56] included
many proposals involving ongoing co-operation between the parties
involved, such as a joint nursing home and transfers of resources
between services. Meanwhile, arrangements were made for the
local authority to provide a research and intelligence service to the
area health authority and the stage has now been reached where the
work of all the health care planning teams is closely linked with
policy planning in the local authority.

The arrangements for joint financing announced in 1976[57] are
encouraging but much remains to be done. At one level there is a
case for much more systematic training of public authority personnel (including local authority members) in the work of the *other*
authorities affecting their area. This could be complemented by
loan, secondment or transfer of staff between authorities to build
mutual understanding of shared problems. At another level local
authorities would do well to consider John Stewart's notion of an
'assertive authority'.[58] He believes that the local authority has the
right to assert itself as the main agency of city government elected
by the people of that city and backed by a political process centring
on city issues. An assertive authority would, *inter alia*, debate
health service and water policies and would expect its representatives
to follow its policies.

So far we have discussed collaboration in terms of joint planning
between public authorities. But the local authority also needs to

consider much more positively how its policies relate to action in the private sector. For too long local government has left economic planning and management solely to the central government when there is a vitally important local dimension particularly in declining areas such as the inner areas of our major cities. Where are the policy analysis reports on housing which have really understood and sought to influence the detailed lending policies of local building societies? Where are the working groups on local employment policy which include representatives of local employers and trade unions? Why is local government shareholding in private companies only being pioneered by a handful of local authorities when it holds out such promise for ensuring implementation of local employment policies? The list of possibilities for a much more outward and enterprising approach by local government is long. Corporate planning has tended to stress the internal management of the authority. It could also be leading the way in exploring new avenues of influence to improve local living conditions and opportunities.

Values

Much of corporate planning practice has played down values and the expression of values through political argument. Possibly because of its business origins corporate planning has stressed the managerial and technical aspects of local government policy making and some elected members have expressed a marked disenchantment with what they see as a professionalization of the political arena.[59] Too often, however, the debate has been couched in terms of management versus politics when, of course, local government must consist of both. The answer is not to attack the idea of corporate planning but to seek new directions for its application which strengthen rather than emasculate the political process. This means that corporate planning must positively recognize the differences in society – the variability of needs, the plurality of objectives, and the conflicts of interest between different sub-groups of the population. All too often the corporate planning policy process has been used to conceal rather than expose the very real political choices which local councillors have to make.

This criticism demands elaboration. At almost every stage of the policy process (see Figure 5) corporate planning practice has failed to be sufficiently discriminating.[60] Thus, the definition of *needs* is usually very crude.[61] Measures often used are population, de-

P.P.A.L.G.—C

partmental records and professional judgements and these all have a part to play. But we need to know more about the *intensity* of needs to give depth to the broad brush illustrations of the *extent* of need. Needs information should not be reduced to overall rates per 1000 population (or whatever) but should present the needs of different geographical areas and client groups so that the political discussion about priorities between competing claims on resources is enhanced. Moving on to *objectives* we again find whole batteries of expressions of intent which are totally sterilized of politics. Any hint of conflict has been removed for who could disagree with statements like 'the council's objective is to provide adequate leisure facilities for the needs of the population'? As John Stewart has observed, objectives pitched at this level of abstraction neither help nor hinder, they neither divide nor unite.[62] Often objectives of this kind have been written by officers and rubber-stamped by members and the all-important debate about values is the casualty. Identifying and evaluating *alternatives* is also manifestly a political activity. But alternatives usually pass through a screening process (often unconscious) in which professional presuppositions and value judgements may reduce the scope of possibilities considerably. In relation to *priorities* there seems to be a general awareness that this *is* a stage requiring political decision but the way possible key issues and priorities are often presented is in terms of broad 'packages' or programmes. There is little or no attempt to suggest who would gain and who would lose. Lastly, we should mention *outputs*. Corporate planning practice aspires to measure policy in terms of output rather than input. But the problem is not simply one of measurement – a more fundamental question is 'outputs for whom'? Given the differences in society the search must be for measures of the differential outputs for different sections of the public. This is not a far-off dream way beyond our technical competence. Many important factors are quantifiable once questions relating to distribution are posed.[63] We can see, then, that each stage of the policy process has, in practice, tended to ignore distributional aspects. It is hardly surprising, therefore, that corporate planning has not been noteworthy for its impact on urban deprivation and other major social issues.

None of this should be taken to be an attack on the *idea* of corporate planning. On the contrary, the great promise of corporate planning is that it can be used to strengthen the local political process. It is the councillor's strongest weapon against the old 'carrying on the same way as we did last year' disease of traditional administration. But the councillor's role needs to be strengthened. He needs better support services, not only secretarial help and more relevant information but also analytical assistance. This latter could, perhaps, be provided by corporate planners. He may also need improved pay and, certainly, a change from the current system of allowances which was rejected as a sensible system as long ago as 1967 by the Maud Committee on Management. But above all, he needs to become involved in the policy making process at a much earlier stage. There is a growing body of evidence which shows that decisions (or non-decisions) are actually made long before the supposedly all-important committee meeting.[64] Commitment to a particular course of action is generated in a complex way over a long period to the point where switching from the preferred alternative involves a whole range of penalties.[65] We need to experiment with a number of different ways of involving the member in the policy/management process. This does not just mean chairmen being 'allowed' to attend the chief officer's management team. It means members and officers getting together, in a variety of ways, and positively sharing ideas on policy making. Of course, there will be conflict but there should be less misunderstanding and mutual distrust.

Learning to learn

Corporate planning has not all been consensual. It has, in particular, involved conflict with traditional methods and the dynamic conservatism mentioned early on in the chapter has employed a number of strategies to resist change.[66] The obvious ones are: ignore it, counter-attack it, contain and isolate it. But a more subtle, and probably more widespread response, has been to absorb it – to de-fuse, dilute and re-direct the energies originally directed towards change. Donald Schon has described this process as 'the governmental bureaucracies' magnificent semi-conscious system for the long-term wearing down of agents of change'.[67] The perfect piece of co-option occurs without the change agent realizing anything has happened. Examples are difficult to quote for absorption is difficult for the insider, let alone the outsider, to perceive. Lord Crowther-Hunt, for example, believes that the Central Policy Review Staff has been virtually absorbed by the Whitehall machine and this is, presumably, based on his experience as a Minister of State.[68] No doubt there are differing views on this. However, most of those who have worked in local and central government will know of promising initiatives which they feel never quite delivered the hoped-for goods. We need to ask why?

Part of the explanation will almost certainly be specific to the particular situation – one or two personalities may have been critical, the timing may have been wrong, an incident may have shifted the political focus and so on. But perhaps there are deeper reasons. Perhaps we have paid insufficient attention to dynamic conservatism and the realities of bringing about change. Perhaps the rational approach, even when coupled with good inter-personal relationships, is not enough to develop a learning organization. Donald Schon believes that recognition of dynamic conservatism explodes the 'rational myth' of intervention which sees social change as a process made up of analysis of objectives, examination of alternatives, and selection of the most promising routes to change. He argues for a complete change of gear in our ideas about public learning:

We must become able not only to transform our institutions, in response to changing situations and requirements; we must invent and develop institutions which are 'learning systems', that is to say, capable of bringing about their own continuing transformation.[69]

The movement towards learning systems of this kind is, inescapably, a tentative and inductive process. Progress is likely to be slow and break-throughs could come from any quarter – quite possibly from sources entirely independent of corporate planning. This idea of learning to learn is taken up again in Chapter 10. The issue is raised specifically at this point for I believe it has profound implications for corporate planning and local government. It is a question which transcends political ideologies for socialist countries are faced with the same problem of developing public service bureaucracies which are sensitive to changing community needs and capable of continuously adapting their own ideas and behaviour. It is no accident that much of the rest of this book is concerned with localized area approaches, for increased delegation to neighbourhoods holds out much promise for developing more humane governmental arrangements which are capable of directing their own self-transformation. But, in a complex industrial society, decentralization and delegation are not enough. We need to learn about learning at all levels of government. Proponents of corporate planning could be in the vanguard.

Conclusion

The introduction of various approaches to corporate planning and management has been a major force in the development of a learning local government. Corporate planning has improved understanding of the inter-relationships of problems in the environment and has stimulated new forms of inter-departmental response. Building on the concepts of PPBS, corporate planning has helped to shift the role of the local authority budget. It is now much less likely to be seen as simply a tool of financial control, for its additional potential, as a key decision aid focussing attention on the results expenditure is designed to achieve, is now widely appreciated. In the mid-1970s almost all local authorities aspired to some form of corporate planning but there are signs of a backlash. Some of the criticisms are undoubtedly misguided as, for example, those put forward by some 'head-in-the-sand' departmentalists who seem to be incapable of taking a wider view or of recognizing the need for change. But, as with all new movements, corporate planning practice *has* made mistakes and needs to learn from them.

In this review it has been suggested that corporate planning practice has often been too mechanistic and too centralized. It has been too concerned with the internal management of the authority and should direct more attention to collaboration with other agencies having an impact on the area. Perhaps most fundamental, it has played down the role of values in the policy process. This could be rectified by paying much more attention to the distributional aspects of policy. By exposing who gains and who loses the *political* process would be strengthened rather than emasculated. There are no insuperable technical barriers to the development of distributional policy planning once the questions are posed. Lastly, and perhaps most intellectually challenging, are questions relating to how we proceed once we recognize the limits of rational approaches to policy making. The whole idea of developing local government institutions which are 'learning systems', that is to say capable of bringing about their own continuing transformation, is wide open and break-throughs could come from any quarter. One set of ideas which holds out exciting possibilities revolve around approaches which take the local area or neighbourhood as their starting point and we explore these ideas in the next chapter.

3 Area approaches

And we are here as on a darkling plain
Swept with confused alarms of struggle and flight
Where ignorant armies clash by night.

Matthew Arnold, *Dover Beach*

Introduction

The aims of bringing local government closer to the people and of adjusting action more carefully to the needs of particular geographical areas within the local authority have a wide appeal. But the current outlook for area approaches does not seem to be very promising. The last chapter touched on some of the forces which tend to work against area approaches: the growing centralization of political and management decision taking within local authorities, the continued dominance of functional (or service) perspectives in patterns of thinking about urban problems and the narrowing of horizons resulting from the need to reduce public expenditure. In addition, there has been fairly widespread experiment with various forms of area approach in both Britain and America since the early 1960s and many feel that the results have been disappointing.[1]

The current danger is that the whole idea of area-based approaches to policy making and management may become discredited in advance of any overall, systematic evaluation of its usefulness. This would be a particularly retrograde step when recent theoretical and practical developments are beginning to close the gap between spatial and social perspectives on urban problems. David Harvey, for example, has argued convincingly that social processes *are* spatial and that we must, therefore, harmonize and integrate social and spatial policies for dealing with city problems or else continue to create contradictory strategies.[2]

The starting point for this chapter is the confusion which surrounds the consideration of area approaches. The aim is to show how this confusion has grown up and try to penetrate this confusion by focussing on the motivations which underlie various area approaches. Attention is concentrated on the British situation but some of the points also hold for American experience. The chapter introduces a number of themes which will recur in the discussion of various area approaches later in the book.

Some definitions

At the beginning of a discussion clarification of terms can be tiresome, but we cannot proceed much further without some attempt being made to define what is meant by area approaches. Such approaches differ between local authorities, between neighbourhoods and between services, and they change over time as objectives and methods are modified in the light of ongoing experience. In these circumstances attempts to provide an overall definition of area approaches are in danger of generalizing too broadly and the following is therefore advanced strictly as *a preliminary definition*:

Area approaches involve gearing the planning and/or management of policies to the needs of particular geographical areas within the local authority and may involve delegating administrative and/or political responsibility for at least part of this work to the local level.

It is important to draw attention to the two 'and/or' phrases. The first points up the linkage between area planning and area management which are opposite sides of the same coin. The word 'planning' in this context is not restricted to land use planning and includes all policy preparation which will affect an area. Too often planning (or policy design) and implementation are seen as two distinct and entirely separate activities. This blinds planners to the political and inter-personal intricacies of implementation and accounts for much planning disillusion. We all know of paper plans destined to gather dust rather than commitment. It also blinds managers and service providers to the relevance of at least part of their work for policy making. Thus, much of the literature on neighbourhood decentralization focusses on questions of service delivery and often fails to recognize the potential of area management for policy learning. Jeffrey Pressman and Aaron Wildavsky in their excellent book *Implementation* could have been writing about British local government:

The great problem as we understand it, is to make the difficulties of implementation a part of the initial formulation of policy. Implementation must not be conceived as a process that takes place after, and independent of, the design of policy. Means and ends can be brought into somewhat closer correspondence only by making each partially dependent on the other.[3]

The preliminary definition therefore deliberately leaves scope for strengthening the bond between area planning and area management.

The second 'and/or' phrase links administrative and political responsibility and permits broadening of the concept of decentralization beyond management delegation to include moves up to and including devolution of some control to another agency or body. Here it is important to clarify the overlapping meanings of decentralization, delegation and devolution at least insofar as they are used in discussions about local government practice.[4] *Decentralization* has two meanings. It is sometimes used to refer purely to the physical dispersal of operations to local offices. In a second sense it is used to refer to the delegation of a greater degree of decision making authority to those officers whose work concerns particular areas. These officers may or may not operate out of local offices. Where they do the two meanings of decentralization are combined. *Delegation* also has two meanings. First, delegation can mean entrusting a greater degree of decision making authority to lower levels within the administrative system. This overlaps with the second meaning of decentralization. Second, delegation can be used to refer to changes in decision making authority within the political system as when authority for certain decisions is delegated to an area committee of councillors. This overlaps to some extent with the idea of *devolution* which involves a transfer of authority to a body which may or may not be separate from the local authority. For simplicity the discussion of these three concepts has been couched in terms of the distribution of *authority*, i.e. the ability to take action without prior confirmation from a higher level. But we also need to consider these concepts in terms of the distribution of *influence*, i.e. the ability to exert leverage on decisions affecting the area. In practice we shall see that most of the area approaches which shift power to the local level have done so by means of decentralization/delegation/devolution of influence rather than authority.

Figure 8 provides a simplified summary of the overlaps between these three concepts. It shows how delegation does not convey the totality of what is sometimes meant by decentralization and devolution. But it also shows that delegation is the more central of the

Figure 8   Decentralization, delegation and devolution

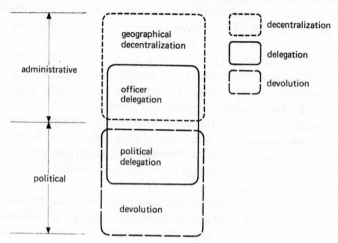

Figure 9   Examples of decentralization, delegation and devolution

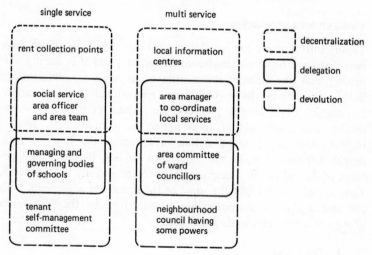

three concepts and that it straddles the administrative and political spheres. This is why delegation is used in the preliminary definition of area approaches given above. Decentralization, delegation and devolution can be used to describe situations within a particular service or situations which involve a corporate or inter-corporate approach. Figure 9 provides illustrations of single service and multi-service situations and, by pointing to concrete examples, should also help to clarify the differences between the three concepts. In general, the usage in this book attempts to distinguish between these three concepts but this is not always appropriate. Sometimes it would be unnecessarily cumbersome and sometimes reference is made to the work of other writers who have used these terms in slightly different ways.

It now emerges that the second 'and/or' phrase in the preliminary definition is at least as important as the first. Clearly administrative delegation, without the legitimacy provided by parallel political devolution can only go so far from the straight and narrow path set down by central direction. In closing this brief discussion of some definitions no claim is made that the review has been exhaustive. The aim has been merely to supply a point of reference from which we can venture into the ongoing debate about area approaches.

Views on area approaches

Taking into account the bewildering variety of policies which have been focussed on neighbourhoods in recent years it is hardly surprising that the debate about area approaches is confused. In Britain initiatives have included: educational priority areas, community development projects, the urban programme, social service area teams, action areas under the planning acts, general improvement and housing action areas under the housing acts, neighbourhood councils, the inner area studies, the area management trials and so on. These are discussed more fully in Chapter 5. Here the aim is to highlight some of the dominant arguments both for and against area approaches as perceived by the four main groups of actors involved. These are:

1   The public
2   Councillors
3   Officers
4   Central government

The discussion which follows involves a drastic simplification of the debate. The point, however, is to show that *despite* such simplification there remains a confusion of different expectations and fears about area approaches.

1   The public

Community pressure for a more open and effective approach to planning and management in local government is persistent. Since the late 1960s residents' action groups, amenity societies and other local pressure groups have become increasingly effective in demanding a say in the preparation of policies which affect their area.[5] This has led some community activists to call for neighbourhood control. George Clark, for example, believes that it is absolutely vital that local autonomy at the neighbourhood level should have statutory recognition and be the starting point for all policies right up to the national level.[6] Apart from group pressure members of the public as individual consumers have come to expect higher standards of service delivery and are more ready to complain if service performance is unsatisfactory. This is particularly so following the steep rate increase of the mid-1970s which raised public consciousness about local government spending.

Various innovations with area planning and decentralized administration can, therefore, be seen as a response to public pressure both for more participation in decision making and for more efficient service delivery. At the same time it should be recognized that area innovations will not receive an unconditional public welcome. For example, an area planning process which distracts attention from the arenas where critical policy decisions affecting the area are really made will assuage few community groups. Likewise, area information centres issuing all kinds of glossy leaflets about services but with a low capacity to actually assist visitors, are unlikely to satisfy demands for more convenient and attentive service delivery.

2   Councillors

The rise of so-called community politics points to the weakness of existing representative structures, and to the decline of local political parties as a means of channelling and articulating public demands.[7] Many local councillors have found that the reorganization of local government into larger administrative units has exacerbated this trend by requiring them to represent perhaps twice as many people as a pre-reorganization councillor.[8] Some, therefore, see new forms of area planning and management as a means of strengthening their constituency role by providing better area information, a forum for discussion with neighbourhood groups and quicker redress in relation to complaints about service delivery.[9] They value across the board area committees for they enable the ward councillor to raise items of local detail, a practice usually frowned on in service committees, and allow him to tackle any aspect of council policy which affects his area. The area committee can also be used to monitor the performance of the council with members being able to draw directly on their own local knowledge and day-to-day experience of the actual impact of council policies and services. The countervailing view voiced by some councillors is that area management has a number of drawbacks. Some believe it would foster parochial thinking. Some are anxious about the role of area committees which have a different political complexion from that of the council as a whole. Others feel that if area committees are added to an existing structure of service committees the burden on the councillor's limited time is likely to be too great.

A quite different political perspective on area approaches revolves around the question of positive discrimination. All the leading political parties subscribe in some degree to the idea of focussing powers and/or resources onto particular geographical areas to sharpen the attack on particular problems or issues. However, depending on the issue involved, there are naturally significant differences of opinion as to the extent of redistribution which should be attempted by means of area approaches. This does not simply consist of a straightforward difference between the political left and right for there are those on the left who argue against redistribution between areas preferring redistribution between groups of the population.

3   Officers

The views of local government officers on area approaches are particularly complicated. This is quite natural for the major responsibility for implementing area approaches, whatever their form, falls to the officers and, over the years, they have built up a wealth of experience of certain kinds of area approach, particularly statutory area approaches (e.g. general improvement areas, conservation areas, etc.) and within-service area organization (e.g. administrative structures within social services and housing departments which are based on delegation of authority to area officers). Besides, 'the officers' can hardly be regarded as a monolithic group because of wide differences in training, status, perspectives on the nature of local government, expectations brought to the job and so on. Given these complexities it is only possible to touch on some of the differing viewpoints.

Some officers see opportunities in various area approaches for improving local government effectiveness. In a time of extreme financial restraint they feel savings can be made by avoiding wasteful uniform policies and prefer to tune policies, budgets and workloads to the needs of different areas. A number of chief officers find maximum delegation of decision making to area level relieves them from 'information overload' and frees them to devote more time and energy to questions of major policy. Others, since they are held accountable for all departmental decisions, prefer to retain a high degree of centralized control and feel that multiservice area-management merely distracts from the departmental job of providing professional services.

Officers working at the local level are particularly aware of the fragmentation of the local authority's approach to particular areas and clients and the job frustrations which ensue. It is often the younger area staff who are pressing for the integration of local policy making on a corporate basis or for the development of inter-divisional co-ordination of service delivery at the area level by, for example, setting up 'one-stop shops' providing several services at one point. It is also here, at the periphery of the organization, where area approaches are most likely to be viewed as a community development strategy seeking to promote partnership between the local authority, other agencies such as the health authority, voluntary groups and local people in either meeting needs directly or in seeking to redirect available resources.

4   Central government

Whilst the prototypes of many area approaches have been developed by local government, central government has played a major role in taking up and developing these ideas and securing their wider application. The sharpening of the impact of policy on particular problems has been an important driving force behind many of the area approaches promoted by legislation, with an important secondary feature being the necessity of safeguarding the rights of the individual. Many of the statutory area approaches (e.g. local plans under the Town and Country Planning Act, smoke control areas under the Clean Air Act and so on) involve adherence by local authorites to precise procedures set out in various statutory instruments and regulations. At its best central government's concern for legal due process in the application of area approaches is a valuable safeguard. Sometimes, however, it seems that central government (and local government for that matter) loses sight of the objectives of a given area approach and comes to see adherence to procedures and the use of particular policy instruments as ends in themselves.

A fairly dominant theme in less legalistic central government initiatives has been the view that area approaches could play a significant role in tackling urban deprivation. This idea, not un-influenced by the American urban programme as we shall see, took root in the mid-1960s with developments such as educational priority areas, social service area teams and community development projects (all considered further in Chapter 5). This accent on tackling urban deprivation, particularly in inner cities, has continued as a dominant feature in area approaches promoted by central govern-ment in the 1970s but with an added emphasis on a corporate approach to these areas. Thus, the inner area studies launched in 1972 were to develop a 'total approach' to urban problems[10] and the Housing Act 1974 also sought to direct co-ordinated action towards particular areas: 'The provisions of the 1974 Act for housing action areas and priority neighbourhoods strengthen the hand of authorities needing to tackle, more effectively than hitherto, those areas of stress where progress depends upon a determined concentration of effort. This area approach, integrated with other programmes designed to meet various social needs, is central to the Government's policies.'[11] The accent on tackling urban deprivation is an important feature of the current series of trials designed to test out the concept of area management: 'The Government believes that area management in one form or another has an important part to play in the implementation of its urban strategy, and par-ticularly in the attack on urban deprivation.'[12] However, central government views on the role of area approaches in tackling urban deprivation are shifting. There is an increasing emphasis on revitalizing the economic base of declining areas, notably inner city areas, and there is a growing recognition that area approaches should be viewed as an integral part of a wider social strategy against inequality.

Penetrating the confusion

No doubt this short summary has omitted a number of important viewpoints. But this need not concern us unduly for it has already revealed a complex pattern of expectations, hopes and anxieties. The task now is to penetrate this confusion by separating out three overlapping yet distinct objectives of area approaches:

1 Effectiveness – what gets done.
2 Distribution – who benefits.
3 Accountability – who decides.

Each of these objectives is now discussed together with a fourth factor: the geography of area approaches. Taken together these four factors provide a basic checklist for most of the questions that need to be asked about area approaches. Any attempt to impose some kind of order on such a complex subject runs the risk of over-simplifying and of placing insufficient emphasis on the inter-connections between the factors. These limitations are acknowledged at the outset. The following is intended purely as a starting point from which more sophisticated and developed schemes for under-standing area approaches will hopefully emerge.

1   Effectiveness

This is a relatively neutral objective and includes those attributes of an area approach which are designed to relate action more closely to neighbourhood needs, other than by the conscious redistribution of resources. Effectiveness can be improved by changes in responsiveness, service delivery and other actors' behaviour in relation to the area. These three methods overlap but are considered separately. *Responsiveness* is concerned with taking account of the diverse needs of different areas in the planning and review of services and in the allocation of resources. Examples of the way an area approach might improve responsiveness are: better information on area needs by, say, the regular presentation of socio-economic indicators for each neighbourhood, a corporate or inter-corporate approach to planning services for the area which recognizes the inter-connections between problems in the area, and innovation in individual areas on an experimental basis to generate new ideas on how to meet needs. Ways in which an area approach might improve *service delivery* include: the provision of decentralized area offices to ease public access to services, the development of 'one-stop' shops which can provide assistance with a range of services at one point, improved service co-ordination by the establishment of stronger inter-divisional links locally, and increased delegation of authority to local officials. Examples of action designed to form a partnership with *other actors* are: joining with neighbourhood volunteers to provide local services, co-operation with a housing association to facilitate the renovation of property in a housing action area, and working with building societies to ensure that restrictive lending policies do not become a self-fulfilling feature of neighbourhood decline.

The effectiveness objective in concentrating on what actually happens asks: What are the problems and opportunities in this area? How do they inter-relate? What causes them? What are we currently doing? With what effect? What are we trying to achieve? Are there better or cheaper ways? How can these be implemented?

2   Distribution

This objective overlaps with effectiveness. Indeed it can be argued that all three approaches to improving effectiveness will have distributional effects even if these are rarely recognized. However, it is important to consider distribution as a separate factor partly because it is too often ignored and partly because it shifts the focus away from managerial and towards political considerations. The distribution between groups and areas of the costs and benefits resulting from action by the local authority and other agencies lies at the heart of the local political process. The area dimension is, of course, only one way of considering distributional effects but it is also one that has been seriously neglected. In relation to distribution perhaps three main levels of area approach can be distinguished: no discrimination, limited discrimination, significant discrimination. Discrimination is used here in a positive sense and refers to the degree to which resources, both public and private, are distributed in favour of deprived neighbourhoods. *No discrimination*, then, ignores the distributive consequences of the vast majority of policies. This can work to the serious disadvantage of deprived neighbourhoods. A classic example is provided by much urban renewal of the 1950s and 1960s in Britain and America which focussed resources on particular areas in a way which often worked against the interests of poor residents. Less widely recognized, and arguably of more concern, are uniform policies of provision which conceal wide variations in actual results because of the variation in needs and take-up rates between areas. Examples are grants for further education and usage of library facilities. Area approaches involving *limited discrimination* seek to funnel at least some additional resources and energy into deprived areas as for example, in educational priority areas and housing action areas. *Significant discrimination* occurs when the distributive effect of policies is seen as a major factor in planning and management. Examples of area approaches of this kind are area resource analysis, which seeks to disaggregate public expenditure to neighbourhoods, and the development of area budgets which try to relate resource allocation to the scale of local needs.

The distributive objective asks: What are the relative needs of different areas and groups? What is the actual result of the current allocation of effort and resources? Who gains and who loses? How can a more equitable distribution of resources be brought about?

3 Accountability

This objective is concerned with the degree to which an area approach devolves responsibility and power to the local level. There are significant gradations of citizen participation reflecting the increasing degree of local autonomy. Douglas Yates ranks seven elements of decentralization as follows: (a) stationing officials in localities to find out what is going on in the field; (b) seeking out opinions of local people; (c) making local people administrative agents; (d) establishing elected officials at the local level as representatives of local interests; (e) making neighbourhood administrators accountable to local citizens; (f) giving localities control over policy and programmes; (g) giving localities control over fiscal resources.[13] A similar widely cited scale of participation levels is the ladder of citizen participation developed by Sherry Arnstein[14] and Alan Altshuler also refers to community control as a continuum rather than as an absolute.[15] The notion of participation ranging from minimal to significant levels of citizen control is helpful and moves forward from earlier arguments which treated public participation as something to be either accepted or rejected. But all these writers are American and there is a need to adapt the scalar model of local accountability to British local government by introducing the role of the local councillor. Some of the more recent area approaches, and particularly those concerned with corporate management at the area level, seek to strengthen the councillor's constituency role by various degrees of delegation to ward members. These range roughly along the scale suggested by Yates from better information to fiscal control. This kind of area approach challenges the view that the political party in power is somehow a monolithic embodiment of the political will. It recognizes that, whilst councillors might strive for party unity on questions of overall policy, they are different individuals representing different wards having different local priorities.

Seen in this light the scalar model of local accountability can be applied to both members of the public and to the local councillor's constituency role. With simplicity in mind, area approaches with three degrees of local accountability can be distinguished. First, a *negligible* degree is where the local councillor and members of the public have no formal role. Examples of area approaches of this kind are administrative decentralization and policies focussed on areas on the basis of professional assessment of need, such as density controls or frequency of police patrols. A *moderate* degree of local accountability occurs when the local councillor and members of the public have an indirect role. Examples are the wide variety of consultation procedures developed in recent years in relation to local planning, general improvement areas and so on. The key feature is a two-way flow of information in advance of changes but the local input remains advisory. A *significant* degree of local accountability is when some formal responsibility and power is transferred to the local level. Examples include delegation of some expenditure decisions to area committees of local councillors and devolution of certain aspects of management policy to joint council/ tenant committees for housing estates.

The accountability objective asks: What is being delegated? How does this affect central–local power relations? Whose influence grows? Who decides what?

4   Geography

It is important to draw attention to the surprisingly neglected geographical dimension of area approaches. Much confusion has been caused by a failure to clarify, first the size of area referred to, second whether the approach relates to particular areas or applies to the whole of the authority, third, how the boundaries of the areas were defined. First, the *size of the area* is critical. Some area approaches may relate to only a few streets (e.g. a general improvement area under the Housing Act could have a population of less than 100 people) whilst others may relate to large sections of a city (e.g. social service area teams might serve a population of between 50 000 and 100 000 people). Second, there is a marked difference between the *selective or blanket* approach, the former implying some form of special treatment whilst the latter implies a standardized way of dealing with all areas of the authority. Finally, the *definition of boundaries* may be related to a variety of criteria including: public perceptions of neighbourhoods, the administrative desire to bring about coterminality of different service areas, the relationship to electoral boundaries to clarify political accountability, the incidence of physical, social and economic indicators of community well-being and so on.

The geographical dimension asks: How many areas? How big are they? Is the whole authority covered? How were the areas chosen and the boundaries defined?

Having separated out four key aspects of area approaches it is important to stress again the need to take account of their inter-relationships. Two examples of widely cited urban problems will suffice to demonstrate this point. First, the alienation of the public from local government continues to cause a great deal of concern. This is, of course, an extremely complex issue which raises a string of questions about remoteness, distrust, dissatisfaction, hostility, powerlessness and so on. In considering whether area approaches may be able to reduce alienation it is immediately apparent that all four factors – effectiveness, distribution, accountability, geography – could be involved.[16] A second example is provided by urban deprivation. In considering how area approaches can assist in any attack on this problem one is again faced with complex inter-relationships between all four factors. And that is not all for it is also

Figure 10   Aspects of area approaches

effectiveness	responsiveness service delivery other actors
distribution	no discrimination limited discrimination significant discrimination
accountability	negligible degree moderate degree significant degree
geography	size of area selective or blanket coverage definition of boundaries

essential to understand the relationship of a given area approach to the major functional spending programmes of government and to the market forces operating in the private sector. To pursue area approaches in isolation from these wider processes is to ignore many of the most important factors affecting the future of an area.

Clearly the design, orchestration and implementation of area approaches is a complex task. We need to think more clearly about the nature of area approaches and the precise objectives we expect them to achieve. Figure 10 is an 'at a glance' checklist of the main strands emerging from the earlier discussion, not because it gives the whole story, but because it provides some insight into what is involved. It reminds us that some of the objectives of area approaches may be in conflict. For example, how far can the objective of local accountability be pursued before it comes into conflict with the desire to redistribute resources between areas? Does local control mean rich neighbourhoods remaining rich and poor remaining poor? Conversely, does equity between areas mean remote decision-taking? These questions are fundamental. They were raised in Chapter 1 in relation to the autonomy of local government and they will re-appear in the next part of the book, particularly Chapter 7.

The checklist has two uses. First, it introduces and crystallizes a number of themes which will recur in the discussion of area approaches in Chapters 5 and 6. Following these reviews of experience an attempt is made to develop the checklist into an analytical framework for area approaches in Chapter 7. Second, the checklist has a more immediate and practical use. In conjunction with the sets of questions raised in the text (see italics), it can provide a starting point for those local authorities wishing to assess their own area-based approaches to policy and management. Which aspects are given priority in your authority? Are these the right ones?

Conclusion

Area approaches have potential for forging improved links between planning and implementation and between managerial and political change. But there is a great deal of confusion in the ongoing debate about area approaches. This confusion can be reduced by separating out three overlapping yet distinct objectives of area approaches: effectiveness, distribution, accountability and by clarifying the geography of different approaches. These four aspects provide a checklist of some of the main themes to be developed in the next part of the book which reviews experience with area approaches in Britain and America.

Part Two
Area approaches in Britain and America

Area approaches seem to have considerable promise for improving local government's ability to perceive community problems and to respond to these differing and changing problems at the appropriate organizational level in a timely and effective manner. During the last fifteen years or so the central governments of Britain and America have experimented fairly widely with various forms of policy focussed on neighbourhoods. Part Two deliberately widens the scope of the book to include American developments, not because this is likely to provide ready answers, but because there are both important parallels and important differences between urban policy making in the two nations. Merely to juxtapose the experience of the two countries is illuminating.

Chapter 4 sets the scene by comparing the local government systems of Britain and America. Neither is perfect but they both have strengths which the other lacks and there are therefore opportunities for each system to learn from the other.

Chapters 5 and 6 deal in turn with British and American policies for neighbourhoods. An attempt is made to get beyond the sweeping claims and condemnations which have sometimes been made of these policies by linking discussion to the three underlying objectives of area approaches outlined in Chapter 3: effectiveness, distribution, accountability.

Chapter 7 is short and to the point. It summarizes some of the main lessons to be derived from experience in Britain and America and presents an analytical framework for area approaches.

4 Local government in Britain and America

The American city is not governed by a single hierarchy of authority in which all lines are gathered together at the top in one set of hands. On the contrary, from a purely formal standpoint, one can hardly say that there is such a thing as a local government. There are a great many of them.

Edward C. Banfield and James Q. Wilson in *City Politics*, 1963

Introduction

The purpose of this chapter is to compare and contrast the local government systems of Britain and America by focussing attention on American city government. This is an ambitious task for one chapter but is worth attempting partly because it puts each system in a new perspective and this, in itself, could spark off new ideas, and partly because it is important to provide a context for the more specific British–American comparisons which follow in later chapters.

Before proceeding further a note of caution is in order. Comparative government is a fascinating but treacherous field for comparison of the governments of just two countries is enormously complicated. This is partly because it is virtually impossible to divorce the form, processes and nature of government from the society they were set up to regulate. At the end of his major work on comparative government S. E. Finer concludes that: 'It is *unthinkable* [his emphasis] that anybody can understand the way in which a country is governed without first knowing something about the geography and about the people, their social structure and their history.'[1] This is not to suggest that politics is the same as sociology but it does draw attention to the complexity of cross cultural comparisons and should lead us away from simplistic parallels. Finer was talking mainly about national government but, if anything, a comparison focussing on the local government of two countries is even more tricky. This is because there are likely to be substantial differences between different cities within each country under examination. In his analysis of American city government L. J. Sharpe remarks: 'Nowhere is this more true than in the United States where each state has evolved over a lengthy period its own inimitable style of urban government and where within each state urban areas have adopted different forms so that even within one state more variety may be apparent than in other national systems.'[2] In these circumstances the objectives of this chapter must be modest – to provide a broad outline of the main features of the two local government systems and to focus on some of the more significant differences in city government. Readers wanting to establish a fuller understanding are invited to follow up the references for this chapter on pages 327-32.

The chapter is divided into two main sections. The first is a fairly factual description of local government in Britain and America, and the second is a looser discussion which attempts to assess the relative merits of the two systems by looking more closely at certain key characteristics.

Description

This section deals with the following overlapping aspects of local government – structure, form, politics, finance, and policy making and budgeting.

The structure of local government

Local government in the USA is so fragmented that it is more helpful to think in terms of local government*s*.[3] Leaving aside the fifty state governments there are, to British eyes, a staggering 78 000 local governments in America – county governments, cities, towns and townships as well as school districts and special districts for all sorts of purposes from sewage disposal to mosquito abatement. All these political units are governments in the sense that they have the power to raise money and to spend it. Of the 78 000 local governments some 38 000 are *general* local governments. These are most nearly comparable with British local authorities for they are elected and raise and spend funds on a wide range of programmes. School districts and special districts deal only with one function of government and many of the special districts are not elected: a loose parallel can be drawn with British health and water authorities which, instead of being elected, are appointed by central government and have narrower terms of reference than local authorities.

Tables 2, 3, and 4 compare local government arrangements in America with those in England and Wales. Table 2 provides a breakdown of the number and types of local governments in America. Table 3 shows how the British Local Government Act

Table 2   *Local governments in the United States, below state level*

Type	Number	
Counties	3044	
Municipalities	18 517	
Townships	16 991	
Total of general local governments		38 552
Special districts	23 885	
School districts	15 781	
All local governments	78 259	

Source: US Department of Commerce, Bureau of the Census, Census of Governments, 1972. (*Note*: figures relate to 1967)

Table 3   *Local authorities in England and Wales*

Old (pre April 1974)		New (from April 1974)	
County Councils	58	Metropolitan County Councils	6
County Borough Councils	83	Metropolitan District Councils	36
Borough Councils	259	County Councils	47
Urban District Councils	522	District Councils	333
Rural District Councils	469		
SUB TOTAL	1391	SUB TOTAL	422
London*	35	London*	35
TOTAL	1426	TOTAL	457

* Local government in London was reorganized by the London Government Act 1963 into thirty-five authorities – The Greater London Council, The Inner London Education Authority, thirty-two London Boroughs and the historic City of London.

Note The health and water services were also reorganized with effect from April 1974 but, as they are controlled by central government, they fall outside the local government system. There are ten regional water authorities, fifteen regional health authorities (including Wales) plus a lower tier of ninety-eight health authorities.

Table 4   *Comparison of the number of local authorities in England and Wales and the United States*

	Number of local authorities	Population in 1974 (millions)	Number of local authorities per million population
England and Wales	457	49	9
United States	38 552	212	182

1972 reduced the number of local authorities in England and Wales from 1426 to 457 when it came into force on 1 April 1974. Because the scope of local government activity in the two countries is far from identical Table 4 presents a necessarily crude comparison which should not be taken too literally. Nevertheless it does illustrate a dramatic difference: in America there are twenty times as many general local governments per head of population as there are in England and Wales. This is only the beginning for the picture of a large number of units is further complicated by geographical and functional overlaps. In any metropolitan area there are several levels of government criss-crossing one another and forming a seemingly random spatial pattern usually unrelated to social geography – as when core cities are governed by institutions which are separate from those which run their sprawling suburbs. In addition there is no clear hierarchy of control in the administration of government functions many of which are shared between tiers. For example, in some cases local governments get federal aid indirectly through state governments but in others federal aid will pass directly to the cities or to school districts. There is no clear division of powers between levels. A helpful metaphor is provided by one student of federalism who described it as a marble cake rather than a layer cake.[4] The arguments for and against this confusing, or 'crazy quilt', pattern of American local governments are considered later in the discussion on fragmentation in local government.

Form of city government

City government as used here refers primarily to what goes on in city hall. In both Britain and America this is only a part of city governance but it is usually the most important. American city governments usually observe the principle of the separation of legislative from executive power. There are three basic forms. Most large cities use the *mayor–council* form of government, in which the mayor shares power with an elected city council. There are strong – and weak – mayor governments depending on the actual distribution of powers. In the strong-mayor form the mayor shares responsibility with the council for policy making but he alone has administrative responsibility. He appoints department heads and makes up the budget and is the dominant force in the city government. Council members may be elected in either partisan or non-partisan elections. As we shall see in Chapter 8 both Boston and New York are examples of cities with a strong-mayor form of government. The *council–manager* form, which from its inception in 1910 has been favoured by municipal reform groups, carries the separation of powers a step further. Administrative authority is, in theory, separated from politics and placed in the hands of a professional manager who is employed, usually by a non-partisan council, to implement its policies. Approximately half of the smaller cities (population 25 000 to 50 000) have adopted the council–manager form including Dayton, Ohio which appears as one of the case studies in Chapter 8. The third, and relatively rare, form of city government is the *commission* form in which the voters elect a small commission (usually five members) which exercises both executive and legislation functions. Each commissioner is the chief executive of one of the city departments and the commission makes policy collectively. This form is usually non-partisan and is more popular in the west.

As touched on in Chapter 2, the reorganization of local government in England and Wales in 1974 introduced a two-tier system of counties and districts.[5] In the six main conurbations outside London the relationship between the tiers differs from the remainder of the country as the metropolitan districts exercise the majority of local government powers. The two authorities of Stockport and Liverpool, looked at more closely in Chapter 8, are both metropolitan districts. The metropolitan counties have an essentially strategic planning role. Outside the metropolitan areas the counties have greater responsibilities for direct services as well as strategic planning and the districts have fewer powers. All local authorities have the same basic organizational form which consists of a council elected at partisan elections which is served by a staff of professional officers. Councils are usually quite large in number and committees of elected members are formed, usually on a functional basis, to oversee the work of the officers. There is strictly no political patronage in the appointment of officers who continue in post regardless of changes in the political control of the council.

City politics

It is only possible to touch on a few key features of city politics[6] in the two countries: machine politics, size of councils, role of parties and community action.

Machine politics   Machine politics grew up in the United States during the nineteenth century and was (and still is in some cities) a system of party organization that depends crucially upon inducements which are both specific and material.[7] Working-class people, especially immigrants unfamiliar with American ways and institutions, have always been the mainstay of the machine. Basically, the old-time neighbourhood bosses dispersed personal favours and patronage jobs in return for votes. The reform reaction to the machine gathered momentum at the turn of the century and, as mentioned earlier, sought successfully in many cities to introduce non-partisan elections and to transfer governmental responsibilities from the corrupt world of local politics into the hands of expert administrators. But the reform movement also had important consequences for area approaches to policy making in American cities for it strove to introduce at-large, as opposed to district, constituencies in order to eradicate 'narrow' neighbourhood-based interests. Several writers have dispelled the myth that the machine was an early experiment in participatory, neighbourhood-based democracy arguing that it was a highly centralized, near autocratic system as the word 'boss' implies.[8] But, for all its many weaknesses, the political machine was rooted in localized power and, with its demise, American city politics has been deprived of a base for political organization and co-ordination which could resist the rise of executive-bureaucratic imperatives which are increasingly dominating the political sphere.[9]

The increase of officer power at the expense of political control is not unknown in Britain. As was discussed in Chapter 2 it has sometimes been a side-effect of the introduction of new forms of management into British local authorities. But politicians in British local government have a much stronger geographical base than many of their American counterparts for they are all elected on a district (i.e. ward) system. This is not to suggest that the local roots of political parties in Britain are all that healthy,[10] but it does mean that the British councillor can speak *with legitimacy* on behalf of a given area or interest. As we shall see this is a feature which some of the more recent experiments with area management have attempted to strengthen.

Size of councils City councils in Britain are considerably larger than those in America. In accordance with the Local Government Act 1972 the Local Government Boundary Commission for England is responsible for the review of local electoral arrangements. After consultation with the local authority associations and the political parties the Commission has stated that the membership of county councils should be within the range of sixty to a hundred members and that in metropolitan districts the range should be fifty to eighty. American councils are much smaller and may have as few as five members and special districts may only have two. It is difficult to produce overall comparative figures showing the ratio of population to councillor. However, Table 17 in Chapter 9 relates the size of council to size of population in the five case study cities and these figures are illustrated in Figure 30. This data needs to be interpreted cautiously. First, the three American examples are core cities which, being less fragmented than local governments on the fringes of metropolitan areas, have considerably higher populations than most local government units. Second, the ratios leave out elected school boards and special districts. Even so the illustrations do show that the high ratios of population to elected councillor in America contrast sharply with the low ratios in Britain.[11] At the extreme they show that a New York City councillor has to 'represent' thirty-six times as many people as a Stockport councillor i.e. 177 000 as against 4900 people. Dayton provides a less extreme, and not uncommon, American example with each councillor 'representing' 41 000 people. In Chapter 3 it was noted that, following the 1974 reorganization into larger units, many British councillors have found themselves representing perhaps 5000 constituents. Many councillors feel that this is too many and hanker for the days when wards were much smaller. One is bound, therefore, to question how responsive American urban councillors can be. Surely they are too few in number to encompass the divergent interests within each city.

Party politics   A further, and major, difference between city politics in the two systems is the existence of the Labour Party in Britain. The reasons for the absence of a social democratic party in the United States are complex and cannot be entered into here. But it is interesting to note that various writers have suggested that at-large elections form part of the explanation, not least because of the greater cost of conducting at-large campaigns.[12] Possibly resulting from the weakness of the left in America is the popularity of non-partisan elections. This contrasts sharply with the party political approach which plays an important and growing role in British local government.[13] In a number of local authorities the policy committee is composed wholly of the leading political figures of the majority party and it is argued, by some, that strong, central party control is necessary to the politicization of local government.[14] In a number of authorities the leader of the party group is becoming less faceless, generally more 'available for comment' and increasingly influential as an individual. Interestingly, this might be viewed as the beginning of a move towards the American strong leader (or strong-mayor) form of city government in which those at the centre of power are more visible and, perhaps, more accountable.

Community action   Finally, a developing feature of city politics on both sides of the Atlantic is the spectacular upsurge, since the 1960s, of community action or grassroots groups. The sheer diversity of activities of this kind defies concise description and it is only possible to touch on these movements here. Janice Perlman has provided a very useful review of American community-based activity and has classified a large sample into three broad groups: those which use *direct action* to pressure existing institutions and elites to be more accountable; those which seek power *electorally* in order to replace the existing elites and institutions; and those which bypass existing centres of power by forming *alternative institutions*.[15] To some extent a similar taxonomy could be used to review British experience. An alternative perspective has been provided by various writers who discern two broad types of community action in terms of origins and motives.[16] First, there are those with *affluent origins*. In the 1960s the acquisition of a growing range of consumer goods turned people's attention to 'public goods', such as peace, quiet, and local character, which they could not readily buy for themselves. The community had to act together to improve or defend the quality of its environment. Second, there are many community action groups with *disadvantaged origins*. Much interventionist local authority action, for example slum clearance, urban motorway construction and redevelopment, has been directed towards the relatively disadvantaged parts of urban areas. The community had to act together either to remove the threat or to improve sensitivity in the management of the process of change.[17]

This rapid increase in direct pressure from the electorate is one of the most significant recent developments on the local government scene, on both sides of the Atlantic. Small-scale organizations of various kinds are becoming increasingly effective in mobilizing community feelings to win local victories and demonstrate that authority can be challenged. These growing forces are posed against the insensitive behaviour of a variety of large-scale organizations in society, including multi-national companies and private industry as well as the various public authorities. But, there is no escaping that much of the criticism is directed at local government which is often accused of being unresponsive to community needs and wishes. As we shall see, many of the area approaches developed in both Britain and America have attempted to respond to this widespread demand by people for a bigger role in decision-making processes which affect their lives.

Local government finance

There are three major kinds of taxes that citizens pay in the United States: income taxes, sales taxes (and other taxes on consumer goods) and property taxes. Each of the three main levels of government tends to rely on one form for most of its revenue. The federal government gets over four-fifths of its revenue from income taxes, state governments get about two-thirds of their revenue from sales taxes, and the localities get almost nine-tenths of their revenue from property taxes.[18] In particular areas there are wide variations from these overall proportions. The federal income tax has a number of advantages over the state and local taxes based on sales and property: it provides more money, it is progressive, it is more flexible. Many states and some cities have introduced income taxes of their own but in most cases political pressures have kept the tax rates very low. In America there are always exceptions! For example, local income taxes are used fairly extensively in Ohio and Dayton, one of the case studies in Chapter 8, derives a third of its income from a

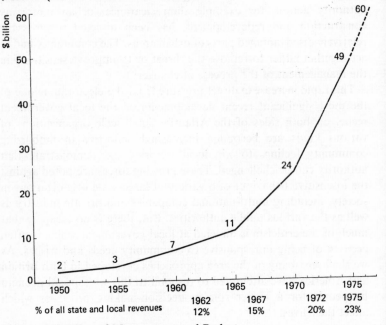

Figure 11 Federal aid to state and local governments
$ billion (i.e. one billion = 1000 million)

| % of all state and local revenues | 1962 12% | 1967 15% | 1972 20% | 1975 23% |

Source: US Office of Management and Budget

city income tax. Sales and property taxes, as with rates in Britain, lead to inequality among the states and among the localities for wealthy communities can raise more revenues when the needs of poorer communities may be greater. This partly explains the increasing role of central government and, of course, brings us straight back to the whole question of central government–local government relationships discussed in Chapter 1. Figure 11 shows how federal aid to state and local governments has grown dramatically in dollar amount, particularly during the 1970s. Federal aid has also grown significantly as a proportion of all state and local revenues and approached the level of a quarter in 1975. The equivalent figure for Britain is, however, considerably higher at 45 per cent.[19]

In Chapter 1 it was suggested that there is scope for reducing the level of detail in some aspects of British central government financial control. The relatively new forms of federal aid – revenue sharing and block grants – are therefore of particular interest for they seek to reduce detailed federal scrutiny and to enlarge local discretion.

There are, basically, three forms of federal aid.[20] Prior to the mid-1960s virtually all federal aid took the form of *categorical grants* which were provided to fund specific programmes. In their enthusiasm to draw attention to the new forms of aid some writers seem to forget that categorical grants still account for some three-quarters of total aid and that there are some 500 grant programmes for which state and local governments are eligible. Categorical grants remain of central importance. *General revenue sharing* involves the granting of federal funds with few restrictions to state and local governments and was introduced by the State and Local Fiscal Assistance Act 1972 for a five-year period. The level of funding has been at about $6 billion a year so that general revenue sharing has provided about 11 per cent of federal aid in recent years. The funds can be used for tax relief or any of the normal local government activities and the approach can be compared with Britain's rate support grant. In September 1976 legislation continuing the general revenue sharing programme until 1980 at slightly higher funding levels ($6·85 billion a year) won overwhelming approval in Congress.

Beginning in the late 1960s a variety of *block grants* emerged and these now constitute an important, middle sector in the federal assistance of the 1970s. In 1976 block grants overtook general revenue sharing in terms of size providing $6·9 billion or 12 per cent of federal aid in that year.

There are now five main block grants: in health, Partnership in Health (PHA) grants; in criminal justice, Law Enforcement Assistant (LEAA) grants; in welfare, Social Services (SSA) grants; in manpower, Comprehensive Employment and Training (CETA) grants; and in community development (CDBG) grants. Most of the block grants came into being by merging previously separate categoricals. The basic features of an American block grant are:

- it authorizes federal aid for a wide range of activities within a broad functional area;
- it gives recipient jurisdictions fairly wide discretion in identifying problems and designing programmes to deal with them;
- its administrative and fiscal reporting requirements are designed to keep federal intrusiveness to a minimum, whilst recognizing the need to ensure that broad national goals are accomplished;
- it is distributed by formula and this reduces grantmanship and provides some sense of fiscal certainty for grantees;
- its eligibility provision is fairly specific, relatively restrictive, and tends to favour general purpose governments.

The Transport Policies and Programmes (TPPs) described in Chapter 1 provide the nearest British equivalent and the idea of extending this block grant approach is being widely canvassed. Given the broad range of policy areas to which the block grant has been applied in America there would seem to be a strong case for studying these initiatives much more closely than seems to be happening at present. One programme – the Community Development Block Grant – will be touched on again later in the book. It consolidates a range of categorical programmes relating to urban renewal and environmental change and passes to local government the responsibility for assessing needs and establishing local priorities. A number of cities, including those discussed in Chapter 8, have attempted to ascertain neighbourhood priorities on how the funds should be spent. By comparison British budgeting for public spending on physical and environmental renewal is hopelessly disjointed.

Policy making and budgeting

Generally speaking greater intervention in the market processes of the urban system is a feature which distinguishes British policy making from American approaches. For example, control of physical development is considerably more sophisticated in Britain, our public housing record is more impressive, and the Community Land Act 1975 gives local authorities power to bring development land into public ownership before disposal (this, *inter alia*, is designed to restore to the community the increase in the value of land resulting from development). It would, however, be wrong to believe that Britain is always more interventionist – for example, American pollution control powers are both more comprehensive and restrictive than Britain's.[21]

Turning to the allocation of public resources the annual planning budgetary systems of British and American cities seem to have much in common. This is hardly surprising for they share the same heritage. Chapter 2 provides more detail on the evolution of the PPBS (planning-programming-budgeting-system) approach following its enthusiastic introduction into the federal government during the mid-1960s. The formal PPB system was often found to be too rigid and the approach has been modified substantially in practice. Nevertheless local government officers from Britain and America can find a deal of common ground in the way they have tried to establish a coherent framework for decision making – by setting objectives, developing programme structures, measurements of need, resource forecasts, performance criteria and so on. There are parallels too in the way policy work is often undertaken by inter-divisional groups of officers (or task forces as they are known in America) frequently assisted by staff from a central unit (such as a corporate planning unit in Britain or an office of management and budget in the United States). On the whole the annual budgetary choices in both countries tend to be made between functions. There is only the beginning of an awareness of the need to take account of other dimensions when considering the distribution of resources. One of these is, of course, the area dimension but, even in the five cities which have pioneered area management we shall see in Chapter 8 that area budgeting is not highly developed.

A difference in budgeting between the two countries results from Britain's economic crisis of the mid-1970s. From 1974 onwards British attention has shifted away from unachievable objectives to agonizing reappraisals of how to make the best use of existing resources. The mid-1970s also saw American local government wrestling with reduced budgets, but my impression from visiting several city halls in 1976 was that their problems were less serious than those faced in Britain – the outstanding exception being New York City. This may, however, be a question of timing for there are those who believe that a number of other American cities will face financial crisis during the late 1970s.

Political involvement in the policy making process probably differs more between cities than it does between the two countries. Some British authorities have made serious attempts to involve elected members at an early stage whilst others wait until a final report is prepared before seeking political reactions. In strong-mayor cities political involvement in policy work is continuous but in council–manager cities there may be little overt awareness of the political nature of policy making.

Corporate planning in the sense used by the Bains Committee (see Chapter 2) is a peculiarly British phenomenon. The discussion on fragmentation which appears below shows how it has been the American tradition for the politician, if anyone, to integrate policies. Not surprisingly therefore Americans often find great difficulty in grasping the concepts of corporate and inter-corporate planning as they apply to local government. The distinction drawn by Daniel Moynihan between policy and programme is helpful here: essentially programmes relate to a single part of the urban system whilst policy seeks to address the system in its entirety.[22] Moynihan believes that the structure of American government and the pragmatic tradition of American politics have resulted in a definition of public policy in terms of programmes and that this has inhibited the development of true policy. He urges the development of a policy approach which encompasses the largest possible range of phenomena and concerns. It would flatter policy planning in British local government too greatly to say that such an approach is already in hand, but it does seem that moves in this direction are considerably more advanced than in America. Supporting evidence for this is provided in Chapter 2.

Discussion

We have now built up a broad picture of the British and American local government systems and several interesting similarities and contrasts have emerged. But what are the relative merits of the two systems? How well equipped are the two systems to recognize the true complexity of problems in the community and how able are they to respond to these differing and changing problems at the appropriate organizational level in a timely and effective manner?

Before venturing further two qualifications should be made – one about evidence and one about values. There has been, with the notable exception of the study by L. J. Sharpe which is drawn on heavily below, little recent work in this vein. Sharpe, himself, points out that we lack much accurate information and he admits frankly that his own assessment of American city government 'sometimes has to make some fairly hefty bricks with very little straw'.[23] The limitations of the available evidence need, therefore, to be acknowledged at the outset. The point about values is obvious, but often goes unrecognized, and this concerns the cultural bias most of us will bring to questions of local government. To restate a simple point made in Chapter 1, Britain has a *unitary* government in which all local governments are subordinate to, and exist at the pleasure of, the central government. America has a *federal* form in which the constitution guarantees the survival of the states and in which real powers remain in the states.[24] To borrow the terms coined by Aaron Wildavsky most of us will probably possess either a 'federal' or a 'hierarchical' bias and this is likely to colour our approach to the issues which follow.[25]

Two opposed perspectives

The ideas of 'federal' and 'hierarchy' can provide us with a broad structure for the discussion which follows for they point towards two opposed perspectives which occur with some consistency in the literature.[26] To summarize two stereotypes, American city government is often seen as an experimental, open, participatory system in which power is fragmented and limited to the ratification of agreements reached by conflicting groups. By contrast British city government is seen generally as a conservative, closed, placid, autonomous system which attempts to be comprehensive in the name of the public interest. Wildavsky has identified two political economies which crystallize these two perspectives: one uses market metaphors – competition, conflict, bargaining – and the other uses bureaucratic metaphors – hierarchy, co-ordination, consistency.[27] He calls these the conflict–consent and the co-operative–coercive models. Although Wildavsky does not refer explicitly to America and Britain as we assess city government in these two countries we are, to some extent, comparing these two models. For the purpose of probing the two broad perspectives more deeply the following aspects of local government are discussed in turn[28] although, in reality, they interweave: fragmentation, innovation, openness, conflict, participation, bureaucratic influence and distributional effects. Conclusions are provided at the end of the chapter.

Fragmentation

The degree of fragmentation in local government is of central importance in understanding the two systems and is therefore discussed more fully than other aspects.

Some arguments against fragmentation The Royal Commission on Local Government in England which sat from 1966 to 1969 provides a fund of arguments against fragmentation many of which are advanced in the ongoing American debate. For example: the importance of recognizing the interdependence between town and country; the inter-relationships between services and the dangers of planning these in isolation; the need for a certain minimum size if authorities are to command the resources and skilled manpower necessary to provide services with maximum efficiency (the Commission said around 250 000 population) and so on.[29] In the American situation political, financial and racial arguments are more evident and these carry particular force when applied to the cities. The Advisory Commission on Intergovernmental Relations has criticized fragmentation of government in metropolitan areas in the following gloomy tones:

Political responsibility for governmental performance is divided to the point of obscurity. Public control of government policies tends to break down when citizens have to deal with a network of independent governments, each responsible for highly specialized activities. Even when good channels exist for registering public opinion, each government is so circumscribed by its powers and in the area of its jurisdiction that important metropolitan action is virtually impossible for local governments to undertake.[30]

The city problems of financial fragility and racial imbalance are worsened by the current arrangement of boundaries which encourages 'white flight' to the suburbs. When the white middle class leaves the city it crosses a political boundary into another community. It loses its right to participate in city government but, and crucially, it no longer pays taxes to the city.[31] It would be a misguided reformer who argued that changing the boundaries would end the problems but it *would* improve the city tax base, so providing greater opportunities for redistributing resources, and it would encourage integration. Reference to bussing must be made to clarify this latter point. In July 1974 the Supreme Court ruled against cross-bussing between Detroit and its suburbs favouring the principle of local control of schools over equality of opportunity in education. If city boundaries were drawn more widely to include metropolitan areas, the core cities and suburbs would not be considered separately for bussing purposes. This, in turn, would weaken the drive among the white middle class to leave the city since it would make less difference to the schooling of their children.[32]

To summarize the case against fragmentation, the metropolitan areas are social and economic units sharing problems. The current pattern of American local government does not cause these problems but it does make them worse for it frustrates effective and accountable government.

Some arguments for fragmentation   The case for fragmentation uses both theoretical and practical arguments. Aaron Wildavsky has presented a strong case for the dispersal of power at the local level on grounds of principle: 'If there is a federal principle it cannot be limited to relations between a national and state governments. If it is good for power to be divided and shared, that principle must also prevail in relationships between states and their cities, counties and special districts.'[33] He goes on to challenge the idea of reorganizing American local government.

The most deeply ingrained assumption on the relationship between governmental structure and policy outcomes is that rural and urban problems are traceable to the large number of overlapping jurisdictions, governments and special authorities that exist in America. The most critical issue in organisation theory for area development, in my opinion, concerns conflict–consent versus co–operative-coercive models of organization. Are externalities to be taken into account by internalizing them in ever-larger organizations to coerce co-operation, or through facilitating a 'crazy quilt' pattern as a multitude of conflicting interests bargain out their differences in the mixed-motive game we call the political process? Which alternative generates the most information on preferences? Imposes fewer costs? Inculcates the most dynamism? Leads to integrative solutions?[34]

This view can draw support from Charles Lindblom's classic attack on centralized decision making in which he argues that partisan mutual adjustment is an appropriate way of dealing with competing community interests, and that such mutual adjustment involves a rational assessment of alternatives.[35] But the argument runs deeper and takes us to the heart of the American political tradition which is that authority lies always in the popular will. It is from this starting point that Aaron Wildavsky, Robert Dahl[36] and other American political scientists argue that fragmentation contributes to local pluralism and hence to local democracy. The political focus is on the individual and there is seldom any conception of the public interest in an indivisible sense. Instead the public interest emerges in a pluralist fashion, with policy resulting from an open and continuous contest between opposing groups in a free political market place. As Sharpe observes, this tradition sees divided government always as a positive good:

Divided government is not only preferable as between horizontal levels, but also within each level; and not only does division itself promote democracy but it also promotes competition between the divided elements of each level. This competition also safeguards democracy by never allowing one agency to dominate, each checking and balancing the other.[37]

The practical political advantages of the dispersal of power and influence have been presented by Banfield and Wilson. They see the politician as a kind of broker who arranges the terms on which the possessors of the bits and pieces of power will act in relation to one another:

> In most cases there is no *formal* mechanism by which all these (local) governments can be brought together to co-ordinate their activities or to decide jointly on matters of general interest. In most sizable cities, collaboration among governments is essential to all important undertakings, but it must be arranged – if it can be arranged at all – informally, and therefore usually, by means of a political process.[38]

There is an implication here that fragmentation strengthens political control at the expense of more formal, bureaucratic influence. However, it was suggested earlier in the section on city politics that this is probably not so. Professionalization of services, the expansion of bureaucratic structures and the political insulation of bureaucracies have increased the power of central administrators and citywide professional elites at the expense of the machine which was rooted in localized power.[39] Bureaucratic influence is touched on again below.

A separate argument for fragmentation is that, contrary to widespread belief, there are few economies of scale for most services. Niskanen and Levy conclude that the evidence of all major studies is overwhelming: 'There do not appear to be any significant economies of scale in the provision of local government services (other than water and sewage services) above the level of the smaller cities.'[40] This does, however, seem a little sweeping and there are several studies available which suggest the question of scale is more complex.[41] Even so it is, perhaps, true that the performance of large-scale organizations has often not been up to expectations. Further points against reorganization into larger units are the potential remoteness of the new authorities, the general confusion created for the public by boundary changes and the high administrative costs of executing the change.

To summarize the case for fragmentation, partisan mutual adjustment is seen as an appropriate way of dealing with diverse community interests which is likely to be more democratic and less costly than large-scale, comprehensive local government units. My own view on fragmentation is provided at the end of the chapter.

Innovation

In view of the vast array of electoral arrangements, representative systems and decision-making structures of American cities, it is difficult to deny that American urban politics are more experimental than British. The introduction of corporate planning in some British authorities has developed as a force for innovation but even corporate planning has become standardized to some extent. Certainly too many local authorities threw away the golden opportunity afforded by local government reorganization. As argued in Chapter 2 at least some reached for the Bains Report and used it as a blueprint. The result is that American observers continue to be startled by the lack of variety in British approaches to urban management. The blame lies with both central and local government in Britain. Sometimes local government just isn't bold enough but sometimes there are central constraints which can, and should, be questioned. For example, as Brian Keith-Lucas argues:

Why should local authorities be so tightly controlled in their constitutions? For too long our local authorities have been tied to archaic institutions, instead of working out for themselves how best to run their communities' affairs. If a city council thought that its business would be better run if it had an elected 'strong mayor' on the New York pattern, instead of the conventional Father Christmas figure of an English mayor, it should be able to go ahead. Similarly, if a council decides that the present local government electoral system – the 'block vote' – is indefensible (as it is) and wants to replace it by proportional representation, why should it not be able to do so?[42]

Openness

American city government is undoubtedly more open than British. The media play a much more important role in transmitting and interpreting information on the activities of city government. For example, council meetings are televised on local stations either as they happen or within a few hours. The status of the local press is higher in the United States for exposure to the public gaze is seen as a major strength of American democracy. By comparison British urban politics is shrouded in secrecy. There are exceptions and some authorities are according a greater place to the press in the processes of local government. But these moves are generally modest for there remains a fairly widespread suspicion of the media in British local government.

Conflict

British local government may appear more placid but this is probably more a question of style than content.[43] The very openness of the American system means that conflict when it does occur is usually in public view. An additional factor is that British social habits and the accent on formal procedure in council meetings tend to moderate the tenor of political conflict. The truth is, however, that politics is probably just as contentious in British as it is in American city councils. Perhaps there is nothing comparable with the racial conflict found in American urban politics, certainly the strength of feeling generated by issues such as bussing is likely to catch the British observer by surprise. But housing and education are just two services which touch fundamental aspects of equality and provide the basis for sharp party conflict in many British council chambers. These local conflicts often reflect the conflicts in Westminster whereas there is probably a less direct link between central and local party political argument in the United States.

Participation

At first glance American urban government seems to be more participatory than the British. But, of all the attributes considered so far, this is the most dynamic and any observations are likely to date rapidly. For example, reference has already been made to the growth of community action and grassroots activities of various kinds. These developments have rendered anachronistic much of the literature on participation of even the early 1960s. Take, for example, the view of Banfield and Wilson writing in 1963: 'The spread of knowledge about politics may also reduce the amount of well-meant but often harmful interference by citizens in the workings of political institutions. A public which understands the nature and necessity of politics may perhaps be more willing than one that does not to allow politicians to do their work without obstruction.'[44] Who is to say that current observations on participation will not also seem well out of touch a few years from now?

At the same time we can say that the American political tradition, with its central notion that all authority should derive from the people, does seem to provide greater opportunity for pressure groups to influence policy. But we need to take this further and inquire how far the practice of group activity extends beyond the middle and upper classes. Schattschneider provides us with a delightful turn of phrase: 'The flaw in the pluralist heaven is that the heavenly chorus sings with a strong upper class accent. Probably about 90 per cent of the people cannot get into the pressure system.'[45] Again, however, we need to know that Schattschneider was writing in 1960 and it is almost certainly true that there are now a great many more working-class pressure groups.

Nevertheless, the view that the American system is more participatory needs qualification. Reference has already been made to the size of councils which suggests that the American representative system is less participatory than the British because of the high ratios of population to elected councillor. A further factor touched on earlier is the greater opportunity in the British system for area interests to be represented. Kenneth Newton suggests that the ward system not only affords greater possibilities for participation in general, but also provides local area interests better opportunities for getting them directly represented on the council than is possible in American cities.[46] Other points brought out by L. J. Sharpe which question the participatory character of American urban government are that both the frequency of elections and the average turnout of voters are lower than in Britain.[47]

Bureaucratic influence

The traditional view is that the bureaucrat in American urban government is weaker than his British counterpart. This is because the public interest emerges in a pluralist fashion from open political conflict whereas, in British cities, 'the policy-making process is less open and the public interest is viewed not so much on the resultant of opposing group interests, but more as the "right way" to tackle a problem, given the particular circumstances. This means that greater autonomy is granted to the full-time professional expert by the council and the electorate.'[48] This ties in, Poulson and other corruption scandals notwithstanding, with the greater public trust of government and respect for public officials in Britain. It is also true that British urban authorities employ far more full-time professional experts than their American counterparts to the point where Sharpe's description of the British system as 'obsessional professionalism' is not that easy to refute.[49]

But a number of points have been touched on earlier which suggest that the American bureaucrat is in fact more influential than the British. With the demise of the political machine it is difficult for even a strong mayor to establish political authority over the bureau chiefs of quasi-independent agencies (or 'islands of functional power' as they have been aptly described). Moreover in the non-partisan cities the elected leadership carries even less weight, certainly far less than the political leadership in a British city who usually command the support of a disciplined party. But the city manager arrangement itself is perhaps the most conclusive evidence showing the strength of the American bureaucrat, for 'the formal duties of a city manager involve a concentration of power in the hands of a non-elected official that would be viewed as intolerable in Britain'.[50]

To a certain extent considering the *relative* strength of bureaucracy in British and American city government may blind us to a broader and more disturbing realization – that bureaucratic influence is substantial in both countries and seems to be growing. The contradiction of contemporary urban politics – of streamlining in the management and administrative spheres coupled with weakening in the political sphere – should be of central concern to both British and American local government. Yet very little is being done, in research or practice, on either side of the Atlantic, to understand this problem or develop firm and positive proposals for the revitalization of local politics.

Distributional effects

Local government in both countries has failed to get to grips with distributional effects. There are, perhaps, two sets of issues which need to be placed more firmly on the local government political agenda, particularly in the cities. These are the distributional effects of, first, private and, secondly, public investment. There can be little doubt that local government politicians need to concern themselves much more positively with the economic development of their locality and with the way decisions on private investment enhance or hinder local life-chances. The decline of inner city areas is, for example, inextricably linked with their declining economic base. Secondly, there is a need for much greater attention to be paid to the distributional effects of public policies and programmes on different groups and areas within the local authority. A renewed focus on distribution could help to revive local politics but little substantive progress has been made in either country.

The reasons are complex but are at least partly bound up with the issue of bureaucratic dominance and associated deep-seated notions about the nature of government administration. *Inter alia,* these notions tend to assume the existence of an undifferentiated society, place high importance on uniformity and standard procedures, and usually attach great weight to professional views. They sustain patterns of information flow which usually ignore the differences in society. This promotes habits of political decision making which are concerned with what shall (or shall not) be provided rather than with who gets what.

Fortunately the 1970s are witnessing a few developments which, in their different ways, may begin to shift the focus of attention back towards the political process. Within the political arena itself the astonishing rise in community action on both sides of the Atlantic is probably the single most significant trend. But there are also signs that, in at least some urban authorities in Britain, strong party political leadership is beginning to assert itself more forcefully. Perhaps the cutbacks in public expenditure and services have helped to raise political consciousness. Within the field of policy research there are also one or two shifts of emphasis in some quarters which are trying to throw more light on political questions. One strand, for example, is provided by the neo-marxist studies such as those produced in recent years by Britain's national community development project. These, *inter alia,* raise the intensely political question of increasing governmental control of private capital as the central plank in any strategy seeking to stem inner city decline.[51] Another strand is provided by those studies which have attempted to expose the distribution of public services and goods to different groups and areas within the local authority.[52] We certainly need to think more deeply about the dimensions within which budgetary choices are made. The functional dimension (i.e. choice between services or programmes) if used in isolation cannot hope to get to grips with the distributional effects of government policy. Much of this debate is being conducted by academics and researchers in both Britain and America but some attempts are being made to carry the issues into the arena of practical local politics.[53]

Finally, the view that policy analysis is an entirely dispassionate and value-free process is wearing pretty thin in both countries. Again, certain academics and researchers are a little ahead of local government practice. Not only have they shown that information and data can never be understood in isolation from the ideas and values which give them meaning,[54] but they have also made progress in replacing the so-called 'scientific' approach to policy research. In particular, it is now increasingly recognized that the controlled experiment approach to the improvement of public policy should give way to more open-ended forms of policy learning.[55] The role of evaluation should be more that of a positive steering mechanism than an instrument of critical review. We return to these exciting ideas on public learning in Chapter 10 but, at this stage, we have to record the almost total absence of such approaches in current local government practice in both Britain and America.

Conclusion

This review has cast some doubt on the two stereotyped views of American and British urban government outlined earlier. In particular, whilst the American system is more open and innovative it is perhaps not as participatory as many have imagined. Conversely, the British system whilst it needs to be less secretive and much more experimental may have a greater asset in the ward councillor than it has previously recognized. This is partly why the attempts to strengthen the councillor's constituency role in the various area management experiments, including those in Stockport and Liverpool, are of particular interest. It is also significant that these initiatives seek to combine political and management innovation and are therefore working to bring about a better balance between the political and bureacratic spheres. The revitalization of local politics is needed in both British and American city government and it has been suggested that one way to bring this about is to focus more attention on local economic planning and to pay more attention to the distributional effects of government policies and programmes. The so-called 'scientific' approach to policy research should give way to new, more open-ended forms of policy learning which attempt to unite planning and implementation into a single action process.

But what about the grand questions raised by fragmentation? What can we conclude about federal versus hierarchy? Before attempting to answer this we must distinguish between decentralization and fragmentation. Some see decentralization as a process in which power is devolved from centre to locality with fragmentation meaning a horizontal division of powers based on functional rather than geographical distinctions.[56] This conceals some of the complexity of fragmentation in American local government (for functional units often relate to territories which differ from those of other functions) and it fails to capture the confusing consequences of fragmentation. But it does help to make it clear that it is perfectly possible to argue for less fragmentation – for a more intelligible local government system in America which has clearer lines of accountability – without saying a word against decentralization.

My own opinion, therefore, is that American city government is too fragmented. In its current form it usually leaves politicians too weak to control the bureaucracies and the citizen totally confused so that even the 'federal' goal of responsiveness is sacrificed. A simplification of the system could clarify lines of accountability without involving a significant concentration of power for this could be dispersed on an areal rather than on a functional basis. This links to one of the broader themes of this book which is the need to strengthen territorial power *vis-à-vis* functional power and this applies equally in Britain and America. The scene is now set for the following two chapters which review British and American attempts to relate urban policy to geographical areas.

5 Neighbourhood policies in Britain

Like the Roman, I seem to see the river Tiber foaming with much blood.

Enoch Powell in his speech on immigration
and the government's Race Relations Bill, 20 April 1968

Introduction

This chapter is concerned with the development of area approaches in Britain and, in particular, with the various government policies which have attempted to discriminate explicitly between geographical areas.[1] Such policies have a long history but have moved into the political limelight during the last ten years or so because of the widespread experiment with new forms of policy focussed on relatively small areas or neighbourhoods. These include educational priority areas, community development projects, the urban programme, action areas under the planning acts, general improvement and housing action areas under the housing acts, the inner area studies and the area management trials. Some of these initiatives, particularly those which address themselves to the problems of urban deprivation, have been strongly criticized. The sort of objections raised are that deprivations are not as spatially concentrated as many have assumed,[2] that the root causes of the problem cannot be tackled effectively by compensatory planning for particular areas,[3] and that the underlying political motive is to show maximum concern at minimum cost.[4]

There is force in these arguments, but at least part of the disenchantment with some of the area policies addressing urban deprivation has been caused by unreasonably high expectations as to their likely impact. Too often they have been seen, or even portrayed, as a ready answer when they are more helpfully viewed as part of a wider social strategy against inequality. As pointed out in Chapter 3, the current danger is that the whole idea of area-based approaches to policy making and management may become discredited in advance of any overall, systematic evaluation of its usefulness. This chapter is a small contribution towards filling this gap. It aims to provide an *overview* of British experience with area approaches which is developed in the light of the three underlying objectives of area approaches identified in Chapter 3: (1) effectiveness; (2) distribution and (3) accountability.

Most of the chapter is concerned with policies which discriminate *explicitly* between areas but it is important to remember that these account for only a small proportion of total government spending. The publicity they receive should not obscure the fact that almost all government policies have spatial implications – every recipient of a service or benefit is resident somewhere, and every physical improvement or development has a geographical location. The spatial implications of the major functional policies are poorly understood, particularly at the micro or neighbourhood scale. This is one of the factors which has worked against improved understanding of the distributional effects of policy.

Macro policies

Before moving down to the sub-local authority level it is important to mention the major national policies which discriminate between larger areas. Indeed, a great weakness of several of the small area policies discussed below results from a failure to appreciate how they tie in with these broader policies. For example, many of the special area policies focussed on the inner city have been pursued in isolation from regional economic policy when both have been directly concerned with questions of deprivation.

In Britain the main thrust of area policies has been, and in financial terms still is, at the macro level. In economic policy there are a whole range of regional controls and incentives which apply to the different grades of depressed area. For example, Industrial Development Certificates (IDCs) were introduced in 1947 to control the distribution of factory developments and, in 1966, a new system of investment grants was introduced to encourage employers to locate their operations in the Development Areas. With the introduction of the European Economic Community aid programmes an international dimension has been added. The regional policies, with their focus on the reversal of industrial decline, have been overtly distributional. The policies *have* brought jobs to the depressed regions but there are question marks against the cost-effectiveness of these policies. Recent moves demonstrate a desire to tune economic policy to the needs of smaller areas – for example, inner city areas.

In urban development the new towns represent probably the most explicit example of area discrimination, and in environmental planning the national parks are a good example of the efficacy of imposing discriminatory controls on particular geographical areas. These macro policies, including the regional economic policies, have a history of thirty years or so and are operated substantially outside the local government system. New towns and national parks have sought to improve the effectiveness of various government policies by designating specific areas for special treatment. None of these macro policies set out to increase local accountability. On the contrary, the new towns can be accused of reducing local democratic control because, within the designated area of a new town, wide-ranging powers are bestowed on an appointed board which is accountable to the local population only through Parliament.

Central government discriminates explicitly between areas by its arrangements for financial support to local government. The rate support grant tries to channel available national resources to local authorities in a way designed to compensate those authorities faced with unusual burdens. Less familiar, but no less important, are recent moves to improve health service resource allocation. A number of studies have revealed a serious maldistribution of health service resources in relation to needs[5] and the Department of Health and Social Security is trying to rectify this. The consultative document on priorities for health and personal social services is a first attempt to discriminate between various 'health care planning groups' at national level[6] and the resource allocation working party, within the DHSS, is attempting to improve the distribution of resources to the different regions and areas of the country.[7]

As discussed in Chapter 1, the Layfield Report on Local Government Finance goes to the political heart of spatial discrimination when it raises the whole question of who should decide policies for particular local authority areas.[8] The choice between a central or local emphasis for responsibility is complicated by the growing interest in various forms of regional management and/or devolution. At least one piece of evidence submitted to the Layfield Committee advocated regional budgets as a means whereby disparities in the quality of life between regions could be significantly reduced.[9] The debate engendered by the preparation and publication of the

Layfield Report shows that policies for areas are not usefully considered in isolation from the political and administrative arrangements required to implement them.[10] Many area approaches have failed to grasp this crucial connection between area and power.

Physical and environmental planning

Policies for spatial discrimination at the micro level have been more numerous than those at the macro level and, at first, were mainly concerned with improving the impact of policy on the local physical environment. The concepts of the clearance area (under housing legislation) and the comprehensive development area (under town planning legislation) have long histories. For decades these approaches have produced a major impact in terms of physical change but social and economic consequences have often been neglected. Despite their frequent location in deprived areas their impact on urban deprivation has been questionable. Certainly physical change *was* needed in many of these areas but the pursuit of physical change in isolation from other policies has often shifted rather than solved problems. A further drawback is that physical change was usually imposed without any form of public consultation so that, in more recent times, clearance and redevelopment have met with widespread community opposition.[11]

Smoke control areas introduced by the Clean Air Act 1956 have been particularly effective in raising environmental standards. It is no surprise, therefore, that the Control of Pollution Act 1974 employs a similar area-based approach by providing local authorities with power to declare noise abatement zones. Other important area approaches to physical conditions are environmental areas and conservation areas. The former is a concept developed in the Buchanan Report[12] and refers to an area having no extraneous traffic within which considerations of environment predominate over the use of vehicles. The latter aims to protect and/or enhance the appearance of areas of special architectural or historic interest by designation under the Civic Amenities Act 1967. These small area approaches to pollution, traffic control and conservation have frequently resulted in a significant improvement in the effectiveness of environmental policy. The same is, as a rule, true for the whole apparatus of land use and density controls which constantly discriminate between areas. However, as with clearance and redevelopment, there has been a failure to assess the impact of these policies in social and economic terms. The wholesale removal of small businesses from inner city residential areas because they are 'non-conforming uses' provides a classic example. More than that, there has been little or no attempt to grasp the distributional effects of town planning and environmental policies. For example, variations in residential density are justified in town planning because their impact is judged more in physical than in social terms.[13]

Public involvement at the local level

However, physical planning practice has at least attempted to wrestle with the question of local accountability. The new planning concepts set out in the report of the Planning Advisory Group[14] reached the statute book in the form of the Town and Country Planning Act 1968. Increased opportunity for public participation was a major feature of the new planning system and in 1969 the Skeffington Committee reported on the best methods, including publicity, of securing the participation of the public at the formative stage in the making of development plans for their area.[15] This development, despite its shortcomings, is significant because it represents the first official recognition of the need to integrate public opinion into the planning process. Within the planning profession there is a continuing interest in developing planning aid (an approach Americans would probably call advocacy planning) which demonstrates a desire to ensure that disadvantaged groups engaging in the planning process are able to obtain independent professional advice and support.

The informal community action referred to earlier was complemented by an upsurge of interest in neighbourhood or community councils. On reorganization the government accepted the need for community councils in Scotland and Wales and, in 1974, circulated a consultation paper on the proposition that statutory status should be made available to neighbourhood councils in the unparished areas in England.[16] A decision on this latter issue has yet to be taken. Other forms of consultative machinery have developed in recent years in relation to other public services. For example, since 1974 community health councils have been established in every health district to represent consumer interests in the health service. Pressure from parents for more say in schooling is another important development and is considered further below.

Judgements as to the efficacy of these, and other developments in public participation at the local level vary enormously, partly because of the great differences between various initiatives, but also as a result of the different values brought to bear in the assessment. For example, those who reject prevailing social values, goals and institutions see these attempts at public participation as part of a package of measures designed to support capitalism by obscuring the structural inequalities of British society.[17] Others, often following first-hand experience, may not reject prevailing values but are disillusioned because they see the process as one of manipulation and not of genuine dialogue. Yet others feel that the overall movement has had some success in the demystification of government and the opening up of new citizen involvements.[18]

There is, however, a measure of agreement on the scale at which public involvement is likely to be most effective. Direct experience with public participation and the findings of social and psychological research point in the same direction and suggest that people are most concerned with local matters that directly affect their 'home' area than with city-wide issues. The implication is that if the effects of policies can be spelt out in terms of their impact on small areas then public involvement in policy making is likely to be promoted. But how small should the areas be? Great caution is needed here for simplistic connections are too often made between physical and social conceptions of 'neighbourhood'.[19] On the basis of his own research Terence Lee suggests that a meaningful neighbourhood is likely to contain from 5000 to 7500 people.[20] The government consultation paper on neighbourhood councils suggested that the populations served should be 'very local, say 3000–10 000 population, preferably nearer the lower end'. The Association of Neighbourhood Councils has suggested that neighbourhood council populations could range from 5000 to 15 000.[21] There can be no hard and fast rules but it seems likely that areas with a population of less than 15 000 are most significant to local residents.

During the late 1960s, at the same time that the new ideas on physical planning were taking root, a wave of other initiatives rapidly broadened the scope of policies focussed on small areas. The following are now discussed in turn: education policy, social services and community work, the urban programme and area approaches to housing policy.

Education policy

The problems faced by schools with substantial numbers of immigrants from the Commonwealth stimulated the first significant development in spatial discrimination within education policy. Section 11 of the Local Government Act 1966 empowers the Secretary of State to pay 75 per cent grant on the full cost of staff whose activity is attributable to the difference of language or custom of recently arrived Commonwealth immigrants, and proportionate costs, calculated on a formula basis, of services in which individual officers cannot easily be identified. By 1974/75 £43 million had been paid out in section 11 grants. The basic requirement is for a local authority to show that more than 2 per cent of its schoolchildren have parents who were born in the New Commonwealth and arrived in the UK within the past ten years. A drawback, therefore, is that the grant excludes areas of earlier settlement, notably Liverpool. In practice section 11 is generally used as a language teaching grant although some authorities have used the grant more widely.

The Plowden Committee[22] reporting in 1967, called for the identification of *educational priority areas* where the schools should receive special help. The American urban programme clearly influenced the committee which insisted on the compensatory principle and asked for positive discrimination in favour of deprived schools going well beyond an attempt to equalize resources. The full recommendations of the Plowden Committee were not implemented but three developments did result. First, in 1967 £16 million was allocated over two years for a special building programme to replace old and unsatisfactory school buildings. Second, in 1968 a system of additional allowances for staff in 'schools of exceptional difficulty' was introduced. This was originally £75 per annum but has been increased in an attempt to keep pace with inflation. At January 1977 it stood at £276 per annum. The Burnham Report 1968 set out the criteria used to designate schools eligible for these allowances:

- the social and economic status of parents
- the absence of basic amenities in the homes of children attending the school
- the proportion of children receiving free school meals
- the proportion of families on supplementary benefits
- the proportion of children with linguistic difficulties.

A third strand was a special study, directed by Dr A. H. Halsey, of five of these educational priority areas (EPAs). Action research projects in each area sought the most practical and effective ways of improving the education of children living in deprived areas. The detailed findings of this research have been published in five volumes. The first volume[23] provides an overview of the project and came to the following main conclusions:

1   The educational priority area, despite its difficulties of definition, is a socially and administratively viable unit through which to apply the principle of positive discrimination.
2   Pre-schooling is the outstandingly economic and effective way of raising educational standards in EPAs.
3   The idea of community schools, put forward by Plowden, could be a powerful method of community regeneration.
4   There are practical ways of improving the partnership between families and schools in EPAs.
5   There are practical ways of improving the quality of teaching in EPA schools (much of the work was devoted to the development of new curricula which were better suited to the interests and needs of working-class children).
6   Action-research is an effective method of policy formulation and practical innovation.
7   The EPA can be no more than a part, though an important one, of a comprehensive social movement towards community development in a modern urban industrial society.

Detailed results published in subsequent volumes are, to some extent, contradictory. The researchers in Deptford concluded that the majority of individually disadvantaged children were not attending EPA schools and the majority of children who were in EPA schools were not disadvantaged.[24] The implication was that resources should be concentrated on groups of disadvantaged children rather than on schools. Even then the authors were doubtful as to whether disadvantaged children would benefit from improvements in schools unless there were considerable changes in their home and community environment. This fairly negative view of the impact of innovations based on the school was challenged by the researchers in Yorkshire who suggest that the changes initiated in their project had been of real benefit to the children affected.[25] In particular, they emphasized the value of pre-school education.

In 1974 the Educational Disadvantage Unit was set up by the Department of Education and Science to act as a focal point for the exchange of advice and information on measures to combat the effects of disadvantage and to influence the allocation of resources in favour of those areas where children were suffering from educational deprivation. In July 1975 the Unit established the independent Centre for Information and Advice on Educational Disadvantage which provides an information service and initiates special inquiries into good practice.

This brief summary of the evolution of education policy may give the impression that the search for improved effectiveness and for re-distribution of resources within education have been the guiding lights during the last ten years. There has been some valuable work, particularly in individual schools, but the resources devoted to innovation and the impact of positive discrimination on overall education policy have both been minimal. This point is well brought out in a collection of essays on urban education policy put together by Frank Field.[26] This gets well beyond the 'comprehensive versus grammar school' debate and raises important questions about both the content of education policy and the relationship of education policy to other urban policies.

Interestingly, it seems likely that our third underlying theme of accountability will take on an increasingly important role in approaches to education. At national level the habit of secretiveness in the way the Department of Education and Science reviews education policy has been firmly challenged.[27] Shirley Williams took over as Secretary of State for Education in September 1976 and 1977 saw the launching of the 'great public debate' on education. Meanwhile, local parental pressure for more involvement in the running of schools has grown, fuelled, to some extent, by certain experiments in progressive education which went 'wrong' – notably the William Tyndale junior school, in inner London.[28] The Taylor Committee, which reported in 1977 on the government and management of schools has intensified the debate between those who see the professional judgement of the head and staff as paramount and those who hold that the local community should play a significant role in the planning and execution of education policy.

Social services and community work

The year after the Plowden Committee advanced the idea of educational priority areas the Seebohm Committee concluded that, in general, the new social service departments should be administered through area teams concentrating their activity in areas of special need.[29] The size of the teams should be around ten to twelve workers and should serve a population of between 50 000 and 100 000. The Committee shared the view of the Plowden Committee that, to achieve equality, resources must be *unevenly* distributed to counter-balance the gross inequalities which already exist. The Committee also stressed the importance of delegating a substantial measure of authority to the area teams. Ideas about the organizational structure of social service departments are changing and developing[30] but the importance of an area approach remains central. The reasons are multiple – ease of co-ordination and communication, pooling of skills, enhanced responsiveness – but two ideas are worth emphasizing: access and community.

First, there has been a strong emphasis on the idea of providing a comprehensive social work service from area offices situated where they were most accessible, at the local level. *Access* is defined broadly and goes beyond geographical convenience to include a whole range of psychological factors which work against take-up of services by those in need. Thus, area offices will generally seek to improve information (its availability and intelligibility), reception procedures and the attitudes of 'front-line' staff. Often following on from social service initiatives there have been attempts to develop the 'one-door' philosophy of providing several services at one point. These have sometimes been linked with other agencies such as Citizens' Advice Bureaux. However, much remains to be done by local government as a whole to improve public access to services. In particular there would seem to be a case for a complete review of the local advice industry. This might be expected to reveal an imbalance between the provision of centralized, specialized, often costly, advice services – for example, consumer, housing, planning, legal and other advice – and smaller, cheaper, neighbourhood centres integrated with local services. Certainly the planning and co-ordination of advice services is fragmented and haphazard. Perhaps Britain (and America) can learn something from the more purposeful attempts at 'retailing government services' which are being tested in Australia.[31]

Second, the idea of a '*community*' approach has been proclaimed far and wide to the point where the current danger is that the term may become devoid of meaning:

Sociologists in search of the meaning of 'community' have so far come up with ninety-four different definitions. Their diffidence has not prevented politicians and professionals from using it as a kind of 'aerosol' word to be sprayed on to deteriorating institutions to deodorise and humanise them. Thus – at a stroke – schools are transformed into community schools, planners into community planners, doctors into community physicians, approved schools into community homes – and paper delivery boys into communicorps.[32]

But perhaps we should not be too cynical. Certainly government can be accused of promoting a 'community' approach to social services as a means of shedding its responsibility for the disadvantaged, but there remains a strong case for 'community' as opposed to institutional care purely because it is often the best way of providing the most suitable help to many clients. In any event a high level of domiciliary support can be as expensive as residential care. Generally speaking 'community' or 'self-help' approaches are locality-based for they attempt to key onto and develop existing neighbourhood networks and feelings of cohesion. An insight into these approaches can be provided by considering the development of community work which spiralled between the mid-1960s and mid-1970s.

At risk of over-simplifying we can discern three approaches to community work.[33] First, the *social pathology* approach emphasizes self-help and may be seen as an extension of social work practice from casework to group work within the community. Family Advice Centres often pioneered this approach.[34] Many, but not all, community workers now reject this method on the grounds that many of the difficulties experienced by 'problem families' and 'problem areas' do not arise from personal or family handicaps so much as from external factors such as low income, bad housing and poor environment. A second approach centres on the idea of *social planning* which was the main message of the 1968 Gulbenkian Report on community work.[35] In this approach the community worker may well be employed by the local authority but will not necessarily work in the social services department.[36] His task is likely to centre on bridge-building between the various authorities and the local community and may involve the promotion of neighbourhood councils to voice neighbourhood views. To some extent he will be concerned to thread together the work of various departments at grass roots level and, with this interest in the integration of local services, this kind of community work has affinities with corporate planning.[37] A third approach hinges on *conflict* and sees deprived neighbourhoods in terms of the competition between different interest-groups in the city, and in the wider economy, for shares of the scarce resources of jobs, housing, and government services. This approach is overtly political and is directly concerned with the re-distribution of resources, benefits, power and influence.[38] Thus we can see that community work is so diverse that it encompasses all three of our underlying themes with, perhaps, a changing emphasis from effectiveness to accountability and, finally, to distribution.

The urban programme

There are two main strands to the urban programme and both have been developed by the Home Office: urban aid and the national community development project (CDP). Some of the ideas were already germinating in the Home Office during the mid-1960s but the introduction of the urban programme was unmistakably triggered by Enoch Powell's infamous 'Rivers of blood' speech delivered in April 1968. This heightened racial tensions particularly where immigrants had settled in large numbers, mainly in the inner cities. The urban programme was announced by the Prime Minister in a major speech on immigration and race relations in May 1968 and was put into effect by the Local Government Grant (Social Need) Act 1969 and by the introduction of the CDP, also in 1969.

The aim of *urban aid* was to help local authorities, by 75 per cent grant support of certain approved projects, to attack 'needle points' of deprivation. It has been observed that this assumes, first, that these points can be defined and, second, that the approach offers a solution which somehow with minimal expenditure will go to the roots of deprivation.[39] Actual central government expenditure on urban aid for the period 1968/69 to 1974/75 was £55·⁻ million and estimates for the period 1975/76 to 1978/79 total £85·4 million.[40] The total for the ten-year period from 1969 is, therefore, in the region of £140 million. There can be no denying that £14 million per year is an unrealistically low level of spending when set against the objectives of urban aid stated by James Callaghan, the then Home Secretary, when introducing the legislation: 'The purpose of the bill is to provide for the care of our citizens who live in the poorest or most overcrowded parts of our cities and towns. It is intended to arrest, insofar as it is possible by financial means, and reverse the downward spiral which afflicts so many of these areas.' But, for all its weaknesses, the urban programme has tried to avoid providing more of the same services and has had some success in stimulating innovation. It signalled the beginning of slightly more flexible approaches to small areas.

The national *community development project* was focussed on twelve deprived areas ranging in population from 8600 (Glyncorrwg) to 46 000 (Canning Town). The Home Office described the aims as 'a modest attempt at action research into the better understanding and more comprehensive tackling of social needs, especially in local communities within the older urban areas, through closer co-ordination of central and local official and unofficial effort, informed and stimulated by citizen initiative and involvement.'[41] The CDP concept was a major breakthrough in policy making for a number of reasons. But perhaps the two most important are that the approach was (a) unfettered by a particular legislative framework, and (b) seen as a learning experiment for higher levels of policy making – the twelve project teams were to attempt, *inter alia*, 'to identify needs and possible solutions which are beyond immediate local action but merit feeding back to wherever policy is formed.'[42]

In 1973 the project teams collaborated in the preparation of an inter-project report designed to explore common themes.[43] This identified three models of social change: consensus, pluralist, and structural conflict. There has been a mixture of approaches in the twelve projects but most of them have turned to the structural or class conflict analysis as the most satisfactory explanation of the problems found in their areas. The report concludes that the CDP areas are not isolated pockets suffering an unfortunate combination of circumstances and a major response is therefore required from central and local government. At the same time the CDPs do *not* reject the area approach as a means of learning about urban problems: 'From its small area base, CDP can map the points at which private and public policies are having negative and unequal effects.'[44] Each CDP was to run for a five-year term and the project has been phasing down during recent years. Some valuable analytical work on particular issues has been completed by individual projects. However, the CDP publications have become more and more overtly political. The Home Office decided to close down the project's Central Information and Intelligence Unit from 1 October 1976. The final action project is scheduled to close in March 1978. In terms of the three underlying motives of area approaches CDPs have, as discussed in relation to community work above, tended to evolve from effectiveness through accountability to arrive at a distinctive position on the question of distribution.

Area approaches to housing policy

We must return a final time to the mid-1960s to understand the roots of area approaches to housing policy. The 1964 Housing Act was a first, feeble attempt to develop an area approach to older housing by concentrating the take up of standard grants into particular areas. Structural improvement was not, however, included and the procedure was cumbersome and relatively ineffective. In 1965 the Milner Holland Report on London's housing conditions called for the designation of areas of special control in which bad living conditions would be attacked comprehensively and assisted by an enlargement of local authority powers.[45] The Denington Report appeared the following year and argued that halting the decline of the nation's older housing stock was in the economic national interest.[46] Thus, a combination of social and economic motives resulted in the 1969 Housing Act which introduced general improvement areas (GIAs), the logic being that effort and resources devoted to house improvement provide a better return when directed to the up-grading of whole areas – the houses and the environment.

The original government circular on area improvement does refer to areas of housing stress and, a point widely overlooked, suggests that the social reasons for taking action in such areas may be imperative even if the economic prospects are doubtful.[47] However, the GIA approach was designed mainly to achieve physical and environmental change in a reasonably responsive way in areas of older housing.[48] It was not designed to tackle the many social problems inextricably linked with the areas of worst housing. This latter objective is a primary aim of the Housing Act 1974 which introduced the housing action area (HAA) and priority neighbourhood concepts. Housing action areas should be areas of housing stress where bad physical and social stress interact and where intense activity will immediately follow declaration. Priority neighbourhoods are designed to prevent the housing position in or around stress areas from deteriorating further.

At first sight it would seem that housing action areas, with their special grants covering up to 90 per cent of house renovation costs, might be an effective way of diverting resources to where they are most oeeded. But doubts have been raised.[49] Both GIAs and HAAs are focussed on very small areas. The Department of the Environment has suggested that the size of successful GIAs has been typically 200 to 300 houses and goes on to suggest that a typical HAA should also be of this order of magnitude.[50] During an era in which council and housing association acquisition and improvement work is restricted by lack of funds and in which local authority mortgages are being cut back, there is a danger that GIAs and HAAs will become pockets of renovated housing located within wide zones of deteriorating property.[51] A further danger is that these initiatives may change the housing function of these small areas and, in particular, may diminish the supply of cheap furnished rented accommodation.

The dominant underlying motive of area approaches to housing policy has been the desire to improve the effectiveness of government action. In particular, official guidance in recent years has stressed the importance of focussing on areas of housing stress and of developing a corporate approach to urban renewal.[52] Strengthening local accountability has also been a feature. Public participation in the implementation of GIAs has sometimes been fairly extensive and in some authorities there has been experiment with tenant involvement in council estate management. Because there is an element of positive discrimination in favour of GIAs and HAAs, by means of higher rates of grant, it is also possible to argue that housing policy has involved an element of spatial re-distribution. But, as with EPAs, the amount of resources being funnelled into these areas is minimal when set against housing spending as a whole.

Comprehensive approaches

A recurring theme in the development of the various area approaches discussed above has been the need to integrate separate policy initiatives. But the importance of adopting a comprehensive approach to urban problems received a particular boost from an extremely imaginative small area project launched and sustained by Shelter – the national campaign for the homeless. In 1969 Shelter expanded its concern from the literally homeless to those parts of the city where homelessness principally occur. The *Shelter Neighbourhood Action Project* (SNAP) was a three-year experiment lasting from 1969 to 1972 in one of the most deprived areas of Liverpool. The final report of the project suggested that urban decline was a *total* problem and set out the case for a completely transformed, comprehensive urban programme.[53]

The project had a direct impact on Peter Walker, then the Secretary of State at the Department of the Environment. In July 1972

Walker announced his intention to carry out studies to 'develop a total approach to the improvement of the urban environment'.[54] Three studies were quickly carried out to assist the new local authorities in their overall approach to urban problems,[55] and three *Inner Area Studies* (IAS) involving action-research extending over several years were established. The latter resemble CDPs in that they are concerned with practical work in a particular neighbourhood sponsored by a central government department but closely integrated with the local authority. An important difference is that private consultants are employed. The aim is to look at the study areas as a whole from the point of view of the people living in them and to derive lessons on powers, resources and techniques.

The IAS reports published so far suggest that the area approach has provided a valuable focus for across-the-board study and the summaries of the consultants' three final reports point up some significant trends.[56] But, at around £½ million each, one is bound to question whether these research studies represent value for money. There would seem to be serious limitations on the role that consultants can play in tackling problems of such inter-organizational complexity. A true, 'total approach' depends heavily on the capacity of *existing* governmental institutions to establish relevant, ongoing working relationships. Outside consultants, simply because they are 'outside', would seem to be ill-equipped to play a major role in this process.

In parallel with the Inner Area Studies the Home Office, in collaboration with a wide range of other government departments, was also developing ideas on how to develop a comprehensive approach to urban problems. In November 1973 Robert Carr, the then Home Secretary, established the Urban Deprivation Unit within the Home Office to study 'the real nature of urban deprivation and the problems underlying it'. In 1974 the unit conceived the idea of *comprehensive community programmes* and this approach was outlined by Roy Jenkins soon after Labour came to power: 'A selected number of local authorities in England, Scotland and Wales whose jurisdictions include areas of acute urban deprivation would be invited to prepare comprehensive community programmes (CCPs) . . . The CCP would identify the whole range of economic, social and physical or environmental problems of the area and propose action to deal with them focussing on what could be achieved within five years.'[57]

As originally conceived the CCPs were to concentrate on small areas each having a population of about 10 000. However the approach was modified radically and now applies to the whole local authority area. This is partly because deprivation is not necessarily concentrated in small areas and partly because the emphasis has moved toward the re-direction of the major programmes and policies of central and local government to those most in need. The approach is being developed with a small number of local authorities, notably Gateshead Metropolitan Borough Council, but it is too early to draw conclusions at this stage.[58] What we can say is that the area aspects of deprivation will form only one input into a comprehensive policy review process. This process will involve the two tiers of local government, the regional economic planning board, the area health authority and all the other branches of central government having an impact on deprivation.

Area management

Over the years individual services have introduced various forms of area organization. The area team system developed by social services departments has already been mentioned. Housing departments are also often organized spatially with area housing managers having responsibility for those council estates located within a particular part of the city. Parks, libraries, street cleaning, refuse collection, health inspection, development control and schools are some of the other services which are often administered on an area basis. In one sense these are all forms of area management but here the term is used to refer to those approaches which seek to integrate the management of separate services at the local level and to involve local councillors in decisions affecting their ward. This idea of a corporate or, more radically, an inter-corporate approach to the planning and delivery of local services is still in its infancy although many authorities are beginning to show an interest in the potential of the approach.

Almost certainly the first British local authority to develop this idea was the former County Borough of Stockport when, in 1971, it introduced a number of changes, including area sub-committees, designed to relate the work of the authority more explicitly to the needs of particular geographical areas. This development is discussed fully in Chapter 8. Here it is worth mentioning the involvement of the management consultants Booz-Allen and Hamilton who, following their work with Stockport, recommended a slightly different form of area management in a report for West Norfolk District Council. This rural area has a population of only around 100 000 but it is geographically large. The consultants therefore recommended a system of three area committees, to discuss area needs and advise the central Policy Committee on priorities, and three area managers to be responsible for the effective and efficient management of decentralized services in each area. The area managers have line responsibility for several local services and are members of the authority's management team of chief officers.[59]

The Inner Area Study in Liverpool took a strong interest in area management and drew up a set of proposals for testing the concept in 1973.[60] This initiative, coupled with the experience of Stockport, Norfolk, and one or two other authorities, encouraged the Department of the Environment to promote the current series of area management trials. The trials are being carried out in six local authorities at present: Stockport, Liverpool, Kirklees, Dudley, Haringey and Newcastle. The purpose is to test the application of area management to a variety of problems, geographical characteristics and organizational patterns – both political and administrative. The Department sees area management as 'a means of adapting local government organization so that it can respond more sensitively and effectively to the particular needs of areas. It is a means of identifying priorities and objectives at area level, seeing their relevance locally and putting them in their district-wide context.'[61]

The Institute of Local Government Studies at Birmingham University has been commissioned to study the trials. This monitoring project began on 1 June 1976 and will continue for a maximum of four years. The purpose of the research is to provide information which throws light on the benefits which might be secured by area management and to assess possible problems and practical implications. The first interim report on the project deals with the objectives and structures of the various schemes and reveals a healthy diversity of approaches.[62] Stockport and Liverpool are discussed fully in Chapter 8 and the other trials can only be touched on here. *Kirklees* is developing a system of 'area care' for the whole authority which is divided into five areas. Initially the main accent is on improving the information service to the public. In *Dudley* the area management project is focussed on one priority area, Brierley Hill, and involves a working party of fifteen councillors and a team of ten officers. The project has an annual fund of £8000 to spend on environmental improvement but the main objective is to experiment with new and better ways of using existing resources. Area management in *Haringey* is also related to a single, deprived part of the borough – Green Lanes. There is an advisory committee of councillors but, as yet, no formal inter-departmental group of officers. Instead the officer element comprises an area management unit within the planning department and the main accent is on community development and the generation of a local input into central decisions. In *Newcastle* area aspects are one part of a broader approach to urban stress known as 'top priority'.[63] In 1976 the Council published a Green Paper setting out its ideas and priority area teams are now active in twelve of the city's twenty-four wards. These joint teams of ward councillors and officers hold public meetings to decide on how centrally allocated funds should be spent in each ward. The total amount open to local discretion was £120 000 in 1976/77 but a substantially larger sum was to be made available in 1977/78.

These examples show that area management is more closely related to the role of the elected member than any of the small area policies so far discussed. This is because considerable importance is attached to the councillor's constituency role: in area management ward members often serve on some form of area committee which is concerned with a geographical area rather than a service function. This implies a growing awareness of the need to integrate management and political processes at the local level as well as the centre of the authority.

Area management could also be used to forge new links between the implementation and generation of policy. Elsewhere I have discussed the growing concern about the limitations and relevance of the official statutory view of local planning and hinted at the potential for collaboration between new forms of local planning and area management.[64] Some authorities are already developing wider problem-solving approaches which edge towards the idea of continuously reviewed area corporate plans coupled with annual area budgets. Broader approaches to local planning of this kind could give purpose and direction to area management initiatives which are always in danger of becoming absorbed in the minutiae of service co-ordination and delivery at the expense of developing a capacity for policy learning. There are important training implications here, not least for the education of local planners. At a time of 'no growth' local planners with a good grasp of area management could make a significant contribution to the better use of limited resources.

If service co-ordination and/or management are to be effective then the size of the area served will need to be considerably bigger than the upper limit of 15 000 people suggested earlier as a basis for improving public involvement. The Liverpool area management scheme, for example, relates to an area with a population of 60 000 and this is in line with the Seebohm Committee view that area teams might serve a population of 50 000 to 100 000.[65] These different requirements should lead us away from the search for an 'ideal' size of area. Stockport provides one example of a multi-levelled approach. The borough is divided into three operational areas for the purpose of service co-ordination (populations range from 84 000 to 114 000). These areas are sub-divided into a total of eight area committee areas (populations 24 000 to 49 000). At the 'grass roots' level there are twenty-three community or neighbourhood councils (populations 3000 to 12 000). Maps and more details of both Stockport and Liverpool are presented in Chapter 8.

Policy for the inner cities

The most recent and, arguably, the most significant area initiative relates to inner city areas as a whole. In September 1976 Peter Shore, Secretary of State for the Environment, made a major speech on the problems of Britain's inner urban areas. Since that date, and at the Prime Minister's request, he has been chairing a special ministerial committee on inner city problems. The main purpose is to give an inner city focus to the hitherto fragmented government and local government policies, programmes and budgets which impact on the inner city. A major conference on the inner city was held in Bristol in February 1977 and three members of the Cabinet Committee attended – Peter Shore, Reg Freeson, Minister for Housing and Construction, and Gordon Oakes, Minister for Education. Reg Freeson expressed his hopes as follows:

[The Cabinet Committee] comprises Ministers from every relevant Department under the chairmanship of Peter Shore. For the very first time Government is now looking at inner urban problems as a whole. Its immediate task is not to prepare some long-term grand design, but to seek practical ways to act now. The more major reforms can come later. This inter-departmental approach is itself a major and, I hope, the decisive step forward. At last urban renewal is coming from the periphery right to the centre of politics.[66]

All three ministers emphasized the importance of improving the local economies of the inner city areas and all stressed the need for much greater policy integration – at Whitehall, at the level of the local authority and at the level of the neighbourhood. But perhaps most significant was their unanimous view that solutions rested with the main programmes of government. They felt that there would remain a role for small-scale priority area projects but that significant headway would not be made until the main programmes – education, housing, social services, transport, planning, industry, manpower, environmental services – were re-deployed.

These views were given formal expression in the White Paper, *Policy for the Inner Cities* published in June 1977.[67] This stressed the need to strengthen inner area economies as well as unify and re-direct the main policies and programmes of government. The Comprehensive Community Programme, being pioneered in Gateshead, is seen as providing lessons for authorities faced with concentrations of deprivation in their inner areas, including those cities which are to enter into a special partnership with central government to regenerate their inner areas.

Synthesis

This chapter has shown that British policies for neighbourhoods have been hopelessly fragmented. Figure 12 provides a simplified picture of the way these various policies have evolved over the period 1964 to 1977. This shows how area approaches in town planning, housing, social services and education have all been pursued in relative isolation. Fortunately, the figure also reveals a growing emphasis on approaches designed to combat this weakness. The comprehensive community programmes, the Cabinet Committee on the inner city and the area management trials are all striving to integrate diverse policies and relate them more effectively to the needs of particular localities, whether it be at the level of the authority, the inner city or the neighbourhood. These initiatives are to be welcomed, but it should be noted that they have been largely stimulated by central government and are being pursued in only a few local authorities at present. There would seem to be a great deal of scope for more widespread innovation by individual local authorities in the realm of policy integration particularly at the level of the neighbourhood.

The various national events shown in Figure 12 provide reference

Figure 12   Evolution of neighbourhood policies in Britain (1964–77)

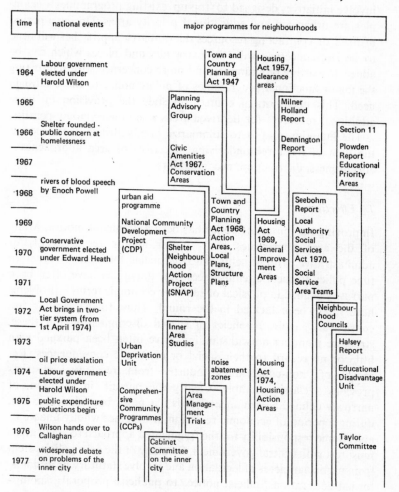

time	national events	major programmes for neighbourhoods
1964	Labour government elected under Harold Wilson	Town and Country Planning Act 1947 / Housing Act 1957, clearance areas
1965		Planning Advisory Group / Milner Holland Report
1966	Shelter founded - public concern at homelessness	Dennington Report / Section 11
1967		Civic Amenities Act 1967. Conservation Areas / Plowden Report Educational Priority Areas
1968	rivers of blood speech by Enoch Powell	urban aid programme / Seebohm Report
1969		National Community Development Project (CDP) / Town and Country Planning Act 1968, Action Areas, Local Plans, Structure Plans / Housing Act 1969, General Improvement Areas / Local Authority Social Services Act 1970. Social Service Area Teams
1970	Conservative government elected under Edward Heath	Shelter Neighbourhood Action Project (SNAP)
1971		
1972	Local Government Act brings in two-tier system (from 1st April 1974)	Neighbourhood Councils
1973		Urban Deprivation Unit / Inner Area Studies / Halsey Report
1974	oil price escalation / Labour government elected under Harold Wilson	noise abatement zones / Housing Act 1974, Housing Action Areas / Educational Disadvantage Unit
1975	public expenditure reductions begin	Comprehensive Community Programmes (CCPs) / Area Management Trials
1976	Wilson hands over to Callaghan	Taylor Committee
1977	widespread debate on problems of the inner city	Cabinet Committee on the inner city

points to help fit the area approaches into a time frame. Perhaps two points are worth emphasizing. The first concerns race. Enoch Powell did not, of course, generate the urban programme single-handed. But he did catapult the issue of race relations onto the national political agenda and this has now developed into a wider and growing concern about the problems of the inner city. The second issue concerns the national economy. The country is still reeling from the escalation in oil prices of 1974. Most of the area approaches were conceived before the era of 'no growth' and often involve initiatives designed to 'top up' existing programmes – examples are urban aid and educational priority areas. During a period of fixed or contracting resources relevant area approaches will need to be less concerned with the extra bits and pieces which can be added to existing programmes and more concerned with redirecting the major functional programmes of public policy to those most in need. This does not, of course, preclude the provision of large additional resources for deprived areas when the economy permits.

The intention now is to summarize briefly British experience in the light of the three underlying objectives of area approaches – effectiveness, distribution, accountability.

1   *Effectiveness*

Improving the impact of policy has been a dominant motive. Many of the area approaches focus power and/or resources and/or administrative arrangements onto particular localities in order to tune policy to local circumstances. But intentions have often been narrowly defined in physical or social or economic terms – problems have rarely been tackled in the round. Thus, town planning has consistently involved policies of spatial discrimination but these, structure planning notwithstanding, have often been pursued with little or no regard to their social or economic consequences. Removal of 'non-conforming' industry from residential districts provides a classic example. Clearly the pursuit, in isolation, of narrowly defined environmental ends has never been desirable but, during a period of economic recession, it becomes wholly unacceptable. Some responsibility for the fragmented approach to small areas must rest with central government. So many of the area policies stem from particular pieces of legislation and involve statutory procedures, formal declarations, official notices to publicize proposals, submission of schemes to Whitehall and so on.

We need to ask whether area approaches of this kind focus too much attention on the administration of procedures and how far they blinker local analysis and action. Possibly the greatest strength of policy making based on small areas is that it enhances understanding of the *combined* impact on an area of all policies. Seen in this light small area policies cannot be viewed separately from the larger issue of power relationships between central and local government. Should central government through, for example, the statutory local planning and housing-area processes continue to exercise a major role in the way a local authority relates its activities to particular neighbourhoods? Or should local authorities be given greater discretion to develop their own policies for areas, subject to resource constraints, but unhindered by detailed procedural requirements?

2 Distribution

In considering the usefulness of area approaches in pursuing distributional ends it is important to distinguish between learning and action. Experience suggests that the *learning* process can often be highly effective if related to fairly small areas whereas the *action* process required to bring about change will often depend on policy decisions taken at higher levels within the governmental hierarchy. This is not to belittle the value of schemes designed to delegate more discretion to the local level but rather to recognize that, in many cases, effective action will require more fundamental changes in overall policy.[68]

As touched on in the introduction, it is the major functional policies rather than the area focussed policies which consume most resources and have most impact on the quality of life. It is surprising, therefore, that most local authorities are completely ignorant of expenditure variations within the geographical area covered by the authority. The small amount of research which has been completed has revealed serious territorial injustice.[69] There is, then, a need for more research into the distribution of resources between fairly small areas to enlighten decisions not only on how money is spent but on where and in whose interests. There remains a general dearth of easily captured small area statistics and yet it is a comparatively simple task to introduce geographical coding into ongoing record keeping, including records relating to expenditure.

3 Accountability

A striking feature of recent area-based policies has been their attempt to involve the public, an objective almost completely absent from the policies developed before 1968. There are sharp differences of opinion as to how valid the various developments in public participation have been. But there is considerable agreement that policies related to an area with a population size of less than 15 000 are most likely to attract public interest. Area-based policies have shown repeatedly that the public do not compartmentalize community problems into the various service divisions adopted by government for the purpose of administration. Much frustration has been caused by the failure of many authorities to develop a corporate approach in their dialogue with the public about area problems and plans.

In some authorities the local ward councillors are taking a more positive role in public involvement and, given that participation usually exposes essentially political conflicts, this is a welcome development. At the same time it is disappointing to note that, even in those authorities with developed systems of area management, there is relatively little delegation of authority to area committees, community groups or local officers. In an era of resource constraints increased delegation would seem to be a promising way of ensuring better value for money by exploiting the knowledge of those closest to the problems on the ground.

Conclusion

Since the mid-1960s there has been widespread experiment with new forms of policy focussed on neighbourhoods. But most of them have been pursued with little or no understanding of the relationships between them, or of the way they relate to the major spending programmes, let alone the way they influence market forces in the private sector. These area-based policies are coming increasingly under attack. Peter Townsend has even argued that, because of the labelling of areas, some of the area deprivation policies scare off potential development and actually intensify local problems.[70] However, the spatial dimension remains important and public policy makers would be unwise to reject the value of various forms of area approach for they retain considerable potential for opening up fresh possibilities for change. First, they can promote new ways of learning about problems and opportunities in the city and the efficacy of current policies. They can cut across functional patterns of thinking. Second, they can bring important new perspectives to bear on the *combination* of processes which coalesce to give rise to our most serious problems of urban deprivation. Third, they can, by relating policies to areas which are meaningful to local residents, assist in the renovation of management *and* political processes at the local level.

6 American approaches to neighbourhoods

> come senators congressmen
> please heed the call
> don't stand in the doorway
> don't block up the hall
> for he that gets hurt
> will be he who has stalled
> there's a battle outside raging
> it'll soon shake your windows
> and rattle your walls
> for the times they are a-changing
>
> Bob Dylan. Released January 1964
> Lead track on 'The times they are a-changing'

Introduction

Federal policies for neighbourhoods have seen striking developments since 1960 and have had a considerable influence on British approaches. The major stimulus for new federal initiatives was provided by President John F. Kennedy who launched a rational and hopeful reform programme within the United States soon after he was elected. It is a bitter irony, and one felt deeply by Dylan himself,[1] that the President was shot in November 1963 only a few weeks after 'The times they are a-changing' was recorded. But the currents for change were strong and remained so throughout the 1960s. Whilst the sit-ins and freedom rides of the late 1950s and early 1960s led by Martin Luther King were soon to achieve their major legislative objectives in the form of the Civil Rights Act 1964 and the Voting Rights Act 1965, unrest, particularly in the cities of the north, was to grow. Civil disorders started in 1963. More disturbances occurred in 1964 and the serious riots in the Watts area of Los Angeles took place in August 1965. Disorders peaked with 167 occurrences reported during the first nine months of 1967.

The National Advisory Commission on Civil Disorders found that:

'White racism is essentially responsible for the explosive mixture which has been accumulating in our cities since the end of World War II.'[2] And the importance of racism was also stressed by some black leaders.[3] Certainly British readers need to make an effort to appreciate the significance of racial conflict in influencing federal neighbourhood policies but the point can be overstated. Racism is important but urban violence is more helpfully viewed as a response to frustration with wider aspects of the urban system including the relative lack of opportunity caused by social, economic and political disadvantage.[4] P. Lupsha has placed particular emphasis on the political causes of urban violence: 'It is an anger directed at the inability and inadequacy of the political system and its institutions to live up to their promise . . . to process demands, and to make allocations in a responsive and responsible manner.'[5] It is not surprising, therefore, that Peter Marris and Martin Rein in their analysis of the American poverty programme suggest that it was concerned with an issue more profound even than poverty – the viability of democracy itself.[6]

This chapter focusses initially on federal initiatives. It starts with urban renewal, reviews the major President-led programmes of the 1960s and discusses the 'new federalism' of the 1970s. Federal initiatives are only part of the story and, towards the end of the chapter, an attempt is made to review wider developments in American approaches to neighbourhoods. As with Chapter 5 the aim is to provide an *overview* of American experience with area approaches which is developed in the light of the three underlying objectives of area approaches identified in Chapter 3: (1) effectiveness, (2) distribution and (3) accountability.

The qualification in the introduction to Chapter 5 bears repetition here. This chapter is concerned mainly with policies which discriminate *explicitly* between areas but it is important to remember that these account for only a small proportion of total government spending. The publicity they receive should not obscure the fact that almost all government policies have spatial implications – every recipient of a service or benefit is resident somewhere, and every physical improvement or development has a geographical location. The spatial implications of the major functional policies continue to be poorly understood, particularly at the micro or neighbourhood scale. This is one of the factors which has worked against improved understanding of the distributional effects of policy.

Urban renewal

Since the Housing Act of 1949 the federal urban renewal programme has provided local renewal agencies with federal funds and the power to condemn slum neighbourhoods, demolish the buildings, and resell the cleared land to private developers at a reduced price. In addition to relocating the slum dwellers in 'decent, safe and sanitary' housing the programme was intended to stimulate large-scale private building, provide new tax revenues for the cities, and re-vitalize downtown areas by halting the exodus of middle-class whites to the suburbs. During the early 1960s the programme met with increasing protest from slum dwellers who found support at the local level from the growing civil rights movements. By the mid-1960s a substantial body of literature had built up which was strongly critical of the programme primarily on the grounds that it was positively detrimental to the urban poor.[7] None of the slum dwellers who were dispossessed could afford to move into the expensive new apartments and, because almost two-thirds of the cleared slum units were occupied by negroes, the urban renewal programme has often been characterized as negro removal. In too many cities urban renewal was a form of negative discrimination – away from the poor and to the rich.

The Housing Act 1954 amended the 1949 Act and established seven new guidelines (known as the 'workable programme') which had to be met as a condition of receiving federal funds, one of which was a programme of citizen participation in the planning and execution of each project. This requirement might have been expected to strengthen local accountability but, on the whole, membership of advisory committees concentrated heavily on representation from real estate, construction and business groups, particularly chambers of commerce, as well as some community-wide housing and planning groups; representation from the project areas was almost totally absent.[8] Sherry Arnstein, in her famous paper 'A ladder of participation in the USA', suggests that at the meetings of these citizen advisory committees communication was a one-way process in which the officials educated, persuaded and advised the citizens, not the reverse.[9] She concludes that urban renewal is a prime example of 'manipulation' – the bottom rung of the ladder.

In 1968 the Department of Housing and Urban Development attempted to improve public involvement in the urban renewal programme by requiring the establishment of Project Area Committees (PACs) comprised of residents of the area affected. In some cases the opportunity was taken to develop an influential role for the PAC. For example, in Springfield, Illinois, between 1971 and 1973 members of the PAC were involved in interviewing applicants for positions relating to the urban renewal project.[10] However, for the most part, the urban renewal programme has a poor record for public participation. It remains an example of limited resident input and maximum retention by officials of decision-making responsibility. A parallel can be drawn with the generally low level of public involvement in the clearance and redevelopment process in Britain. However, the urban renewal programme is significant for it was the first in a series of federally funded programmes requiring some degree of public participation.

The grey areas project

During the late 1950s staff members of the Ford Foundation's Public Affairs department were concerned about the deteriorating inner areas or 'grey areas' of American cities and were equally convinced that broader approaches than physical renewal were needed.[11] Beginning in 1961, the Foundation made sizeable grants to city governments and independent social action agencies in five cities and one state. Apart from these six experiments, which constituted the grey area projects, the Foundation contributed to a similar project in New York's Lower East Side, Mobilization for Youth. All the projects directed their activities toward the general social environment of depressed neighbourhoods and were particularly concerned to develop broadly based social programmes involving inter-agency co-operation. In this respect they were the forerunners of the model cities programme discussed below.

The grey area projects focussed on the needs of young people and were influenced by a relatively new interpretation of the causes of delinquency developed by Richard Cloward and Lloyd Ohlin.[12] This saw inequality in economic and educational opportunity, rather than individual pathology, as the real problem and justified a wide scope of intervention. Direct participation in the projects was low for they were run by boards and staff representing established organizations, city government, and reform-minded citizens drawn mainly from the ranks of upper income groups.[13] Although a prime objective of the projects was to re-establish a sense of community in poor neighbourhoods relatively few of the board members came from the neighbourhoods served. We may conclude that the grey area projects were primarily concerned with improving the effectiveness of intervention by trying to re-open opportunities for deprived individuals and groups. Less emphasis was placed on redistribution of resources in favour of the deprived and on establishing arrangements to ensure local accountability.

The President's Committee on Juvenile Delinquency

When he was elected John F. Kennedy was eager to give substance to the campaign slogan of 'a new frontier' by a series of innovative programmes. Soon after his inauguration in 1961 he established the President's Committee on Juvenile Delinquency and Youth Crime which was to review and co-ordinate federal activities bearing on juvenile delinquency and to stimulate experimentation and innovation in this field. In the early stages the Committee was influenced by the interpretation of delinquency developed by the grey area projects. Indeed, Lloyd Ohlin, who was co-director of research at Mobilization for Youth, was appointed to help develop the federal programme. Inspired by a common philosophy the grey area projects and the President's Committee introduced a similar range of experiments. Both concentrated their resources in a few selected projects hoping they would serve as demonstrations of new approaches. Both tried to make the institutions affecting slum residents more responsive. Both introduced a wide range of measures – educational innovations, vocational training, legal aid and community service centres. By the end of 1964 there were sixteen projects funded by the Committee under way.

All the delinquency projects sought to involve the affected populations in policy formulation but such involvement was more frequently in an advisory rather than a decision-making category. In one study of the projects Melvin Mogulof found that in none of the policy making coalitions did the involvement of neighbourhood representatives approximate more than 10 per cent of the governing body.[14] At the same time the grey area projects and the President's Committee both attempted to extend to the people of the neighbourhoods at least a measure of control over the projects which served them. This idea of local accountability was to be taken up and pursued vigorously by many of the agencies in the community action programme.

The community action programme

The programmes of the Ford Foundation and the President's Committee heightened public awareness that poverty remained a serious problem in the United States. In 1963 President Kennedy stated his intention to include anti-poverty measures in the 1964 legislative programme. The day after the assassination President Johnson asked for work on these proposals to be kept moving. Early in 1964 he established a task force to develop proposals for a 'war on poverty'.[15] Soon afterwards the Office of Economic Opportunity (OEO) was created to lead the 'attack'. Community action was only one part of the anti-poverty strategy which came into force with the passing of the Economic Opportunity Act in August 1964. Other elements included the Job Corps, work-training programmes, special rural programmes and Volunteers in Service to America (VISTA).

But community action was a central feature. It was defined by the Act as a programme which combines the resources of an area in actions which promise to reduce poverty or its causes – 'through developing employment opportunities, improving human performance, motivation and productivity, or bettering the conditions under which people live, learn and work'. This action was to be organized by a public or private non-profit agency, and to be 'developed, conducted and administered with the maximum feasible participation of the residents of the areas and members of the groups served'. The President gave his personal support and the community action programme grew quickly. Federal spending was on quite a different scale from that of the President's Committee on Juvenile Delinquency which in 1964 cost less than $30m for the sixteen projects.[16] The federal expenditure on community action agencies was $237m in 1965 and $628m in 1966.[17] Note, however, that these sums were spread around hundreds of agencies with the result that grants to particular neighbourhoods were often scarcely larger than those provided by the President's Committee on Juvenile Delinquency.[18] As federal support grew the Ford Foundation phased out the grey area projects and most of the projects funded under the juvenile delinquency programme were transferred to the Office of Economic Opportunity.

Exactly who coined the phrase 'maximum feasible participation' and what they meant is a matter of differing memories. Daniel Moynihan (a member of the task force on the war on poverty) suggests that the phrase was intended to ensure that persons excluded from the political process in the South and elsewhere would participate in the *benefits* of the programme.[19] This view conflicts with that of Richard Boone (also a member of the task force) who saw the desire for maximum involvement as part of a continuing thrust towards localism – the right to local decision making in planning and operating anti-poverty programmes.[20] In practice, OEO staff pushed for as much representation of the poor as they could obtain through their power to withhold grants with the result that, as early as the spring of 1965, protests from city governments about the tactics of the new community action agencies were already pouring in. A group of mayors led by Richard Daley of Chicago met with Vice President Humphrey and voiced their concern. The President and Vice President sided with the mayors and the Budget Bureau soon passed the word to the OEO to keep the role of the poor in policy making to a minimum.[21]

Nevertheless, the revolutionary notion that representatives of the poor should have seats on the boards of community action agencies had taken hold. By the end of 1965 OEO's informal policy was to require at least one third to be representatives of the poor. In 1966 Congress passed the Quie Amendment which made this requirement legally binding. This was a Republican amendment which, as Howard Hallman observes, was motivated more out of mischief to embarrass the Democrats than dedication to the theory of participation.[22]

There is now an extensive literature on the 'war on poverty' much of which was focussed on the controversial community action agencies which assumed widely diverse roles in the over 800 communities in which they were established. Approximately 90 per cent took the form of private non-profit organizations, and most of the others were part of local government. The degree of citizen participation varied considerably and this makes generalization difficult. Robert Yin and Douglas Yates have suggested that the community action programme acted only as a *partial* impetus for decentralization. This is because citizen participation took place in citywide organizations, not neighbourhood-based ones, and citywide boards determined policy.[23] Nevertheless, the programme did provide opportunities for new groups of participants to gain first-hand experience of public policy making and Richard Cole, whilst acknowledging the existence of tight control of community action agencies by city hall in a few areas, concludes that the programme as a whole did promote the mobilization of the political power of the poor.[24] Ralph Kramer reached a conclusion somewhere between these two views in his analysis of five agencies in the San Francisco Bay area: whilst there was no substantial shift in the distribution of power, nevertheless a new decision making structure with an unfulfilled political potential had appeared outside the existing institutional framework.[25]

Despite the promising start the programme was soon in decline. A discerning analysis of the reasons for the attrition of the programme is provided by Peter Marris and Martin Rein in the epilogue to their book.[26] They conclude that the war on poverty was planned with very inadequate resources, for fear of over-committing the president on a politically doubtful issue. This led to a strategy of community action whose conflicting interpretations then alienated support, confirming the initial doubts. By 1967 it seemed doubtful whether the programme would continue at all. At the last possible hour of the 1967 session Congress authorized another two years of the programme, but only just.[27] In his first message to Congress in February 1969, President Nixon proposed that OEO should give up responsibility for its established programmes and concentrate all its energies on its innovative role of devising programmes to help the poor.[28] The programme was allowed to continue in diluted form during Nixon's first term, but the Office of Economic Opportunity was gradually dismembered with most of its programmes being transferred to other federal agencies. For example, Head Start was placed with Health Education and Welfare, legal services now operate under a Legal Services Corporation and manpower programmes were transferred to the Department of Labor. Even so the vast majority of the local community action agencies still exist and function drawing funds from a new Community Services Administration and from other federal and local agencies.

In summary, the Economic Opportunity Act did not achieve its ambitious objective of eradicating or significantly reducing poverty in America. But the emphasis on the failure of the programme in this respect has obscured some of the lasting benefits of the programme for governmental responsiveness. These have been touched on by Howard Hallman who suggests that the community action programme:

accomplished unstated objectives related to bringing groups and neighborhoods more fully into the local governmental and political system.

Minority group professionals advanced rapidly in administrative positions, and quite a few transferred to top governmental jobs and some gained elective office. Large numbers of poor and near-poor people got jobs as non-professionals, and many of them moved up career ladders. The community action programme also built an institutional network in poor neighborhoods that were deficient in services and lacked effective community organizations.[29]

Set against the high expectations the impact of the community action programme was disappointing, but it did challenge local government bureaucracies to improve their performance, it did involve some redistribution of resources and it did strengthen public involvement in some cities.

The model cities programme

Although the war on poverty set out to include a very broad scope of operations it did not give much attention to the physical environment of cities; housing, community facilities, and transportation systems. In 1965 Congress established the Department of Housing and Urban Development (HUD) which was designed to bring together the federal programmes concerned with the environment of cities, a move to be emulated later in Britain by the establishment of the Department of the Environment in 1970. A task force set up in October 1965 to advise the President on the work and organization of the new department recommended the model cities programme[30] as the grand unifier and co-ordinator of all federal urban grants. The President wanted swift action and the serious riots in the Watts area of Los Angeles the previous August strengthened the sense of urgency for more direct action to meet the needs of the inner city poor. In January 1966, the President called on Congress to enact 'a massive demonstration cities program' to rebuild or revitalize slum areas. The Demonstration Cities and Metropolitan Development Act was passed in October and had a strong neighbourhood focus. Resources and services were to be channelled into small specific areas. Thus, the model cities programme was more concerned with territorial discrimination than the community action programme.[31]

In the first draft of the task force report funds were to be concentrated in thirty-six cities but this was extended to sixty-six in the final report.[32] With so many 'experiments' the validity of the programme as a demonstration was questionable even before the proposal reached Congress. Here there was strong political pressure to spread resources even more thinly with the result that the programme eventually comprised 150 model cities agencies. The grants were to be in two stages – first, to meet up to 80 per cent of the cost of planning, and second, to carry out the plans. Some $12 million were allocated for planning in each of the first two fiscal years (1967 and 1968) and the amount spent on implementation grew from $200m in 1968 to over $300m in 1969 and over $500m in 1970 and 1971.[33] Thus the level of annual federal expenditure on model cities was roughly on a par with OEO's budget for community action. Relative to the problems being tackled Marris and Rein suggest that this is a trivial level of expenditure: they point out that New York City spends three times as much on welfare.[34] But compared to previous and more recent policies the model cities programme did, because funds were focussed on small areas, enable poor neighbourhoods to make relative gains in the share of federal funds.

The model cities programme seemed to place control firmly in the hands of local government and can be seen as a retreat from the more radical approach to citizen participation attempted by the community action programme. Instead of 'maximum feasible participation' the early guidelines from HUD sought to develop 'means of introducing the views of area residents in policy making'.[35] Nothing was said about board membership. Some of the staff within HUD, particularly Sherry Arnstein, pushed for a stronger approach to citizen participation and the HUD guidelines were modified. This set in motion actions which generally increased the role for residents of model neighbourhoods. However, as with the community action programme, it is difficult to generalize because of the variations between projects. Some writers suggest that neighbourhood residents played a limited role in relation to city hall[36] whilst others have shown that, in some cases, residents gained a *de facto* veto power over local programmes.[37]

Bernard Frieden and Marshall Kaplan identify two themes winding through the entire history of the programme:

Model cities was an attempt to respond to the crisis of the cities and at the same time to improve the management of the federal grant-in-aid system. These twin purposes led to an emphasis on concentrating federal resources in selected poverty neighborhoods across the country and to a further emphasis on making the full range of federal categorical aids readily available to the participating city governments. Both purposes ran counter to deeply ingrained ways of managing programs in Washington. As a result, the attempt to establish local model cities agencies as a single point of entry for federal aid, to earmark categorical funds, to simplify federal reviews, to provide effective technical assistance, to make the categorical systems more flexible, and to undertake systematic evaluations of the results all fell far short of early expectations.[38]

But, whilst the difficulties of reversing the administrative practices of federal bureaucracies account for much of the disappointment with the model cities programme, these authors also question the seriousness of the nation's commitment to solve the problems of the cities, the poor and minority groups.

With the inauguration of President Nixon in January 1969 the future of the programme was uncertain. The Nixon administration was developing its own strategies around the concept of a 'new federalism' in which power, funds, and responsibility would flow from Washington to the states and local governments. However, the model cities programme was never as controversial as community action and, since the programme was originally designed to last five action years after planning was complete, the Nixon administration was content to let it run its course. There was, however, one significant change when, in 1970, HUD developed the idea of 'planned variations' to the model cities programme. When implemented in 1971 it allowed the programme to go citywide in twenty selected cities and gave the city halls a larger voice in all related federal programmes through a device called 'chief executive review and comment'. This was a step in the direction of revenue sharing. As we shall see in Chapter 8 it was also an important factor in the development of neighbourhood priority boards in Dayton.

Revenue sharing and block grants

The three basic forms of federal aid – categorical grants, general revenue sharing, and block grants – are discussed in Chapter 4 in the section on local government finance. *General revenue sharing* was introduced in 1972 and can be seen as a reaction against the federal programmes of the 1960s which tended to concentrate decision making, even on local programmes, in Washington. In theory, general revenue sharing was to bring government closer to the people by enabling them to exercise a greater influence in determining local priorities and distributing federal funds. In practice, it has increased discretion for established local governments to allocate funds as they see fit. The federal legislation and administrative regulations put little or no pressure on local officials to open up government procedures to greater community involvement and there are fears that firm control by local government may work against an equitable distribution of these resources.:

Low income and minority groups do not appear to be receiving a fair share of General Revenue Sharing funds. Surveys show that most of the money has gone to capital expenditures, public safety and transportation. Other funds have been used to reduce property taxes or to keep taxes from rising. Very little, approximately four to six per cent, has been spent on social services for the poor and aging, housing and community development.[39]

In 1976 Congress approved a continuation of general revenue sharing until 1980. It remains to be seen whether there are sufficient safeguards to ensure that local government responds adequately to those in need and dispossessed of power.

There are now five main *block grants*: in health, criminal justice, welfare, employment and community development. As with general revenue sharing these enlarge the discretion of local governments and should, therefore, contribute to a more effective use of resources since priorities can be set locally by those closer to the problems on the ground. However, questions have been raised about the looseness of the requirements relating to public involvement and about the degree to which disadvantaged groups are helped. Interestingly, criticism has also been voiced by some state officials who feel that the 'new federalism', of general revenue sharing and block grants, is diminishing their role to the disadvantage of small communities outside the big cities: 'From a state point of view, the decentralization theme of the new federalism was roughly synonymous with a "cut the states out of the action" strategy.'[40] These different reactions remind us of the great importance of getting to grips with central government–local government relationships (see Chapter 1) and, also, point up the very real conflicts between our three underlying objectives of effectiveness, distribution and accountability. One of the block grants – the Community Development Block Grant – deserves closer consideration for it involves a particularly interesting approach to planning and budgeting for the physical environment of urban neighbourhoods.

The community development block grant

Title 1 of the Housing and Community Development Act 1974 established the community development block grant programme which consolidated seven existing categorical grant-in-aid programmes: urban renewal, model cities, water and sewer facilities, open space, neighbourhood facilities, rehabilitation loans and public facilities loans.[41] In this way the programme simplifies administrative procedures considerably: a single application and review process replaces seven sets of detailed programme requirements. The programme differs from the federal initiatives discussed earlier in several ways. First, local elected officials, rather than special purpose agencies, have responsibility for determining community development needs, establishing priorities and allocating resources. This is, of course, a double-edged attribute: some welcome the restoration of control to local government, others are concerned that low income groups lacking political weight will lose out in the local competition for resources. Second, the funds may be used anywhere within the local government's jurisdiction and need not be focussed on a particular neighbourhood. There are vague requirements that the programme should serve the needs of low and moderate income people and/or tackle the problem of slums but it is difficult to see how this can be monitored. Third, as a general rule public participation is more limited than it was in the model cities programme for HUD's criteria can be met by superficial citizen involvement. The discretion is, however, with the local authority and as we shall see in Chapter 8 both Boston and Dayton have made serious attempts to gather neighbourhood views on how the block grant should be spent. Fourth, aid allocations are based on a statutory formula using three measures of need. This reduces the role of grantmanship and political influence in sharing out federal funds and should provide a firmer context for the preparation of future budgets.

The allocation arrangements, however, present problems as well as advantages.[42] The total federal aid budget for community development will remain about what it was before the 1974 Act but it will be divided differently. Unlike general revenue sharing, the funds are not granted to all the 38 000 odd general local governments in the country. Instead they are concentrated in about 500 'metropolitan cities' (central cities and other cities with a population of 50 000 or more within metropolitan areas) and some fifty urban counties. These communities will be entitled to formula allocations, provided they meet programme requirements. The formula takes into account population, overcrowded housing and the extent of poverty, with the poverty factor given double weight. Many cities, particularly those that have been aggressive consumers of federal aid, will be worse off under the formula. Transitional grants which gradually reduce over a five-year period and cease in 1979 will cushion the shock but there can be no doubt that the distribution of federal aid for community development will change drastically as a result of the block grant approach. As we shall see in Chapter 8 Boston, whose aid will be cut by approximately two-thirds, is one of the big losers.

It is still early days so that it would be unwise to make sweeping conclusions about the community development block grant at this stage. But, given the growing British interest in block grants, it would seem to be a programme well worth further investigation. One of the exciting aspects of the programme is the great opportunity it offers for entirely new, creative approaches to community problems. Because of its flexibility it provides scope for the development of new partnerships between community groups and local government in the design of programmes tailored to meet the needs of particular neighbourhoods.

Approaches to neighbourhoods – the wider scene

So far we have concentrated on federal initiatives but, before discussing the most recent neighbourhood legislation, it is useful to review briefly other developments in approaches to neighbourhoods. For convenience, these developments are considered under two broad headings: community design experiments and neighbourhood organization.

Community design experiments

American architects and planners were among the first professionals to attempt to open up the design and planning processes. For example, in the mid-1960s they developed advocacy planning. This involves professionals advocating the neighbourhood or resident viewpoints against that of the government bureaucracy.[43] In the late 1960s this approach also developed in Britain and has become a standard feature of public inquiries into road schemes, redevelopment plans and other proposals. More recently some professional activists on both sides of the Atlantic have become less concerned with arguing on behalf of the disadvantaged and more concerned with passing on skills so that the residents can handle their own affairs. The central idea that there are alternative ways of viewing the same planning problem – which depend on different perspectives and different sets of values – remains.

Public participation in planning does not always have to centre on the gladiatorial combat of the public inquiry or public hearing. American institutions seem to have been more willing to experiment with direct forms of community involvement and Britain may be able to learn something here. For example, one idea which has been used fairly widely in the USA is the charrette process. This is a relatively new approach to community planning which brings together citizens, agency officials, technical experts and elected representatives to resolve complex community problems in an accelerated manner.[44] 'Charrette' is an architectural term meaning a creative, yet deadline-oriented process. It has been used mainly as a prelude to the design of a building (e.g. a community school or health centre) but it can also be used for formulating neighbourhood policies.

Essentially the process involves two or three months' groundwork to establish an agenda of problems and to intensify local involvement. This culminates in the charrette which may last about fourteen days. During the charrette perhaps a hundred residents are paid their normal salary to discuss the various problems in groups, supported by professional advisers, with anyone joining in during the evenings. This may sound a lavish approach to public involvement but American experience suggests the approach is cost-effective. Designs are more successful and residents see projects conceived in this way as really a part of *their* community. Which British local authority and/or health authority will be first to innovate with the charrette process? The slow-down in capital building programmes provides an excellent opportunity for it creates more time for experiment and has, to a certain extent, reduced pressure on architectural design time.

Charrettes are only one example of the more innovatory approaches to community design being attempted in the USA. Others are the community design centres found in several cities which provide a wide range of planning and design services to groups of residents from low income areas,[45] the 'take part workshops' developed by some progressive architectural firms,[46] and the fairly widespread experiment with videotape as a design tool.[47] It would be misleading to suggest that these approaches to community design are flourishing in every city, let alone every neighbourhood. But there can be no denying that the American commitment to a more imaginative, and less paternal, style of community involvement in many projects and plans is more widespread than in Britain.

Neighbourhood organization

At the municipal level attempts to decentralize services to neighbourhoods have proliferated. Many of these have occurred within services, such as health, safety and education, and have occasionally involved radical experiments in neighbourhood control as happened in New York City's experiment in school decentralization.[48] Some initiatives have involved more than one service and include developments in multi-service centres and little city halls.[49] More detail on particular examples of decentralization is provided in Chapter 8 in the discussions on area approaches in Boston, New York and Dayton.

At the neighbourhood level a kaleidoscope of initiatives are taking place. Many of them derive strength from the long-standing American tradition of small units of government as a means of securing public participation in politics and voluntary activity for community improvement. These concepts have been updated and reasserted by a number of authors in recent years.[50] The initiatives themselves take many forms. Some originate with community protest and develop into community organization in the way promoted by Saul Alinsky.[51] Some are neighbourhood organizations stemming from the initiatives of the Ford Foundation and federal government discussed earlier and are mainly concerned with social services in deprived areas. Some, known as community development corporations, are more explicitly concerned with economic development and may receive aid from the Federal Office of Economic Development funded by the Community Services Administration. Yet others are highly active and progressive organizations which operate without substantial government funding, such as the Adams-Morgan Organization, Washington DC and the Sto-Rox Neighborhood Corporation just outside Pittsburgh.[52]

Added to these are a range of new expressions of neighbourhood power which take the form of either charter revisions or city ordinances. These aim to weld some kind of neighbourhood council or community board onto the basic structure of municipal government.[53] A charter constitutes the legal framework and ground rules within which a city can conduct its affairs. Charter revisions are not brought about swiftly but they are likely to endure. City ordinances and council resolutions can show results more quickly but are less secure. Howard Hallman has suggested that the various efforts to establish community boards have three major differences from most of the initiatives of the 1960s.[54] First, they are aimed at middle-class citizens as well as residents of poor neighbourhoods. Second, they are citywide in scope and do not focus only on selected target areas. And third, they are mostly advisory and rarely provide neighbourhood boards with control of budgets, staff and programme policy. A useful across-the-board review of American community-based activity is provided by Janice Perlman.[55]

Inextricably wound up with this large variety of local initiatives for neighbourhoods are a cluster of independent national organizations. These include:

    National Association of Neighborhoods
    National Center for Urban Ethnic Affairs
    National People's Action on Housing
    Center for Community Change
    Citizen Involvement Network
    Center for Governmental Studies

They are important not only for their role in sustaining local initiatives and documenting developments in different areas, but also for their direct impact on national policy as several of them are engaged in direct and effective lobbying in Washington. A number of the more recent legislative approaches to neighbourhoods result, at least in part, from this pressure group activity.

Recent neighbourhood legislation

Several recent federal programmes have attempted to increase responsiveness to neighbourhoods. For example, the Comprehensive Employment and Training Act of 1973 explicitly calls for representatives from community-based organizations and the client population to be importantly involved in the planning and evaluation process. However, two federal initiatives have particular significance for neighbourhoods: (1) neighbourhood disinvestment and (2) neighbourhood government.

Neighbourhood disinvestment

'Red-lining' is a term that was scarcely known at the beginning of the 1970s, but, in America, it is now officially recognized that arbitrary refusal by lenders to invest in older urban neighbourhoods is a primary factor in neighbourhood decline.[56] The Home Mortgage Disclosure Act 1975 requires lending institutions to disclose the number and dollar amount of their mortgage loans by either census tract, where readily available at a reasonable cost, or by zip code.[57] The Act represents a considerable victory for the painstaking efforts of scores of community groups to preserve their neighbourhoods. They have gathered statistics to show conclusively that many neighbourhoods have not been getting a fair share of mortgage money.

An excellent analysis of the problems has been provided by two of the leading campaigners for reform – Arthur Naparstek and Gale Cincotta.[58] They criticize existing urban policies and programmes for their failure to recognize the systemic origins of urban decline. They argue that the deterioration of American cities is rooted in certain institutionalized policies, attitudes and practices which lead to discrimination and inequity, go on to outline the cycle of neighbourhood decline from healthy community, through red-lining and disinvestment to urban renewal, and catalogue the critical role of lending policies in this downward spiral. The document also describes the growth of organized community action to tackle this problem. Work by groups began in 1971 and culminated in a direct impact on the Senate Banking Committee which held public hearings into red-lining in the spring of 1975. The receptive chairman of the committee was Senator William Proxmire (Democrat – Wisconsin) who went on to sponsor the Disclosure Act which became law on 31 December 1975 despite a backlash in Congress against new regulatory legislation of this kind. The first statistics available under the new law were made available in the autumn of 1976 and there are indications that some bankers are beginning to atone. For example, the Federal National Mortgage Association, a prime offender, has even started a pilot programme in St Louis to encourage bankers to originate inner city loans.

The Federal response to disinvestment began before the passing of the Disclosure Act with the formation of the Urban Reinvestment Task Force. This is a joint effort by the heads of the federal financial regulatory agencies, including the Federal Home Loan Bank Board, and the Secretary of the US Department of Housing and Urban Development to stimulate the development of local partnerships committed to a co-ordinated reinvestment strategy.[59] The task force is involved in two separate programmes: Neighborhood Housing Services (NHS) and Neighborhood Preservation Projects, with the main accent on the former. The Neighborhood Housing Services approach combines citizens, city government and lenders in a team effort at stemming decline. The approach was pioneered locally in Pittsburgh's Central North Side as early as 1968[60] before being implemented on a national level by the task force which provides technical assistance (and sometimes grants) to local entities interested in establishing a programme. The NHS approach involves selecting target neighbourhoods, increasing public investment in the neighbourhood and establishing confidence in its future through appropriate zoning, systematic code enforcement, a subsidized loan fund for home improvement loans for those unable to afford conventional financing and the involvement of financial institutions to ensure mortage and home improvement loans will be made to bankable property owners in the area. The Neighborhood Preservation Projects also involve a local partnership bringing together neighbourhood residents, the private sector and local government, but these have been developed locally without task force assistance. The role of the task force is to monitor and evaluate those programmes which have promise for replication in other cities. The programmes selected receive modest demonstration grants toward data collection, documentation and support of the project itself.

As a follow-up to the Home Mortgage Disclosure Act, Senator Proxmire has joined with Senator Garn (Republican – Utah) to promote a National Neighborhood Policy Act.[61] The premise is that the banks are not the only forces responsible for neighbourhood decline and that there is therefore a need for a National Commission on Neighborhoods to be established to undertake a comprehensive study of the factors contributing to the decline of city neighbourhoods and of the factors necessary for neighbourhood survival and revitalization.[62] The Commission's work would be wide-ranging and would include analysis of the impact of existing federal, state and local policies, programmes and laws on neighbourhoods as well as trends in public and private investment. The cost of the Commission should not exceed $2 million

American experience with neighbourhood disinvestment suggests that a much more purposeful approach to this problem is needed in Britain. At local level partnerships between local authorities, building societies and community groups could work to 'green-line' neighbourhoods of older housing along the lines of the Neighbor-hood Preservation Projects just described. At national level perhaps the Housing Corporation could develop a wider brief to encompass a firmer role regarding the influence of investment policies by building societies and other financial institutions. Perhaps collaboration will need to be backed by new legislation along the lines of the Home Mortgage Disclosure Act to cajole or require a response from lending institutions. Initiatives of this kind are essential if we are to encourage re-investment in the inner city and yet they have been curiously neglected in Britain – even by the Inner Area Studies discussed in Chapter 5.

Neighbourhood government

Legislative ideas on neighbourhood government do not have the same immediate, practical relevance as legislation on neighbourhood investment but, even though it is politically impractical at present, the proposed Neighbourhood Government Act is thought-provoking. As long ago as 1971 Senator Mark Hatfield (Republican – Oregon) was advocating the introduction of neighbourhood government legislation.[63] He re-introduced the proposal in the form of the Neighborhood Government Act 1975[64] which is designed to encourage neighbourhood control by returning tax monies to the local level. The bill would provide a dollar-for-dollar federal income tax credit for all funds that citizens contributed to local neighbour-hood government corporations.[65] The maximum amount of the credit would be based on the taxpayer's annual income as follows:

Income	Percentage
$10 000 or less	80
$10 001 to $15 000	60
$15 001 to $20 000	40
$20 001 to $25 000	20
More than $25 000	10

If implemented, this would represent a dramatic departure from past practice for, if taxpayers took up the option in large numbers, there would be a massive transfer of funds from the higher levels of government to neighbourhood corporations in the order of tens of billions of dollars per year. Not unexpectedly the proposal has met with great resistance.

One suspects that Senator Hatfield is more concerned to achieve a radical re-think over the centralization of government power rather than to actually implement the neighbourhood government proposal as drafted. In introducing the Act he stressed the need to return to the fundamentals of democratic life, drew on Eric Fromm's theories of alienation and challenged strongly the usefulness of centralized federal bureaucracies.[66] The Neighborhood Government Act is a provocative piece of legislation and deserves wider publicity. However, even despite the scale of income levels built into the Act, there is a danger that the scheme as proposed will work to the advantage of rich neighbourhoods. The Act brings into focus the potential conflict between the local control and redistribution objectives of neighbourhood approaches introduced in Chapter 3.

Neighbourhood policy under President Carter

This review of American approaches to neighbourhoods would be incomplete without some reference to the attitudes of the new administration in Washington. At the time of writing Jimmy Carter has only just moved into the White House so comments can only be tentative. But it does seem that the neighbourhood is an important concept in Carter's approach to politics. The following is from a speech made in September 1976 during his campaign for the Presidency:

We feel most at home where our roots run deep. Neighborhoods and families are the living fiber that holds our society together. Until we place them at the very top of our national policy, our hopes for the nation, and our goals for our private lives, will not be attained. But for too many years, urban policy has been an enemy of the neighborhoods – and of families too. . . . If we are to save our cities, we must revitalize our neighborhoods first. It we are to save our country, we must first give our families and neighborhoods a chance.[67]

The speech includes criticism of urban renewal, low Republican investment in neighbourhoods and of red-lining. It actually advocates a national law against red-lining and it will be interesting to see whether the administration takes this idea forward.

Some political observers see Carter's campaign strategy on

neighbourhood issues as a way round the Catholic hierarchy on the abortion issue. By going directly into Catholic blue collar neighbourhoods and talking about locally experienced neighbourhood problems, Carter seems to have been successful in capturing considerable Catholic support despite his stand on women's rights in relation to abortion. But, whatever the motives, Jimmy Carter is committed to a positive federal policy for urban neighbourhoods. Those concerned with urban policy in Britain, as well as in America, would be wise to keep an eye on federal initiatives during the late 1970s.

Synthesis

Generalizations about American approaches to neighbourhoods should be advanced with caution both because of the wide variety of initiatives and because of the way they have changed over time. Figure 13 provides a simplified picture of the way the various federal policies have evolved over the period 1961 to 1977, together with a handful of the more significant national events which have influenced these developments. In overall terms we can recognize a shift away from the grand designs of the 1960s for intervention by big government – from the years when massive national efforts were expected to do everything from putting a man on the moon to eradicating poverty in America. Vietnam and Watergate are catchwords which symbolize the more recent distrust of policy making in Washington and the success of Jimmy Carter's 1976 presidential campaign owes more than a little to the average American's doubts about federal competence. Urban policy making has reflected these wider trends and the 'new federalism' of the 1970s places much greater reliance on local government to develop policies appropriate to the needs of particular neighbourhoods. The fact that local government officials were accused during the 1960s of failing to respond adequately to those in need and dispossessed of power seems to have been of little concern in developing the new system.

There now follows a brief summary of American experience in the light of the three underlying objectives of area approaches – effectiveness, distribution, accountability.

Figure 13   Evolution of federal approaches to neighbourhoods in America (1961–77)

time	national events	major programmes for neighbourhoods						
1961	President Kennedy the new frontier	Ford Foundation Grey area projects	President's Committee on Juvenile Delinquency				Urban renewal	categorical grant programmes
1962								
1963	President Kennedy assassinated							
1964	President Johnson the great society war on poverty	community action programme (Economic Opportunity Act 1964)		Department of Housing and Urban Development established				
1965	riots in Watts							
1966	widespread civil disorders	Quie amendment		models cities programme (Demonstration Cities and Metropolitan Development Act 1966)				
1967		Congress only just agrees to authorize continuation of the programme						
1968							Project Area Committees	
1969	President Nixon the new federalism	President Nixon proposes to dilute the programme						
1970								
1971				planned variations in selected cities				
1972		OEO dismantled						
1973	President Nixon begins second term Watergate emerges	Community Action Agencies continue in diluted form		general revenue sharing	end of model cities financing		end of urban renewal funding	
1974	President Nixon resigns - President Ford takes over					Community Development Block Grant (Housing and Community Development Act 1974)		
1975			Home Mortgage Disclosure Act 1975					
1976	President Carter elected							
1977								

1 *Effectiveness*

As with British policies for neighbourhoods, improvement of the impact of policy has been a dominant motive. From an early stage there has been an accent, first on co-ordinated planning for neighbourhoods, and second, on research and evaluation to test out the usefulness of the innovations introduced. Taking co-ordinated planning first, we have seen how the grey area projects, the President's Committee on Juvenile Delinquency, the community action programme and the model cities programme each broadened the scope of government intervention. The pattern of American programmes during the 1960s rehearsed, in many ways, the British search of the 1970s for a 'total approach' to urban problems. In terms of their ambitious objectives the programmes of the 1960s were less than successful, but I have suggested that they did improve government effectiveness, if only by stirring up the local government bureaucracies. Even those who are extremely critical of these programmes have to admit that they did have an impact on civil tensions – the cities were not burned down.

Turning to research and evaluation, again the overall impression is that the 'scientific' approach to governmental learning has been disappointing. Part of the problem was that the idea of research and analysis focussed on a small number of projects was not politically acceptable. Thus, for example, the number of model cities projects grew from thirty-six in the original draft to over one hundred and fifty in practice. But a more fundamental problem is the inadequacy of the 'scientific' model of policy research, a point that was touched on in Chapter 4.

The 'new federalism' of the 1970s with its accent on general revenue sharing and block grants might be expected to improve local government effectiveness by matching resources more closely to neighbourhood priorities. These developments are exciting and the community development block grant will be touched on again in Chapter 8. But two qualifications should be made. First, categorical grants still account for some three-quarters of total federal aid. One might reasonably inquire how far this host of categorical programmes continues to work against integrated planning and action at the local level. Second, and on the opposite side of the coin, it is still early days for revenue sharing and block grant programmes and it remains to be seen whether American local government can manage its increased responsibilities sensitively and equitably.

2   Distribution

The redistribution of resources was a major feature of the rhetoric on American urban policy during the 1960s. President Johnson, for example, set out to 'eradicate poverty'. In practice, whilst the sums involved in the various programmes have been, even allowing for differences in the size of the two countries, infinitely larger than the British commitment, they have still comprised a relatively small element of total federal expenditure. As referred to in the introduction, it is the major functional programmes rather than the special programmes which consume most resources and have most impact on the quality of life. It is surprising, therefore, that most American local governments are completely ignorant of expenditure variations within their geographical areas.

The small amount of research which has been completed has revealed serious territorial injustice.[68] The book by Levy, Meltsner and Wildavsky on urban outcomes in Oakland, California, is a particularly important contribution for it begins to develop a new working theory for urban policy planning. It provides three measures of equity: market equity (provide services in proportion to taxes paid), equal opportunity (equal distribution to all) and equal results (equal outcomes from the services). The authors conclude that outcomes in Oakland are inefficient, have a class bias somewhere between market equity and equal opportunity and, as they operate with a time lag, are responsive to yesterday's demands. The authors go on to set out recommendations on how to improve policy for the three services studied: schools, streets, libraries. Sadly, there seems to have been relatively little further work in this vein. Those involved in America's major programmes for neighbourhoods should give their urgent attention to the distributive effects of existing urban policies before embarking on any new programmes. Perhaps the Home Mortgage Disclosure Act, in seeking to influence the *existing* pattern of investment in neighbourhoods, is beginning to point the way.

3   Accountability

Many of the American approaches to neighbourhoods have respected the nation's strong democratic tradition which expects every citizen to play an autonomous part in the determination of his own affairs. The 'voice of the people' was heard loudest during the

heady days of the community action programme with its requirement for 'maximum feasible participation'. This provoked a backlash
from established local government and the direct role of residents in
the formulation of neighbourhood policy has been generally reduced.
For example, the requirements for public participation in the community development block grant programme are easily met.

At the same time reference has been made to widespread innovation with public involvement in the 1970s and to the spiralling
growth of community and grass-roots activities. Apart from their
impact at local level these groups are having an increasing effect
on policy making in Washington. For example, the various national
groupings of neighbourhood organizations had a direct and
important impact on the Senate Banking Committee in 1975 and
can claim a deal of credit for the origination and introduction of the
Home Mortgage Disclosure Act.

Even so it would be unwise to overstate the strength of local
groups. Chapter 4 has already suggested that American local
government is not as participatory as many have assumed and, even
in those cities which are leading the way in neighbourhood decentralization, there is relatively little delegation of authority to local
officers or neighbourhood associations. This would seem to be an
area which would benefit from further experiment. As neighbourhood organizations multiply it is to be hoped that American local
government can respond to their desire for a greater say in a way
that taps and develops local enthusiasm.

Conclusion

Federal approaches to neighbourhoods have evolved rapidly since
the early 1960s. There has been a changing mix of emphasis among
the three objectives of effectiveness, distribution and accountability.
In a pluralistic system with its constantly shifting coalitions and
political alliances this is to be expected but few would disagree that
federal initiatives have fluctuated too sharply. Too often goals have
been changed rather than achieved. Robert Wood has pointed out
this disturbing tendency to *replace* goals rather than *fulfil* them.[69]
And Bernard Frieden and Marshall Kaplan have suggested that
'before we had a chance to make much progress in coping with the
"urban crisis" we replaced it with the "environment crisis" . . . and
now we are on the "energy crisis".'[70] But this chapter has touched

on one or two developments which should give cause for some hope, if not optimism. For example, at one end of the political spectrum we have seen that the residents of the city are becoming better organized at the local level and, at the other end, the new President has committed himself to a positive policy for urban neighbourhoods.

7 Lessons from experience and an analytical framework

Above all, the polarity between centralisation and decentralisation – one masquerading as oppression and the other as freedom – is a myth ... The poles are two absurdities for any viable system, as our own bodies tell us. And yet government and business continue the great debate, to the advantage only of those politicians and consultants who find the system in one state and promptly recommend a switch to the other.

Stafford Beer, *Platform for Change*, 1975

Introduction

The last three chapters have all been fairly long and have included a considerable amount of detail on British and American approaches to urban problems. This chapter is short and, hopefully, to the point. It falls into two sections. The first, without repeating too many of the conclusions from the previous three chapters, attempts to summarize some of the main lessons to be derived from British and American experience. The second elaborates on the checklist presented in Chapter 3 to develop an analytical framework for classifying area approaches.

Lessons from experience

It would be possible to structure the main lessons from experience using the three themes developed in the previous two chapters: effectiveness, distribution and accountability. However, in this section I adopt a slightly different framework and link the discussion to five headings: institutional change, provision of opportunities, management and social science, democratic accountability, political support. An explanation of why these have been selected is called for.

In October 1969, an Anglo-American conference on urban policy convened at Ditchley Park, Oxfordshire. This followed an earlier meeting between Richard Nixon and Harold Wilson at which the two leaders had agreed to 'look together at some of the social and domestic problems faced by their governments'. But, according to one participant, it was not merely an exchange of views:

... the gathering of social scientists and civil servants was invited to endorse a specifically American strategy of reform, which over ten years had grown from a tentative experiment to a national programme. Ironically, the British were grasping towards it, just as the Americans were turning, somewhat disillusioned, elsewhere.[1]

Peter Marris has identified three basic ingredients in the American approach to urban policy.[2] The first was *institutional change* for it was felt that bureaucratic conservatism was the greatest obstacle to reform. Agencies, public or private, tended to be jealous of their jurisdictions and wedded to familiar functions. Thus, the problems were not so much questions of resources but of method. Secondly, poverty was seen as a failure to *provide opportunities* for the poor to enter the mainstream of American society. The reasons were that the agencies of assimilation – the schools, vocational training programmes, social services, political patronage, housing and planning policies – were not responsive to their needs, and the agencies of social control – the police, the probation service and the law – worked against them compounding frustration by insensitive suppression and unequal justice. Third, *sophisticated management* was essential to tackle the complex problems of an urban industrial society. Advanced approaches to information handling and decision-making should be imported from the business world to improve government effectiveness.

To these three intellectual themes we can add two important political elements. A fourth ingredient, then, is the American *democratic tradition* which believes profoundly in the vitality of local autonomy as an expression of personal freedom. Thus, many of the initiatives have involved active participation by the people affected. Lastly, and arguably most importantly, reform has to sustain *electoral support* in the country at large. A government may wish to redistribute resources in favour of deprived inner city neighbourhoods, but in a democracy, these wishes have to be reconciled against the need to retain a sufficient electoral majority to stay in power. The following discussion is pegged to these five ingredients which also characterize British experience.

Institutional change

Innovation has been an important feature of both American and British approaches but it is questionable how far any of the initiatives have brought about institutional change. More often than not the approaches have supplemented rather than re-directed the activities of existing institutions. It is even possible to argue that the various special programmes have distracted attention away from the need to transform our existing institutions. This would, I believe, understate the educational effect of many of the programmes discussed in Chapters 5 and 6. Several of them have provided valuable new perspectives on urban problems and their ideas have not all fallen on deaf ears. But, having said that, there can be no denying the failure to confront the immense capacity of existing institutions to resist, deflect of dilute the energies directed towards change.

The theory of bureaucracy, with its reliance on impersonal relationships articulated by formal regulations, still goes a good way to explaining the problems we confront. Max Weber's classic analysis of bureaucratic administration highlighted its two sides.[3] On the one hand, a disciplined hierarchy of command, in which each official fulfils a specified role, protects the organization from the corruption of personal favours and arbitrary abuse of authority. But it also imposes on an official great pressures to conform, to the point where loyalty to the organization and its routines obscures the original sense of purpose. A spirit of formalistic impersonality may remove hatred and passion but it also kills affection and enthusiasm. The various initiatives we have discussed simply have not paid sufficient attention to analysing the strengths and weaknesses of existing urban governmental institutions, let alone developed coherent strategies for changing their behaviour.

In relation to institutional change our conclusions on the various central government initiatives echo one of the conclusions made in relation to corporate planning in local government set out in Chapter 2. This is that we have failed to get to grips with the dynamic conservatism of institutions and the realities of bringing about change. One way forward is to develop the idea of government institutions as multi-levelled 'learning systems'. This would involve focussing much more attention on ways of developing imaginative and adaptive approaches by and between existing institutions. It would include a new concentration on people and on ways of releasing their creative potential. This idea of creative learning is taken up again in Chapter 10 but, meanwhile, consider this distinction between people and institutions presented by Stafford Beer:

People, considered as individuals, it seems to me, like change rather a lot. Don't you get bored when nothing changes? I know I do. Then just why do we go around saying that there is a resistance to change? Of course, the answer is simple. It is not the living, breathing human who resists change in his very soul. The problem is that *institutions* in which we humans have our stake resist change. Therefore we feel as individuals that we cannot afford to embrace it. And this is an extremely sound argument.[4]

Provision of opportunities

In terms of willingness to mobilize resources in favour of deprived neighbourhoods the American commitment has been considerably greater than the British. Even so American expenditure on its various urban programmes has been a small proportion of total federal aid. However, we must avoid viewing the various urban programmes in isolation from the major national policies designed to redistribute opportunities: incomes, employment, social security, rents, housing subsidies and so on. Viewed in the round the British welfare state has a better record than the United States in terms of the equalization of opportunities. The 1942 Beveridge Report's[5] proposals to defeat the five giants of Want, Disease, Ignorance, Idleness and Squalor were never fully implemented and much remains to be done about poverty in Britain – particularly in relation to the notorious problem of the poverty trap. But the British system still excites admiration in the United States. Interestingly, Peter Marris sees the convergence of British and American strategies in 1969 as a crossing point of social policies at different stages of evolution, with America moving towards a national family assistance plan under Richard Nixon and with Britain ready to attempt a series of experiments in localized situations.[6]

In my view the great mistake is to see the distribution of opportunities as either a national or a local policy problem – it is both. Likewise, it is a mistake to see the issue as one of distribution of opportunities between groups or areas – again it is both. As it happens most of the area policies we have discussed have done relatively little to redistribute opportunities and there is a growing backlash against the spatial approach.[7] There are those, for example, who pin all their hopes on incomes policy. Of course, incomes policy is crucial but redistributing money can only be a part of an effective policy designed to redistribute opportunities. This is because ongoing government policies continue to distribute day in and day out a wider 'social wage' of services, facilities and environment which has a profound effect on opportunities.[8] I have argued that in many instances these services are of uneven quantity and quality with poorer neighbourhoods often receiving poorer services. Even services provided uniformly often conceal a pattern of usage which is far from uniform and which, in reality, increases the opportunities of the better-off – public libraries provide a classic example. The lesson is not to reject area approaches to urban problems but to recognize, first, that they must be concerned to influence radically the ongoing functional programmes and, second, that they must be viewed as part of a wider social strategy against inequality. Both of these lessons require a politicization of area approaches.

Management and social science

Judgements as to the managerial sophistication of the various initiatives must be relative. Compared with what went before few would deny that they represented a move forward. Many of the programmes helped to promote the shift, discussed in Chapter 2, from an administrative to a purposeful approach by urban government. Many of them have embodied a rational planning process in which an attempt was made to relate action more closely to the needs of particular neighbourhoods and deprived groups. A fair proportion of the initiatives, particularly in recent years, have had broad terms of reference and this has enabled some of them to develop new forms of inter-departmental and inter-agency response. More flexible forms of funding are also being developed, such as joint financing in Britain and block grants in America.

Chapter 4 included criticism of the so-called 'scientific' approach to policy research. It is now widely appreciated that the analogy of the neighbourhood as a laboratory for the testing of social policy innovations has serious limitations. Organizational and/or community changes are notoriously difficult to monitor and, even if they can be measured, it is likely to be difficult to separate out sequences of cause and effect, to find out exactly what happened as a result of the programme and to isolate the effects of the programme from other forces and interactions in the social environment. This is not to suggest that the attempts to research and evaluate policy innovations have been a waste of time. Quite the reverse for, despite their limitations, they have sharpened thinking about different initiatives, represent a serious attempt to learn from experience and provide at least a form of feedback on performance. More important, some social scientists are beginning to develop learning models of policy research which differ from the traditional procedures of experimental science. In these approaches settings for innovation and research 'are not regarded as controlled experiments that critically assess the efficiency of a specific innovation in policy but as *an open-ended exploration of a total environment* that promises to lead to the discovery of ways that will recast a given problem situation into a more desirable form'.[10]

We may conclude that the role of management science and social science in the urban policy innovations we have discussed has been variable. At worst they have translated badly into the complex and erratic world of urban policy making and have found difficulty in coming to terms with the essentially political nature of the task. More commonly they have injected an element of intellectual rigour into some of the thinking and may be expected to play an important role in the generation of ideas on how to develop institutions capable of self-directed learning.

Democratic accountability

Many of the approaches have attempted to strengthen local lines of accountability. However, in all three of the previous chapters doubts have been expressed, first, about the degree to which local government in the two countries may be said to be democratic (Chapter 4) and, second, about the degree to which local people have been able to participate in the planning and implementation of the various policy initiatives (Chapters 5 and 6). But, in overall terms, and bearing in mind the extent of public involvement in the 1950s, most would probably agree that the urban strategies of the 1960s and 1970s have had some success in opening up new opportunities for public participation in government decision-making.

On both sides of the Atlantic there has been a spectacular upsurge of community action or grass-roots groups. It is interesting to speculate on how far the British and American governments led or responded to this public pressure for a bigger role in local decision making. But one thing is certain, 'The institutions of representative democracy are no longer accepted so unquestioningly as the only sufficient means of popular control.'[11]

The British local ward councillor remains a major asset to neighbourhood democracy in Britain and this is an important reason why the recent experiments with area management are of interest and why we shall look more closely at some of them in the next part of the book. Neighbourhood decentralization within the United States also has interesting possibilities. But the public pressure for a greater say will have to be sustained. There are powerful centralizing forces in city government in both countries and we shall see that, even in those authorities with a good record for neighbourhood innovation, the degree of delegation to local level has been minimal.

Political support

Arguably the most fundamental question facing both American and British approaches to deprived neighbourhoods and groups concerns the degree to which the balance of voting interests in each nation actually favours serious action on the problems of the inner city and other declining areas. Critics of urban programmes and area approaches on both sides of the Atlantic might usefully ask themselves whether these initiatives were doomed to have a limited impact, not because of political or managerial incompetence, but because this was, in fact, the nation's will.

This dilemma is being thrown into sharper focus by the growing interest in the economic base of declining areas and neighbourhoods. For example, the investment decisions of large corporations (in determining where jobs will be created and for whom) and lending institutions (in determining which parts of the housing stock will receive finance) have a major impact on the economic structure of inner city areas. But both the British and American national economies are in recession and the top political priority is to regenerate industry and 'get the economy moving'. In these circumstances proposals to increase *controls* over the flow of private capital to take account of social costs are unlikely to win widespread political support. However, this does not rule out more modest steps. For example, readily digestible information on the flow of private capital to different neighbourhoods, along the lines of the American Home Mortgage Disclosure Act, would have an impact on private investment purely from the public relations point of view and might be expected to enjoy support from the electorate.

Our review of the initiatives in Chapters 5 and 6 suggests that national rather than local government is more able to withstand the political consequences of helping minorities. The programmes involving positive discrimination in favour of deprived neighbourhoods have been largely the creatures of Westminster and Washington rather than of city hall. This should lead us to look much more closely at the relationships between central and local government (see Chapter 1). By developing a closer partnership it should be possible for each side to comprehend more fully the political strengths and weaknesses of the national and local situations and to design policies which exploit the relative strengths more fully than at present.

An analytical framework for area approaches

In Chapter 3 we identified three overlapping yet distinct objectives of area approaches:

1 Effectiveness – what gets done
2 Distribution – who benefits
3 Accountability – who decides

Separating out these objectives helps to clarify thinking about area approaches, and hopefully has provided some new insights into the policies reviewed in Chapters 5 and 6. The intention now is to develop this checklist of objectives into an analytical framework which could be used to sort and classify various initiatives more rigorously. The typology advanced is by no means a final product but perhaps it will provide a starting point from which more sophisticated and developed schemes will emerge.

In recent years a useful body of American literature has developed on ways of classifying various approaches to public participation and neighbourhood decentralization. The famous ladder of citizen participation developed by Sherry Arnstein firmly established the concept of a spectrum of levels of local influence ranging from minimal to significant control. The eight rungs on her ladder are: (1) manipulation, (2) therapy, (3) informing, (4) consultation, (5) placation, (6) partnership, (7) delegated power, (8) citizen control.[12] Douglas Yates also concentrates on the degree of local autonomy and ranks seven elements of neighbourhood decentralization along a scale which owes a deal to Sherry Arnstein's model.[13] Richard Cole in his analysis of citizen participation puts forward a two-dimensional framework which contrasts intensity of citizen influence with the scope or variety of programmes within the jurisdiction of a particular programme.[14] Robert Yin and Douglas Yates in their major review of over 250 decentralization case studies use two dimensions which they term the client imperative (transference of responsibility and power to those people affected) and the territorial imperative (expenditure of new resources and efforts to a small geographic area).[15] Finally, Allen Barton and his colleagues at Columbia University have developed a multi-dimensional framework which includes the degree of district resident's influence, the range of services involved, the amount of command decentralization to local officials and the degree of service integration.[16]

The analytical framework presented below is the first to contrast explicitly the three objectives of effectiveness, distribution and accountability. It attempts to break away from the unhelpful dichotomy between centralization and decentralization. Instead, the three objectives are each set against a second dimension which reflects the 'strength of the area approach'. A *weak* form of area approach pays little or no regard to area aspects. A *moderate* form takes some account of area aspects. A *strong* form pays substantial attention to area aspects. In this way it is possible for the framework to accommodate a wide range of area approaches including some which may, at first, seem contradictory, e.g. strong approaches to neighbourhoods which involve no decentralization.

The framework is presented as Figure 14. The vertical dimension shows the three objectives of effectiveness (with its three subdivisions of responsiveness, service delivery and other actors), distribution and accountability. The horizontal dimension shows the three grades of area approach. The simple 5×3 matrix which emerges has fifteen cells which, either individually or in combination, can be used to classify most forms of area approach. It should be noted that many area approaches serve multiple objectives and will naturally overlap several cells. The reality of area approaches is, in other words, much more messy than the framework suggests. This is a penalty which any abstraction of reality must accept. But it is worth emphasizing that a framework of this kind always runs the risk of over-simplifying and of placing insufficient emphasis on the inter-connections between the factors.

There now follows a brief outline of each of the fifteen types of area approach presented in the sequence shown in Figure 14. For simplicity all the examples are drawn from British experience.

Figure 14 An analytical framework for area approaches

objectives ↓ / strength of area approach →	weak	moderate	strong
effectiveness responsiveness	1 statutory area policies only	2 area analysis	3 area-based policy making
service delivery	4 minimal service decentralization	5 moderate service decentralization	6 strong service decentralization
other actors	7 city-wide partnerships only	8 scattered local partnerships	9 local inter-agency teams
distribution	10 no conscious discrimination	11 limited discrimination	12 distributive policy making
accountability	13 centralized accountability	14 advisory relationships	15 local accountability

Effectiveness (Responsiveness)

Statutory area policies only   No area initiatives towards policy are taken except those to comply with statutory procedures, e.g. smoke control areas, general improvement areas. Little or no information is collected on area needs or the impact of policies on different areas.

Area analysis   Positive attempts are made to take account of area aspects in the planning and review of services. This might involve regular area profiles of needs and policy impacts and could include attitude research on the views of neighbourhood residents. Alternatively, or in addition, analysis might be focussed on one or two priority areas, e.g. an inter-departmental policy analysis of the reasons for a neighbourhood's decline.

Area-based policy making   The area aspect is seen as critical and steps are taken to develop a corporate or inter-corporate policy making process for each area which is linked directly to the authority's annual budgeting cycle and other policy processes, e.g. the Area Health Authority planning cycle.

Effectiveness (Service delivery)

Minimal service decentralization   No great advantage is seen in an area approach to service delivery. Staff may be located in available area offices and these may be open to the public, but such developments are likely to reflect the accidental location of available accommodation rather than an intentional approach.

Moderate service decentralization   Purposeful attempts are made to co-ordinate service delivery on an area basis. Initiatives could include: relating services more closely to local needs, co-ordination between divisions, better referral systems at the local level, and the development of 'one-stop' shops.

Strong service decentralization   Greater discretionary authority is delegated to local officials and one local official is charged with responsibility for co-ordinating local services. Staff performance may be measured by impact on local problems as well as by departmental criteria relating to professional competence.

Effectiveness (Other actors)

Citywide partnerships only   Attempts by the authority to influence the behaviour of other actors are conducted almost wholly at citywide level through joint committees, working parties, exchanges with community and voluntary groups and negotiation with the private sector.

Scattered local partnerships   Initiatives are taken on an *ad hoc* basis in different neighbourhoods. Examples could include a good neighbour scheme in a particular locality, a strong involvement in local affairs by a voluntary housing association zoned to a particular district, and a facelift scheme/environmental clean up arranged by area planning staff, local councillors, local traders and residents.

Local inter-agency teams   High importance is attached to local partnerships and teams bringing together local officials, ward councillors, representatives of community groups and other interests are actively established in all areas and receive a small amount of financial support.

Distribution

No conscious discrimination No attempt is made to direct resources into deprived areas and the distributive consequences of most policies are ignored. The result will be unintended negative discrimination against poor neighbourhoods. Examples are urban motorways through inner city areas which have obscure benefits for local residents and uniform policies of service provision which disregard differential rates of take-up.

Limited discrimination Policies of positive discrimination are pursued for selected services as, for example, in educational priority areas and housing action areas. In addition, some attempt is made to assess the distributional effects of individual policies by conducting research which attempts to reveal who is benefiting from the current allocation of resources and pointing to possible transfers of resources.[17]

Distributive policy making The distributional effect of all policies is seen as a major factor in planning and management and becomes a more or less standard feature of all policy reports. Area resource analysis would be a built-in feature of budgeting and ward members would receive area profiles showing the local balance sheet of needs and resources. Area budgeting (i.e. allocation of funds to geographical as well as programme areas) may be developed to achieve a more equitable distribution of resources.

Accountability

Centralized accountability Discussion of policy and management issues takes place centrally with little opportunity for an input from local councillors or members of the public. Public relations efforts may be made to persuade local residents of the council's good intentions or to inform them of developments but power and influence rest unmistakably at the centre of the authority.

Advisory relationships A two-way flow of information is established between the centre and the periphery of the organization which enables back bench councillors and local interest groups to be informed in advance about proposals affecting their area and to have a say before decisions have started to firm up. A host of initiatives of this kind have been taken in recent years with, for example, neighbourhood councils, area committees, public meetings, participation in local planning, community health councils, parent-teacher associations, tenants' committees and so on.

Local accountability   Responsibility and power are transferred to the local level. This may involve management responsibility for some council resources in the area, for example, multiple use of a school or, more radically, the deployment of local staff time. It is likely to involve at least some control of fiscal resources even if this is limited to a small contingency sum. A variety of organizational forms are possible: area committees of local councillors, area committees with co-opted representatives of the public, independent neighbourhood institutions (as happens frequently in America) and so on.

Centralization and decentralization: a false dichotomy

To assess the strength of a given local authority's approach to areas it is necessary to consider each objective separately – where does the approach rest on each of the five lines in Figure 14? Because the objectives are different it is quite reasonable for the strength of area approach to vary between lines. Thus, it is quite possible for an authority with minimal service decentralization (cell 4) to claim that it has a strong area approach by pointing out that it has a developed system of area-based policy making (cell 3). Indeed, it is questionable whether all of the strong approaches could be pursued in parallel: for example, could the conflict between distributive policy making (cell 12) and local accountability be reconciled (cell 15)? We can now see that the polarization of debate into two camps – those who are for and those who are against area approaches – is false. It all depends on the objectives a given approach is trying to achieve. Lasting solutions require not one or the other but a blend of central and peripheral approaches.

The simplification of this subtle problem into a misleading dichotomy is a feature of the wider and more general debate about decentralization. Dr E. F. Schumacher, for example, is widely misquoted by decentralists as an advocate of small is beautiful *per se*. In fact, he was at pains to stress that the fundamental task is to achieve smallness *within* large organization:

Once a large organization has come into being, it normally goes through alternating phases of *centralizing* and *decentralizing*, like swings of a pendulum. Whenever one encounters such *opposites*, each of them with persuasive arguments in its favor, it is worth looking into the depth of the problem for something more than compromise, more than a half-and-half solution. Maybe what we really need is not *either-or* but *the-one-and-the-other-at-the-same-time*.[18]

By avoiding the centralization–decentralization dichotomy the analytical framework may assist in the development of thinking about new ways of accommodating the tension between the desire for an overall, comprehensive and equitable approach to the allocation of resources and the desire to make the process of government more democratic and open, more responsive and enterprising.

Conclusion

This chapter has attempted to prise out some of the main lessons from Anglo-American experience with various forms of area approach. We are left, unavoidably, with an overall feeling of disappointment with these initiatives particularly regarding their impact on deprivation in the large cities. But, in their different ways, they have all edged forward our understanding of urban policy making. They have not been without impact and they have helped to open up several promising avenues for change – a number of these have been mentioned. In particular, it has been argued that, despite disappointment, area approaches must not be rejected in favour of broader social programmes. Whether we like it or not urban policy must deal with a socio-spatial system – the city – and area approaches must have a place in any effective governmental response to city problems. An important task then, is to improve the quality and relevance of area approaches. An analytical framework has been presented in the hope that this will assist the development of more penetrating thought about area approaches.

A handful of cities have attempted to experiment positively with various forms of area or neighbourhood management. It is to these that we turn in the next part of the book – not for ready answers but for new ideas that are grounded in experience.

Part Three
Area management case studies

The idea of area or neighbourhood management is attracting growing interest in local government circles. It offers the promise of scaling down large and seemingly remote local government bureaucracies to a more manageable size – a size which elected members, officers and residents can more readily comprehend and operate. It offers the possibility of developing new forms of local government organization which are capable of learning about the needs of particular areas, of responding sensitively and effectively to local priorities and of changing the relationship between those providing urban services and those receiving them. But there is a dearth of first-hand experience. Part Three gets beyond the rhetoric which surrounds area management by presenting hard evidence drawn from the practical experience of five cities which have pioneered new area-based approaches to urban government.

Chapter 8 provides profiles of area management in five case study cities: Boston, New York City and Dayton in the United States and Stockport and Liverpool in Britain.

Chapter 9 compares the five approaches, provides a rudimentary assessment of the schemes and makes a variety of suggestions on how to improve area approaches in local government.

8 Area management in five cities

One failure of past traditions [in Britain] has been the refusal to recognise that there are local communities which have distinctive needs. We have run our cities and our counties as if they were uniform rather than diverse communities.

John Stewart in The Responsive Authority, 1974

The message of this study is that decentralization is a hopeful and viable alternative in urban policy . . . The question for the future is not whether decentralization [in American cities] should be pursued but rather what kind of decentralization should be initiated.

Douglas Yates in Neighborhood Democracy, 1973

Introduction

The case for area management or neighbourhood decentralization is being voiced on both sides of the Atlantic but there is little first-hand experience. The purpose of this chapter is to present hard evidence drawn from the practical experience of five case study cities in America and Britain: Boston, New York City, Dayton, Stockport and Liverpool. These cities have been selected because they have been involved in bold and imaginative attempts to develop new area-based approaches to urban government.

The chapter has an unusual layout for it consists of a separate profile of the approach adopted in each city. Each profile is a self-contained statement. Notes, references and a list of sources are provided at the end of the book (pages 344–51). The profiles have a standard format using the following ten headings:

Introduction
Origins
Aims
Geography
Structure and activities

Planning and budgeting
Service delivery
Local accountability
Distributive effects
Conclusion

Generally speaking the first five headings are mainly factual and descriptive with the last five headings attempting to provide a commentary on the strengths and weaknesses of each area approach. It is stressed that the profiles are *not* intended as a rigorous evaluation of each scheme. That would require an ongoing and many-sided analysis involving assessment of each approach from different vantage points over a considerable period of time. The more limited objective of the profiles is to describe the schemes using a consistent format and to illustrate the differences in emphasis by focussing on those aspects identified as significant in Chapters 3 and 7. Readers not particularly interested in the case studies themselves could skip to Chapter 9 where a comparison of the five area approaches is presented. Reference back to this chapter could then be made as desired.

The five profiles are presented in the following order:

Boston	– Little city halls
New York City	– District management experiment
Dayton	– Neighbourhood priority boards
Stockport	– Area organization
Liverpool	– Area management experiment

Area management profile
Boston – Little city halls

Introduction

The City of Boston, Massachusetts has a population of approximately 638 000 and forms the core of a much larger metropolitan area having a population of some 2·5 million. Boston has a 'strong-mayor' form of government. This consists of a mayor, who is the chief executive officer of the city, a city council of nine members elected at large, which is the legislative body, and a school committee of five members.[1] In July 1968 Boston opened its first little city hall (or neighbourhood service centre). It now has seventeen located throughout the city together with a twenty-four-hour telephone service for information and complaints located in city hall itself. Three little city halls are housed in mobile trailers, others are in local municipal buildings or community centres and four occupy a shop-front location. The halls are run by the Office of Public Service (OPS) which is immediately accountable to the mayor. Despite the fact that the programme, along with many other Boston services, was trimmed in 1976, there remain 105 people on the OPS payroll with some 95 working in the field. The 1976/77 budget totals some $1·22 million with the result that Boston is making the largest *per capita* investment within the United States for this form of neighbourhood decentralization.

Origins

The idea of bringing government closer to the people was a major feature of Kevin H. White's 1967 mayoralty campaign. When he took office in 1968 he set up an advisory group to develop his idea of a 'neighbourhood service department' to deal with problems of communication between city government and the people. In part White's proposal represented a response to the Kerner Commission Report,[2] which was itself a response to the urban riots of the mid-

1960s. However, the proposal addressed the larger problem of 'citizen alienation' which was current in white as well as black neighbourhoods. Among the factors cited as reasons for the high level of alienation in Boston were:

– urban renewal which made reconstruction of the downtown areas its chief priority and dislocated many residents, especially those at the lower end of the economic scale, in the course of neighbourhood renewal projects.[3]

– a fiscal policy which helped to keep the tax rate low but at the cost of neglecting the majority of older residential areas with the result that a serious decline in services and facilities had become apparent.

– an 'at large' city council which tended to deny neighbourhood residents direct participation in city politics.

While these factors contributed to a generally negative attitude toward city government on the part of many residents, they also provided a natural setting for an emphatically neighbourhood-oriented programme. The little city halls openly and positively recognize that Boston remains a city of neighbourhoods each with its own strong ethnic traditions and culture – such as the North End (Italian), South Boston (mainly Irish but also Polish and Lithuanian), Roxbury (black), Charlestown (mainly Irish), East Boston (Italian) and so on.

From the very beginning the idea of little city halls has been closely associated with Mayor White in person. The mayor of Boston is elected for a four-year term and Mayor White has been unusually successful in getting himself elected for three terms in a row. His third election, in 1975, was by a narrow margin but the absence of a break in mayoral support for little city halls continues as an important feature.

Aims

The aims of the little city halls have evolved over the years but the guiding light has been the idea of bringing municipal government closer to the city's residents by improving communication between the two and by providing on-the-spot government and information services. The five major goals of the programme are set out in Table 5.

Table 5   *Major goals of the little city hall programme*

- provide direct services and information to the public
- respond to complaints
- act as a catalyst for increased citizen participation
- improve delivery of city services through close co-operation with line department personnel and through recommendations for departmental change
- *act as the mayor's representative in the neighbourhoods

Note: The sources are the little city hall fact sheets November 1973 and March 1976. The goals were the same in both sources except that the one marked * does not appear in the 1976 (or 1975) fact sheet

In reality, the little city halls are neighbourhood extensions of the mayor's office. Political opponents of Mayor White have suggested that OPS provides a political instrument with which the mayor can further his own career and even build a political machine.[4] This is a particularly sensitive issue during election years and Table 5 shows how OPS deleted explicit reference to the mayor's interest from its stated goals before the campaign of 1975. This does not alter the fact that a major role of the little city halls is to provide eyes and ears for the mayor. Most of the staff of OPS, and certainly all the senior staff including the little city hall managers, are committed to Mayor White's democratic political platform. Many of them gave up a great deal of their spare time to campaign vigorously for his re-election and, indeed, there is an element of political patronage in the appointment of OPS staff. Many of them would be fired if Mayor White was not re-elected. In these circumstances it is difficult to disentangle political and public service goals. This, of course, would be entirely unacceptable in British local government as currently operated. The defence given is that 'good politics is often good government' and, in any event, the managers have not adopted an overtly political role.

Geography

From the outset it was decided that little city halls would serve all of Boston's neighbourhoods and would not be concentrated in poorer or minority neighbourhoods. The locations of the little city halls and the neighbourhoods served mainly by each are shown in Figure 15, and the approximate populations of these seventeen neighbourhoods are shown in Table 6:

Table 6   *Populations of neighbourhoods served by little city halls*

Neighbourhood	Population*
Allston/Brighton	65 000
Back Bay/Beacon Hill/Fenway	66 000
Charlestown	17 000
Chinatown	4 000
Dorchester	80 000
East Boston	38 000
Franklin Field	33 000
Hyde Park	37 000
Jamaica Plain	58 000
Mattapan	27 000
North End	18 000
Roslindale	29 000
Roxbury	36 000
South Boston	38 000
South End	29 000
Uphams Corner	29 000
West Roxbury	34 000
Total	638 000

*Approximations based on 1975 State Census

The boundaries are defined by residents and sometimes they will change in response to neighbourhood opinion. Boston has poor coterminality of service districts with the different departments operating in relation to different sub-areas of the city. In 1976 attempts were being made to introduce coterminality between OPS and the Boston Redevelopment Authority (the equivalent of a British town planning department) to establish better links between little city halls and local city planning work.

Structure/activities

Figure 16 shows a simplified organization chart for the Office of Public Service. The key role is played by the *little city hall managers* who are the middle men between the mayor's office and the neighbourhood. Their duties are wide-ranging and include: representing

Figure 15   City of Boston   Little city halls and neighbourhoods served by each

N

Charlestown

East Boston

North End

City Hall

Allston/Brighton

Back Bay/
Beacon Hill/
Fenway

Chinatown

South End

South Boston

Roxbury

Uphams Corner

Jamaica Plain

Franklin Field

Dorchester

West Roxbury

Roslindale

Mattapan

Hyde Park

———— city boundary
• location of Little City Halls
- - - - approximate neighbourhood boundaries

0   1   2   3   4   5 miles

0   1   2   3   4   5 kilometres

the mayor in the neighbourhood, representing neighbourhood interests in city hall, supervision of little city hall staff, stimulation of neighbourhood participation, promoting special projects, and co-ordinating with other departments including the district planners working for the Boston Redevelopment Authority. In practice the managers work extremely long hours handling a great deal of

Figure 16   Office of public service – organization chart

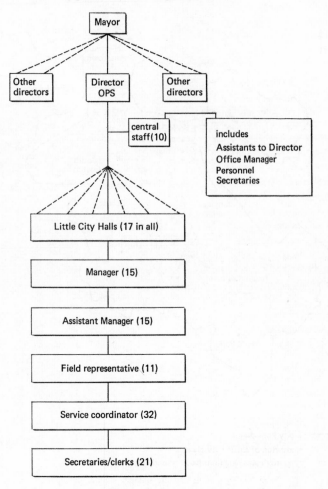

crisis work so that the average manager lasts only two or three years before he 'burns out'. Although he presides over an information and referral service he is not an administrator of municipal services carried out at the neighbourhood level. Thus, his functions are more like a neighbourhood mayor than a neighbourhood manager.

Some of the day-to-day services provided by the little city halls are shown in Table 7. This illustrates the bread-and-butter work which provides the little city halls with much of their legitimacy.

Table 7 *Some of the services provided by little city halls*

- general information and referral
- rent control information and assistance
- year round voter registration
- property and auto excise tax collection, sewer and water payments, assistance in filing for abatements (elderly, widow, over valuation, auto excise)
- income tax services (state and federal)
- assistance to the elderly with a range of services
- consumer advocacy
- referrals for the Housing Improvement Programme
- selective service registration once a year
- notarization of documents
- civil service, including provisional openings, public housing and social security applications, liability claims against the city, electrical permits
- translation/interpretation services
- copies of marriage, birth and death records
- resident parking stickers
- registry of motor vehicles – change of address applications
- residency certification for colleges

Approximately 13 500 calls are made to the little city halls each week so that the number of client contacts in a whole year is more than one per head of the city population. Requests for information or for services directly available through the halls are the primary source of business. About one in six items is a complaint. Over 40 per cent of the complaints relate to housing and the next largest category involves public works problems, such as rubbish collection, street cleaning and road repairs. Attempts are made to handle complaints at the local level through regular contact between the little city halls and line department personnel. This relies heavily on the establishment by little city hall staff of informal links with field supervisors from other agencies. There is no system of neighbourhood cabinets bringing together all field supervisors in an area and, in the absence of any formal authority for co-ordination resting with the little city halls, much depends on the managers' own personal initiative in establishing good working relationships.

Defusing racial conflict is an important part of the little city hall work in the neighbourhoods. This is particularly so since the issue of bussing heightened local tensions. This involves the daily transfer of schoolchildren between black and white neighbourhoods in the name of integrated education. This, of course, is a national issue but feelings have run particularly high in Boston with the result that the city has received considerable national attention. For example, a white working-class group in South Boston known as ROAR (Restore Our Alienated Rights) is an extremely active anti-bussing neighbourhood group which has obtained national coverage for its views. Bussing is a federal policy imposed on cities by the courts. The opposition is not therefore directed at city hall and this has enabled the little city hall managers to adopt a neutral role. Local safety committees of residents were formed with volunteers supervising the groups of children waiting at bus stops, manning telephones to reassure people ringing in about alleged incidents at particular schools and generally co-operating with the police. By providing reliable local information and facilitating co-operation the little city halls have played an important part in quashing rumours and keeping residents calm.

Planning and budgeting

The chief way in which OPS seeks to tune planning and management to neighbourhood needs is by its involvement in the community development block grant programme introduced by the Housing and Community Development Act 1974. As discussed in Chapter 6, this consolidated a number of federal categorical grants and gives greater flexibility to local government in deciding how the funds should be spent. The focus, however, is on physical development activities such as property acquisition and rehabilitation and the construction of public facilities. Instead of giving grantsmanship free rein the funds are allocated to local governments on a formula basis and the amount available to Boston is less than under the previous federal programmes. These gave the city an average of $45 million a year. Community development funds in 1976 were $30·5 million and this is designed to phase down to $11·9 million by 1980. The declining support from Washington has encouraged the city to take particular efforts to match spending to neighbourhood priorities.

In 1975, the first year of the new programme, a decision was taken to use the funds for strategic programmes and projects in all neighbourhoods. The broad goal of the neighbourhood improvement programme (as it is called in Boston) was to have as much impact as possible on neighbourhood preservation and resident confidence.

Prior to formulating the 1975 and 1976 programmes an extensive series of neighbourhood seminars, meetings and public hearings were carried out in every little city hall district. A civic newspaper explaining the programme and asking for community views was prepared in 1975. This included a centre spread, which varied by neighbourhood, with a map of past and planned improvements in that neighbourhood. Over eighty meetings were held to plan the 1975 programme and in excess of one hundred to prepare recommendations for the 1976 programme.

It is, of course, notoriously difficult to evaluate initiatives of this kind but it does seem to have been a genuine attempt to discover and take account of neighbourhood preferences in advance of budget preparation. The 'good politics is good government' dictum applies to a certain extent in that the neighbourhood improvement programme is closely identified with Mayor White. There would be clear political penalties if neighbourhood priorities were totally ignored. At the same time it should be noted that, although the programme does deal with substantial funds ($30·5 million in 1976) it is only a comparatively small part of the city budget which totalled some $256 million in 1976/77. Neighbourhood input into ongoing revenue budgets is virtually non-existent and community input into the district planning process operated by the Boston Redevelopment Authority does not seem to be highly developed.

Service delivery

The little city halls have been particularly successful in improving public access to services. As one field representative put it: 'Any resident can come to this little city hall, speak to someone they're familiar with and get some help with a specific problem or need they have. It's easy to drop in. It's like a den really.' More than 90 per cent of the OPS staff lives in the City of Boston and many live in the neighbourhoods in which they work. A quarter of the staff are from minority ethnic groups and a quarter are bilingual or polylingual (mainly Spanish and Italian). Care is taken to fit staff to neighbourhood and one little city hall manager explained: 'My background, meaning myself as a manager coming in, has a lot to do with how I'll survive in this neighbourhood – how I'll be able to relate to these people.' Many of the staff are young, college educated, 'Peace Corps' types who bring a deal of enthusiasm to the job. The geographical spread of little city halls coupled with the care

in staff recruitment means that city hall does present a more acceptable face to the average city resident.

It is less clear how effective the little city halls are in influencing
the behaviour of the line departments. Where personal relationships
are good there are few problems but, as might be expected, a number
of departments see the little city halls as a nuisance. This can result
in frustration for both clients and little city hall staff: 'It's tremend-
ously frustrating when a person on Cook Street calls three days in a
row because the sewer's still blocked up.' Occasionally little city
hall managers have to go 'up and over' (via the mayor) to coerce
co-operation but this is a last resort, partly because the system
would break down from overload at the top and partly because this
shatters any spirit of partnership which the little city halls strive to
create.

The absence of neighbourhood cabinets to bring field service
chiefs together, the poor coterminality of service districts, and the
lack of delegation to area level are all factors which thwart neighbourhood service management in Boston. In acknowledging the
clear political authority of the mayor it would be wrong to under-
estimate the high degree of control over services retained by departmental heads.

Local accountability

A notable failure in the history of the little city halls programme
occurred in 1969/70 when an attempt was made to set up 'local
advisory councils' which were supposed to function, with and through
the little city halls, as the primary voice speaking for the neighbourhoods.[5] These councils resembled neighbourhood or community
councils in Britain and the Boston experience may therefore be of
particular interest. The experiment failed, with a few exceptions,
because it did not take into account the diversity and effectiveness
of existing neighbourhood groups and because it was an attempt by
authority to impose a particular concept of participation. The mayor
conceded that the project was a mistake but lessons have been
learned. Attempts have since been made to establish more informal
relationships between groups and the little city halls and to relate
the canvassing of opinion to particular programmes as occurs
with the community development block grant programme discussed
above. There have been occasions when managers have asserted
neighbourhood views with considerable impact. Examples of

effective campaigns are prevention of the extension of Boston Airport into East Boston and stopping public infill housing in the inner neighbourhoods. It should, however, be stressed that citizen inputs are strictly advisory and there is no question of devolution of control to neighbourhood level.

Distributive effects

For obvious political reasons distributive effects are played down. The first little city hall was opened in East Boston and this location was selected because it is not a deprived area. Given the political leanings of the mayor and most of his staff one would expect to find the distribution of resources biassed in favour of deprived groups and this may well be happening. At the same time the mayor's political security is fragile and one suspects that a major part of the little city hall effort is designed to sustain his popularity citywide.

Conclusion

Awareness of neighbourhood perceptions of problems is highly developed in Boston but area management is some way off. There is little progress in the development of an integrated approach to either service delivery or planning and budgeting for neighbourhoods but there is an interest in seeing moves in this direction. Eric Nord-linger's study published in 1972 found that 72 per cent of the population wanted to see little city halls continue[6] and there is reason to believe that the programme's popularity continues at a high level. In 1975 over 400 community organizations endorsed the programme prior to the city council's budget hearings. The chief success of Boston's little city halls has been to improve public access to city hall by providing a concerned, local information and complaint service coupled with a few direct services. This basic activity legitimates the work of the managers who serve as the mayor's representatives in dealing with neighbourhood problems.

Area management profile
New York City –
District management experiment

Introduction

New York City and its government are unique. The municipal bureaucracy which serves the city's 7·8 million residents is one of the largest in the world. One way of trying to appreciate its size is to imagine the Greater London Council plus all the London boroughs as one organization. There is enormous diversity within the city and a bewilderingly complex political structure has grown up since the five boroughs – the Bronx, Brooklyn, Manhattan, Queens and Richmond – were consolidated into one city in 1898.[1] In view of this scale and complexity it is hardly surprising that pressures for decentralization to smaller units within the City have grown steadily These have taken many forms ranging from a major push for community control of schools in the late 1960s to a revision of the city charter in 1975 designed, *inter alia*, to increase local control. In this profile attention is focussed on the development of district management.

In 1970, at the start of his second term, Mayor John V. Lindsay established the mayor's Office of Neighborhood Government (ONG) which led an attempt to introduce a new subcity tier of municipal administration to improve the co-ordination and management of all city services at the local level. The key institutional innovation was the creation of district service cabinets, chaired by mayorally appointed district managers, for community planning districts with populations averaging 126 000. A major research study of this district management experiment was conducted by the Bureau of Applied Social Research at Columbia University during 1972 and 1973 and the findings were published in 1977.[2] This study represents the most comprehensive investigation of an area management scheme to date and is drawn on heavily below. In 1974 Mayor Abraham Beame took over and the role of ONG was modified into an Office of Neighborhood Services (ONS) and this change in emphasis is also considered.

Origins

In 1966, when Mayor Lindsay took office, the proliferation of some fifty independent agencies all responsible to the mayor was streamlined into ten new administrations (or 'superagencies'). In this way Lindsay tried to make the city bureaucracy more manageable from the centre but he also took steps to make the organization more responsive. Three should be mentioned.[3] First, neighbourhood city halls were set up in 1966 as store-front operations staffed by a mayoral liaison person who tried to deal with local problems at the local level. These were opposed by the city council as they were seen as political club-houses for the mayor and the city appropriation was blocked. They continued as service and information distribution centres funded by private contributions until 1969. Second, urban action task forces evolved after the public disorders of summer 1966 when Lindsay walked the streets to calm tensions. Essentially they were a mechanism for identifying local leaders and community grievances. Each local task force was chaired by a high-level city official who met with groups of neighbourhood citizens on a periodic basis. The programme grew from thirteen task forces in 1966 to fifty in 1969, and came to include middle-income as well as low-income areas. The third initiative was the neighbourhood action programme, commenced in 1969, which was a special commitment by the mayor to transitional neighbourhoods, i.e., communities in which the ethnic and economic balance was changing rapidly. It was focussed on six areas and involved lump-sum funding of capital projects selected by the community.

Two major deficiencies in the city's ability to deal with local service issues emerged from these experiences of the late 1960s.[4] First, the district-level offices of the various departments did not have sufficient authority to manage resources in a way responsive to local needs. Second, although many of the most intractable issues in a community required a multiple agency response, there was no structured mechanism at the district level to co-ordinate this action.

During the mid-1960s proposals for transferring power in some form to the neighbourhoods had been many and varied. As discussed in Chapter 6 the federal poverty programme and model cities programme often focussed attention on developing 'community control' over local bureaucracies. Arguably of more significance in New York was the passionate demand for community control of the schools which led to bitter conflict between militant blacks and the equally militant teachers' union. This culminated in three strikes by the teachers in autumn 1968. The state legislature ended the dispute in 1969 by requiring the New York Board of Education to create some thirty-two community school districts.[5] Another strand in the public demand for a greater say in local government decision making concerned physical planning. A response to this pressure was made in 1968 when the City Planning Commission established a system of sixty-two Community Planning Districts each with a Community Planning Board.[6] The Boards had an advisory role on planning, site selection and other proposals affecting their districts but had very little power.

At the beginning of his second term Lindsay established the Office of Neighborhood Government (ONG) as part of the mayor's office. The ONG included the two mayoral programmes mentioned earlier – the urban action task force and the neighbourhood action programme – but was also given a mandate to develop a new programme for neighbourhood government. The first public document appeared in June 1970 and represented a direct step towards political decentralization.[7] It called for the strengthening of the sixty-two Community Planning Boards and held out the prospect of their being transformed into elected district councils. Public hearings on this first plan for neighbourhood government showed there was no consensus on the mechanisms for selecting community boards and the plan was shelved. In June 1971 ONG came forward with a revised proposal which played down the idea of political devolution, emphasized administrative decentralization and suggested the programme should be developed in five Community Planning Districts on an experimental basis. ONG took several steps to generate Federal funding. A three-year grant of $1 million was obtained from the US Department of Health Education and Welfare which wanted to promote experiments designed to improve service delivery by service integration. And a three-year National Science Foundation grant to Columbia University of $1·4 million was also obtained to evaluate the experiment and its impact on the quality of life in four communities of the city. The programme was not seen as a high priority by the mayor but, partly because of the federal support, the programme received the go-ahead and operated from January 1972 to January 1974. The approach continued in a substantially modified form under Mayor Beame.

Aims

As might be expected the aims of district management in New York City have evolved over time.[8] Mayor Lindsay in his foreword to the programme published in December 1971 gives an idea of the initial emphasis: 'All cities today face a common problem – making government more responsive to the people . . . Having created the ten administrations to provide consistency and co-ordination on city-wide matters, it is now possible to extend this structure to the Community Planning District level to deal with neighborhood concerns.'[9] From the remainder of Lindsay's foreword it is possible to extract four more specific aims for district management and these are summarized in Table 8.

Table 8 *Main aims of district management in New York City*

– Delegation	– each agency will grant increased authority to their district officers to deal locally with operational neighbourhood problems.
– Co-ordination	– to be improved by three measures:
	1 district service cabinets of local service chiefs providing a formal mechanism for joint planning and management.
	2 district manager to co-ordinate the operations of the various local departments.
	3 coterminality of service area boundaries to be introduced as far as possible.
– Existing resources	– increase the productivity of existing resources rather than add new resources.
– Experiment	– to evaluate the approach in five communities before considering extensions to the rest of the city.

Given that these aims were put forward in 1971 they show considerable sophistication in management thinking. But it is worth emphasizing what the programme did not attempt to do. Public participation was not an explicit aim for it was felt that a great deal must first be done in reorganizing the city's own internal administrative arrangements. Nor did the programme make a major effort to inform the public where to go with problems or to handle complaints. Finally, the programme did not give the district manager line authority over local service managers.

Geography

Great caution is needed in comparing district management in New York City with area management in other cities purely because of differences in scale. New York City is vast. The sixty-two Community Planning Districts have an average population of 126 000 within a range from less than 100 000 to almost 250 000. This means that some Community Planning Districts are larger than the smaller London boroughs.[10] A map of the sixty-two Community Planning Districts is provided as Figure 17. The delineation of the districts tried to strike a balance between identifiable areas (having a sense of tradition and marked by visible physical boundaries) and areas large enough to be efficient for the delivery of services. Five Community Planning Districts were selected for the district management experiment in a way designed to give a good cross-section of communities – by population, income levels, historic sense of community, pattern of agency boundary lines and municipal service needs.[11] There was however, some bias towards larger districts and the experimental districts have higher than average percentages of black populations. The pilot districts are listed in Table 9 and picked out in Figure 17.

Table 9 *Community Planning Districts initially involved in the Office of Neighborhood Government experiment*

Community Planning District	Population (1970)
*Wakefield–Edenwald (No. 13 in Bronx)	119 000
*Washington Heights (No. 12 in Manhattan)	188 000
*Bushwick (No. 4 in Brooklyn)	138 000
*Crown Heights (No. 8 in Brooklyn)	213 000
Rockaways (No. 14 in Queens)	91 000

*These four were subject to extensive research activity by the Bureau of Applied Social Research at Columbia University.

Structure/activities

As implemented there were five key components of the New York plan for decentralized urban administration: district service cabinets, district managers, administrative delegation, coterminality and the central Office of Neighborhood Government.

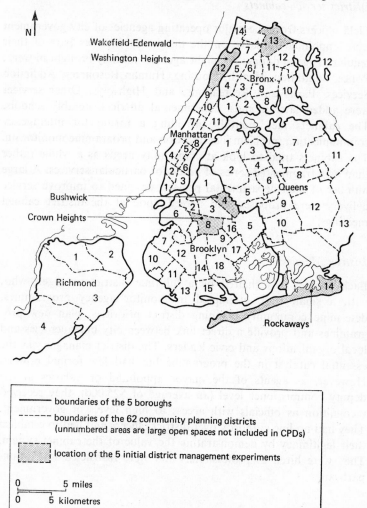

Figure 17   City of New York   Boroughs and community planning districts

N

Wakefield-Edenwald
Washington Heights

Bronx

Manhattan

Queens

Bushwick

Crown Heights

Richmond

Brooklyn

Rockaways

——————— boundaries of the 5 boroughs

- - - - - - - boundaries of the 62 community planning districts
(unnumbered areas are large open spaces not included in CPDs)

location of the 5 initial district management experiments

0   5 miles

0   5 kilometres

District service cabinets

Field officers from the major operating agencies of city government were appointed to serve on the district cabinets as part of their regular assigned duties. The eight agencies initially brought in were: Police, Sanitation, Health, Housing, Human Resources, Addiction Services, Parks and Recreations, and Highways. Other services were added later in most experimental districts, notably schools. The cabinets met monthly providing a forum for interagency communication, problem identification and programme monitoring. The cabinets tried to look at community needs as a whole rather than as a fragmented series of needs for particular services. A large number of inter-departmental projects designed to improve service delivery were proposed and agreed upon at the district cabinet meetings.

District Managers

Each cabinet was chaired by a full-time district manager, who, with a small staff, attempted to monitor agency programmes, determine community planning district priorities, plan new programmes and provide a direct link between city bureaucracies and local organizations and civic leaders. The district manager was the essential catalyst in the programme but had few formal powers. However, as agents of the mayor appointed on salaries at the deputy commissioner level (an average of $25 000), they received recognition as officials with access to high levels of government. They had no line authority over district officers and had to establish their legitimacy by demonstrating the value of the cabinet system. They were hired as professionals and were instructed to be non-partisan.

Administrative delegation

For the district cabinets to function effectively in co-ordinating city services and responding flexibly to the needs of different communities, each agency representative required increased authority over his local operations. For every agency, the key objective of delegation was to grant its district officers full operational control in scheduling and assigning the men and equipment regularly allocated to the area. Additional powers and responsibilities in community relations, planning, personnel, and budgeting were considered in each case. Police Commissioner Patrick Murphy had already developed a model of 'command decentralization', giving precinct captains increased authority to reallocate patrol forces, establish plainclothes anti-crime units, and control corruption. ONG was active in developing similar guidelines for other agencies but with mixed success. Housing and Human Resources only managed to establish weak 'co-ordinators' for their services in the cabinets. In general, the formal delegation of authority was less far-reaching than ONG had hoped.

Coterminality

Almost none of New York City's administrative districts for different services are coterminous with each other and ONG was to lead a move to bring about conformity of service boundaries as far as possible. This is an enormously difficult task for the situation in New York City could hardly be more confusing. Figure 18 shows the district boundaries of just five agencies as they relate to Brooklyn to give an impression of the degree of overlap and non-conformity. Most agencies agreed with the goal of establishing coterminous service districts but were quick to point out the problems and costs such as the difficulties involved in modifying emergency response patterns and the expense of relocating physical facilities. Little progress was made in realigning service boundaries but the issue is still very much alive for the New York City Charter revision of 1975 requires the establishment of coterminous service districts.

Central office

The primary functions of the central office of the Office of Neighborhood Government were to provide an overview of the programme, to play a loose managerial role, to make sure that the activities carried out by district offices fitted the priorities of the overall programme and to develop new methods for strengthening the programme within the mayor's office and with central agencies. Related to the overview function of central ONG is its evaluative function. ONG had a small research staff and co-operated with outside institutions, such as Columbia University, in studies of the experiment in decentralization.

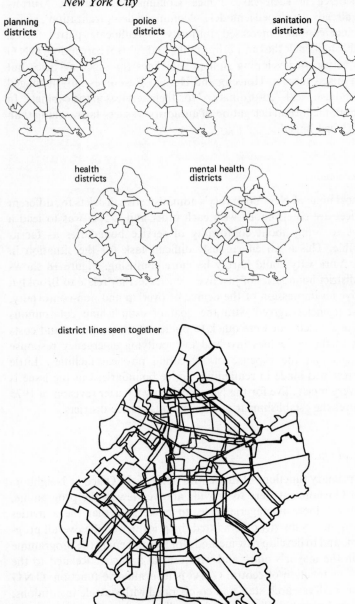

Figure 18 Degree of coterminality of areas among five services in Brooklyn, New York City

planning
districts

police
districts

sanitation
districts

health
districts

mental health
districts

district lines seen together

Source: Preliminary recommendations of the State Charter Revision
Commission for New York City, June 1975, p. 206.

With the inauguration of Mayor Beame in January 1974 a modified approach was applied citywide. The Office of Neighborhood Government was renamed the Office of Neighborhood Services and the programme was diluted with the existing staff being spread around fifty-one district cabinets covering the whole city. These are chaired not by the managers but by commissioners and deputy commissioners of citywide agencies. As the revision of the New York City Charter is implemented the approach will again change. Once coterminous service districts (probably about fifty in number) are established new community boards will be created and these will each employ a district manager who will chair the new cabinet. This new system is due to take effect from 1 July 1977.

Planning and budgeting

Mayor Lindsay's original statement made it clear that an attempt was to be made to develop neighbourhood budgets for both capital and revenue expenditure.[12] These would identify the dollar value of all services going into each of the Community Planning Districts. It was admitted that such a community budget would not come quickly or easily but it was considered that: 'The community budget is absolutely essential as a management tool to make the most sensitive resource deployment decisions for each community.' In practice it proved difficult to bring about major modifications to the city accounting system, partly because of technical constraints but also because of lack of commitment to the idea. In view of these difficulties ONG tested two less ambitious approaches to budget decentralization: block grants for communities and area priorities for different services.

In the first, each district cabinet was granted a capital budget lump sum (usually $250 000 per year) to spend on capital items subject to approval by the Community Planning Board and the appropriate Borough Improvement Board (comprised of the Borough President and City Councilmen representing each borough). The indications are that this approach did provide opportunities for ONG to develop innovative approaches. However, the procedure was vulnerable to political manoeuvring by those opposed to the ONG programme. For example, the Borough Improvement Board in Brooklyn delayed funds indefinitely for the development of play facilities on vacant lots in Bushwick mainly for political reasons.[13]

The second approach to budget decentralization was developed furthest in relation to highways. This involved delegation of influence to the district highways foreman, the district cabinet and the Community Planning Board.[14] Priorities within the district's allocation for resurfacing were set locally subject to approval by Highways central and this almost certainly resulted in a better use of resources. Again, however, political complications set in. Mayor Beame took over in January 1974 and was less interested in delegation to the local level. Agency attitudes changed and Highways cooperation with ONG declined precipitously.

The City Planning Commission has overall responsibility for capital planning and has been particularly aware of the need to develop a geographical dimension to the budgeting process. In March 1973, for example, the Commission requested that each Community Planning Board submit a list of five priorities for capital budget work in their district and the Commission has adopted a similar process for sifting projects under the community development block grant programme introduced in 1974. Some cabinets tried to develop overall plans which integrated physical and operational plans for the district. Probably the best example is that of Crown Heights where the district cabinet prepared a comprehensive capital budget for the fiscal year 1974/75 and negotiated with central agencies to include these requests in the final budget. The process allowed for community input, inter-agency planning and review, and local officer input to central agency budget planning.

Resistance from the higher levels of the centralized departments and the earmarking of city funds for particular programmes (as occurs in many federal and state programmes) both worked against the development of district budgeting. The New York City financial crisis has also been seen by opponents of this approach as another reason for tighter central control. However the advantages of an area input are not diminished and some would say they are enhanced. One researcher pointed to two down-to-earth advantages which would still apply: 'First, the district staff had to think what they were trying to achieve and draw up some kind of a plan for the year ahead. This forced them to step outside the day to day approach to the job. Second, the area inputs did result in some districts getting the specific equipment they needed as opposed to some central allocation of the wrong thing.'

Service delivery

Analysis of sixty-five projects initiated by O N G in four experimental districts suggests that O N G intervened to deal with several deficiencies in the existing departmentalized service delivery system.[15] These were particularly lack of procedures for identifying local issues and priorities (a problem in 65 per cent of the situations studied), lack of resources (65 per cent), lack of inter-agency procedures to deal with the problem (45 per cent) and cumbersome or unreliable operating procedures within and between agencies (43 per cent). Local service officials responded favourably to the experiment: 83 per cent of all members of the five original district cabinets called the monthly cabinet meetings 'very useful' or 'useful'. Co-operation came most easily from agencies with clear line authority down to the district level such as Police, Sanitation, and Parks. In contrast, Health, Housing and Human Resources did not have a unified line authority down to the districts and there was difficulty in establishing a strong cabinet representative for these agencies at the local level. A key factor influencing the success or failure of a district cabinet was the personality of the district manager. The calibre of the managers was generally high and they worked with considerable commitment and skill to bring about increased inter-agency co-ordination and to stimulate hundreds of service improvements which would not have occurred without their presence.

If district management resulted in some improvements in service integration it was less successful in bringing about delegation to local service officials. In 85 per cent of the projects studied, the district manager was involved in trying to get approval from higher levels of city government. This factor, coupled with a lack of strong backing from the mayor's office, resulted in a failure to implement the majority of the service delivery projects developed by the cabinets. An earlier, independent study of the Office of Neighborhood Government also drew this distinction between a vertical change (delegation) and a horizontal change (services integration).[16] It, too, found that horizontal changes were, within limits, unexpectedly successful. In contrast vertical changes were felt to be minimal. This study attached some significance to the fact that district officials have in most cases been career civil servants for many years and have developed firm attitudes to the traditional chain of command. This would seem to point toward the need for retraining of the officials involved.

An analysis of the costs of the local ONG offices and the central office cost allocable to them suggests that the programme cost about $125 000 per district – about $1 *per capita*. An attempt to estimate benefits from ONG projects suggests that due to the non-implementation of many of them, the actual returns may have been less than the costs of operating the ONG. However, crude estimates of the *potential* service improvements which might have been expected from projects blocked at higher levels suggests that there was a significant potential for gain over cost.

Local accountability

As mentioned earlier, the furtherance of public participation was not an explicit goal for the district management experiment. However, the leaders of local organizations were widely contacted and informed about the programme by the district managers and their staffs, and encouraged to make suggestions regarding local needs. In turn the managers relied on these organizations to back requests made of higher level bureaucrats and elected officials. In a sample of community leaders the Columbia University researchers found that 88 per cent reported some contact with the Office of Neighborhood Government in its first two years. In general, community leaders' attitudes were strongly favourable.

Public surveys conducted as part of the Columbia University research project found that only 14 per cent of the public knew of the existence of the local Office of Neighborhood Government. This is not surprising for ONG was concerned with changes within the bureaucracy rather than with publicizing services in the neighbourhoods. The surveys found that the public strongly favours some form of community input into decisions about service delivery and 57 per cent of the general public and 77 per cent of the community leaders believe that local service personnel should make most of the decisions about services in their district.

Distributive effects

Because the programme was an experiment in a sample of districts designed to achieve better use of existing resources positive steps were taken to avoid any diversion of resources into the experimental districts. An analysis by Columbia University of manpower and equipment allocations among all sixty-two Community Planning

Districts in the city and taking into account workload factors and demographic statistics shows that there was not significant diversion of resources to experimental districts from other districts with two exceptions – park maintenance and street resurfacing. As mentioned earlier in relation to planning and budgeting, these were two areas in which all ONG districts were active in seeking improvement and this seems to have resulted in redistribution in relation to these two particular services.

Conclusion

Encouraged by federal financial support New York City undertook a bold experiment in district management between 1971 and 1974. The focus was on changes within the bureaucracy rather than on public involvement in local government decision making. The major research study of the programme by the Bureau of Applied Social Research at Columbia University concluded that the actual impact of the programme was well below expectation. However, the study also concluded that the experiment had a great deal of unrealized potential. With greater mayoral backing and more delegation to local line officials they would have expected the experiment to produce net improvements in services. The study concludes that further efforts along these lines are worth trying if the implementation can be made stronger, the costs kept low, and the political pitfalls avoided.

Area management profile
Dayton – Neighbourhood priority boards

Introduction

Dayton, which has a population of 205 000, is an industrial city in south-western Ohio. It was the first large community to adopt the city manager form of government back in 1914. The city commission (or council) comprises five members (four commissioners and a mayor) who are all elected at large and are part-time.[1] All administrative authority is delegated to the city manager. In 1970 Dayton established a citywide system of six, elected, neighbourhood priority boards to determine municipal spending priorities for their areas. These now provide a regular input into the city's annual planning budgetary cycle and are also responsible for the development of an overall neighbourhood plan. Changes within the city bureaucracy designed to strengthen this area approach include: the establishment of a Department of Housing and Neighborhood Affairs to provide technical assistance and support to the priority boards; the introduction of inter-departmental teams of middle-management personnel serving each priority board area; and the execution of regular public opinion surveys of the population at large regarding the quality of city services. With these initiatives Dayton is making a substantial commitment of city resources in staff time and money to the task of improving the ability of city government to respond to public perceptions of needs and issues.

Origins

The stimulus came from the Demonstration and Model Cities Act 1966 for, in 1967, Dayton was chosen as one of the 150 cities to participate in the model cities programme (discussed in Chapter 6) and the city received an annual $2·9 million appropriation from the US Department of Housing and Urban Development. The project was focussed on the Inner West neighbourhood where racial tensions were running high. This was a run-down, small business and residential area near the city centre, long recognized as a home for minorities, mostly blacks. This community was not extensively involved in drafting the model cities application to Washington and local leaders pressed the city commission for a larger role in the programme. In March 1969 the city commission passed a resolution declaring that the neighbourhood-elected model cities planning council 'will be involved as a full partner in all programs, decisions and planning related to the target area'. The city backed this equal partnership agreement by allocating part of the model cities planning funds to the local planning council so that it could retain its own staff, which would work along with city staff in preparing the programme. The main accent of the programme was on social measures designed to combat deprivation such as provision of a 'one-stop' welfare office in the area, construction of subsidized single-family dwellings, increased youth work, introduction of mini-bus transport for the elderly and so on.

In 1969 the commission appointed a new city manager, James E. Kunde, who was influential in broadening the partnership approach used in Inner West to other parts of the city. On the basis of his recommendations the city commission extended the model cities type process to the remaining five neighbourhoods to give all of the residents of the city an opportunity to determine the priorities for municipal expenditures in their neighbourhoods. Each neighbourhood was allowed to devise its own method for organizing priority boards. Generally membership came from representatives recommended by existing organizations. In only one area was the composition of the neighbourhood priority board initially presented to the city challenged as unrepresentative of the area. Changes were made by area residents to the composition of this board so that it could receive recognition by the city. In the first financial year of the new arrangement (1970/71) the city allocated $200 000 on a *per capita* basis to the areas and each priority board determined how its funds would be spent, subject to final approval and possible veto by the city commission.

In 1971 the Department of Housing and Urban Development chose Dayton as one of the twenty cities to carry out 'planned variations' to the model cities programme. Dayton used the additional annual sum of $5·2 million in four ways: to institute a system of chief executive review and comment which improved communication between the mayor and the federal government, to create state-city task forces to co-ordinate the flow of funds from the state to the city, to simplify rules and regulations in a move towards revenue sharing, and to expand the activities of the neighbourhood priority boards. The city allocated $2·1 million for neighbourhood projects, $2·1 million for citywide projects and the remaining $1 million for staff to serve the boards and take the other administrative steps just outlined. To allocate funds to the neighbourhoods a formula was devised based on total population, substandard housing, poor families, welfare, unemployment and educational level of adults. Within each neighbourhood priority boards were required to give special attention to the needs of low income groups.

So that they would be as representative of their neighbourhoods as possible the five new priority boards held fresh elections by ballot in December 1971. A total of 7442 citizens participated which is 12·7 per cent of those eligible. Elections are held annually although not all seats are contested. Voter turn-out in 1975 was 13·9 per cent and in 1976 was 16·6 per cent. Board size ranges from twenty-four to thirty-six members, most chosen by subdistricts.

Aims

Dayton has a fairly sophisticated programme structure for city services in which all activities are grouped into programmes directed to the achievement of specified goals. Neighbourhood priority boards form a major part of the citizen participation programme which aims: 'to encourage, develop and actively promote citizen input in local government'. Other important elements in the programme are an ombudsman and public opinion surveys. Within this fairly loose overall goal considerable scope is deliberately left for priority boards to fashion their own ideas. These vary by neighbourhood and are evolving over time but it is possible to discern three broad aims and these are summarized in Table 10.

The representative aims of the priority boards naturally come into conflict with those of the commissioners. The commissioners see themselves as elected by the people to make all the decisions on city matters and yet the priority boards can also claim to represent local views. There is an overlap too with the work of the officers themselves. This is because the priority boards are served directly by staff who are based in neighbourhood site offices. Quite naturally these staff (as with many community workers in Britain) are inevit-

Table 10   *Broad aims of neighbourhood priority boards*

– *Policy initiation*
citizens pooling their needs and designating their priorities to policy making bodies (including the city commission, county commission, planning department, board of education etc).

– *Complaint resolution*
referring citizens to the appropriate service and developing an ombudsman function when response is viewed as inadequate.

– *Neighbourhood organization*
citizens joining together to solve their own problems and improve their own neighbourhoods.

ably confronted from time to time with conflict between city and neighbourhood loyalties. These overlaps point to an underlying aim of the priority boards which is to reduce mutual alienation between government and people by bringing the two into closer proximity. Of course there is confrontation and conflict between divergent interests but there is a strong accent in most of the priority boards on citizens and local government working in concert.

Geography

The boundaries of the areas served by the neighbourhood priority boards follow natural geographical features and reflect public perceptions of neighbourhoods. Figure 19 provides a map of the neighbourhoods and Table 11 shows how the population sizes

Table 11   *Populations served by neighbourhood priority boards*

Neighbourhood	Population
Inner-west	19 000
South-west	32 000
North-west	33 000
Fair River Oaks	28 000
North-east	13 000
South-east	79 000
Central business district	1000
Total	205 000

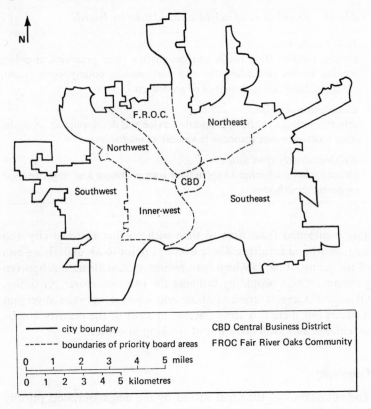

Figure 19   City of Dayton   Priority board areas

N

F.R.O.C.

Northeast

Northwest

CBD

Southwest

Inner-west

Southeast

────── city boundary	CBD Central Business District
- - - - boundaries of priority board areas	FROC Fair River Oaks Community

```
0    1    2    3    4    5 miles

0  1  2  3  4  5 kilometres
```

vary significantly. The six priority boards were joined in 1975 by a seventh – the Downtown Dayton Association – which represents the central business district.

Structure/activities

Figure 20 provides an organization chart for the City of Dayton. It is worth stressing the central role of the city manager who, through the three assistant city managers, exercises direct authority over the service departments. James A. Alloway is the city manager (1977) and he combines a forceful management style with a strong desire to develop a sensitive and concerned organization. The former is illustrated by his annual negotiation of specific performance contracts with service chiefs which spell out responsibilities and

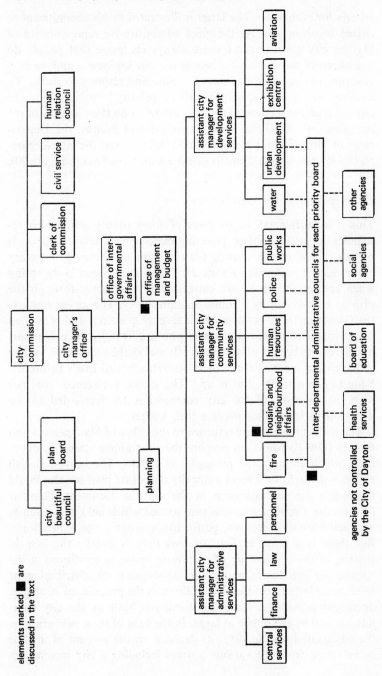

Figure 20   City of Dayton – organization chart

elements marked ■ are
discussed in the text

criteria for evaluation. The latter is illustrated by his commitment to citizen involvement: 'As the chief administrative representative of Dayton city government I must always recognize that people do not interrupt our business – people *are* our business – and we as a government must find the ways to relate and respond to them.' To understand the way the neighbourhood priority boards relate to the city government it is useful to focus attention on three aspects of the organization: the Office of Management and Budget, the Department of Housing and Neighborhood Affairs, and the inter-departmental administrative councils (these are all picked out in Figure 20).

Office of Management and Budget

This is a fairly small department of some twenty staff which resembles a British policy planning/management services unit. It plays a critical role in steering the city's annual planning budgetary cycle which is outlined in Figure 21. The process begins in the spring when community views are canvassed in two ways: through the priority boards and by a public opinion survey. The survey employs the Gallup method, involves about seventy questions and is applied to approximately 800 respondents who are stratified by neighbourhood. As one budget officer put it: 'It makes the most sense to take in the citizen input at the earliest opportunity and that's before the budgets are actually drawn up.' The public preferences together with the concerns of the city commission are forwarded to the departments *before* they prepare their budgets.

The budget requests are returned to the Office of Management and Budget (OMB) who then prepare the programme strategies document which employs the principles of PPBS. The nearest British equivalent would be a local authority corporate plan but this could understate the sophistication of the Dayton document. Familiar features are a programme structure format which links programmes and activities to objectives, performance criteria and expenditure. But there is a more explicit analysis than is usually the case in Britain, of the relationship of each programme to conditions in the community with maps and diagrams showing the distribution of needs and views across the city. In this way the programme strategies document provides a basis for discussion both by the city commission and by the public at large. In the light of these deliberations the city commission finalizes its decision on the amount of finance to be raised from the various sources including a city income tax

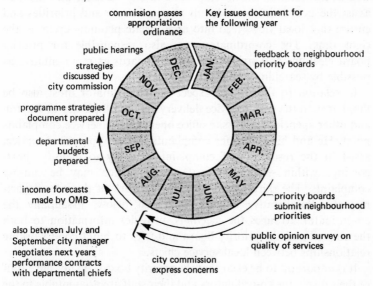

Figure 21   Outline of the city of Dayton annual planning budgetary cycle 1975/76

commission passes
appropriation
ordinance

Key issues document for
the following year

public hearings

strategies
discussed by
city commission

programme strategies
document prepared

departmental
budgets
prepared

income forecasts
made by OMB

also between July and
September city manager
negotiates next years
performance contracts
with departmental chiefs

feedback to neighbourhood
priority boards

priority boards
submit neighbourhood
priorities

public opinion survey on
quality of services

city commission
express concerns

Note Fiscal year is the calendar year

(which provides a third of the city's revenue). A document outlining key issues for investigation in the following year is prepared and area implications are fed back to the priority boards.

Department of Housing and Neighborhood Affairs

The neighbourhood affairs section of this department consists of thirty-five staff and had a 1976 budget of $700 000. These officers work directly with the priority boards and are based in local offices in each neighbourhood. There are six 'community affairs co-ordinators' (one per neighbourhood) who each supervise from three to nine staff and clerical personnel. Their central task is 'to facilitate the development and continuation of the process of citizen participation in decisions made by city government or other agencies that may affect the quality of life in the neighbourhood'. In practice, the co-ordinator's work can be considered in three parts: community development, service complaints and administrative co-ordination. In relation to the first, the co-ordinator works closely with the priority board chairman, board members, and other community organizations by providing technical and administrative support as well as information on developments in city hall. He and his staff assist the boards in their identification of needs and priorities and ensure that local views feed into appropriate planning cycles at the right time. The co-ordinators are also responsible for priority board elections and strive to make the boards as representative as possible by searching out local leaders.

In relation to the second aspect the co-ordinator must also be familiar with the entire service delivery system of the city of Dayton and other agencies for his site office operates as a service complaints point. He and his staff refer complaints to the appropriate service, assist in the resolution of complaints and try to identify short-comings within service delivery systems which may be causing complaints. The third aspect links to the work of the inter-depart-mental administrative councils discussed below. Essentially the co-ordinator arranges the meetings, provides information to both the council and the priority board and tries to build good working relationships between local service chiefs.

It is important to be clear that the priority boards do not have staff of their own – the co-ordinators and their staff are accountable to the city manager. Initially this was a sore point for the original model cities planning council for Inner West had its own staff. The city manager argued that this was a special situation for a low income, black neighbourhood usually left out of previous programmes. As a compromise, the priority boards interview applicants for neighbour-hood affairs jobs who have first been screened by the city.

Administrative councils

In May 1975 an administrative council for each priority board was established. These consist of middle management personnel from major city departments and other agencies. They meet on a once-a-month basis with the priority boards for the purpose of discussing with citizens complaints and issues that adversely affect service provision in the neighbourhoods. As problems are identified during the meetings they are assigned to a particular middle-management member of staff to work on a solution. The departments involved in the administrative councils include: Fire, Housing and Neighbour-hood Affairs, Human Resources, Police, Public Works, Water, Urban Development and neighbourhood planners from the Planning Department. Representatives from other agencies include health personnel (from the Montgomery Health District) and education officers. A chairman, who might be drawn from any department, is designated to co-ordinate the complaint resolution activities of each council. In 1976 the chairmen were drawn from Water, Housing and Public Works. Discussion topics range from immediate problems such as the accumulation of rubbish, roving dogs, and abandoned cars to longer-range concerns including neighbourhood land use policies, support services for the elderly and the rising number of burglaries.

Planning and budgeting

The city's 1976 total budget was $98 million but the priority boards have most influence on the way the community development block grant is spent. As discussed in Chapter 6 this was introduced in 1974 and consolidated a number of federal categorical grants to give greater flexibility to local government in deciding how the funds should be spent. Under the previous grants system Dayton received in excess of $15 million annually but, as the new grant is allocated on a formula basis, the city now receives in the order of $9 million under the community development block grant.

The process for deciding how this money should be spent is an integral feature of the annual planning budgetary cycle discussed earlier and illustrated in Figure 21. Basically each priority board prepares a needs statement setting out long- and short-term objectives. These are presented to a task force (or inter-departmental group) of officers led by the Office of Management and Budget. The task force consolidates the common concerns of the neighbourhoods. In 1975, there were six main areas of concern: (1) community involvement, (2) employment and economic development, (3) housing and environs, (4) social service delivery, (5) crime and delinquency, (6) land use planning. These were broken down into some thirty-three sub-objectives. A total of ninety-three projects were submitted for funding and these were evaluated against the concerns and sub-objectives. Other factors were also fed in including performance of previous projects and social indicator research on housing needs. The task force finalized recommendations on how the $9 million should be spent and forwarded these, via the city manager, to the city commission.

Dayton has gone a dood deal further than most cities in opening up its planning budgetary cycle to neighbourhood influence. The priority boards enjoy a formal role and do influence budgetary choice. Chief doubts surround the work of the task force and, in some ways, these reflect more generally on the city manager form of government. There seems to be a lack of awareness that the sifting and ranking of projects for funding is an essentially political process. The task force does not present policy options to the city commission so that it can exercise a political choice. Instead, the managerial analysis leads to one set of recommendations which tends to conceal the value judgements that have been made about spending priorities. There is some recognition of this problem in Dayton. Efforts are being made to develop ranking systems to expose priority board value structures more clearly. But even the most sophisticated systems cannot shift questions of budgetary choice out of the political and into the managerial arena.

Service delivery

In some areas, such as Inner West, 'one-stop' shops have been provided to give a range of services at one point in the neighbourhood and so ease public access. But the main ways of improving service delivery in Dayton relate to complaints procedures. Both the neighbourhood site offices and the administrative councils spend considerable time receiving and resolving complaints. A great deal depends on the personality and willingness of the community affairs co-ordinators. As one co-ordinator put it: 'The co-ordinator has no supervisory authority over the administrative councils so it's a question of working together. There is, of course, an up and over channel of coercion but that just isn't the way. That way fails to comprehend the co-operative nature of the beast.' Local service chiefs view the administrative councils with mixed feelings. There is enthusiasm about the potential of the councils and pride in small accomplishments but some feel that the councils have tended to get bogged down in the processing of simple service requests instead of tackling problems of more far-reaching significance.

Since the administrative councils have been in operation, at least two city commissioners have noticed a reduction in the number of citizen complaints brought to their office and they attribute this to the work of the councils. More specific performance measures are available. For example, one target is to ensure that 90 per cent of all complaints registered by citizens through the administrative council process are addressed within a thirty-day period. A survey in 1975 of priority board members and neighbourhood residents found that 141 of their 164 complaints were addressed within a month and that the majority were satisfied or highly satisfied with the results (61 per cent for members, 88 per cent for residents). The administrative councils are a young and developing concept. An early progress report is optimistic: 'By facilitating communications between the professionals responsible and the citizens on the receiving end, the city of Dayton hopes to sensitize service providers to the problems of the neighborhoods, to sensitize citizens to the complexities of city management, and ultimately to marshal all its resources in a systematic effort to improve the quality of city life.'[2] The chief danger would seem to be that the councils may be asked to face up to community pressure over issues they cannot control or influence effectively.

Local accountability

Dayton regards itself, with some justice, as a national leader in involving its citizens in governmental decision-making processes. By providing a city presence in the neighbourhoods (in the site offices), by funding considerable support to the neighbourhood priority boards and by building public preferences into the annual budgeting process, Dayton is certainly trying very hard to provide visible opportunities for residents to influence events. In an earlier appraisal Howard Hallman concluded:

Citizens participating in the priority boards have achieved results and gained a sense of satisfaction and accomplishment. Otherwise, they would not be putting in the long hours required. ... Not the equal-partnership arrangement in every neighborhood that first developed under model cities, and not neighborhood government with local boards appointing their own staff and running services. Rather an approach where elected neighborhood boards give their views and city officials listen and respond. A structure for citizen influence rather than formalized power-sharing characterizes the Dayton approach.[3]

During 1976 a task force on community involvement was reviewing the existing system and considering methods of improvement. In the evidence being submitted by all kinds of individuals and neighbourhood groups it is worth drawing attention to two points. The first is the widespread pressure to 'think small'. Priority boards which fostered and facilitated the growth of street groups (or block clubs) were praised whereas those which ignored sub-neighbourhood interests were criticized. The second concerns the pressure to amend the city charter so that the city commission would be elected by districts rather than at large. The five-member commission under-represents certain geographical areas and social groups.

Distributive effects

Evidence on the distributive effects of Dayton's approach is con-tradictory. In its origins with the project in the Inner West the approach was clearly designed to channel resources into a deprived area. When the programme went citywide in 1970/71 the $200 000 fund was distributed on a *per capita* basis and this was obviously not designed to give preferential treatment to poor neighbourhoods. More recently progress seems to have been made in relating expendi-ture to needs. For example, the 1975 allocation of the community development block grant does seem to impact mostly on the poorer neighbourhoods. At the same time it has to be admitted that wealthier areas are often better equipped to exploit the opportunities provided by the neighbourhood priority board system. The degree to which energetic staff support to deprived neighbourhoods can offset in-built disadvantages remains an open question for Dayton.

Conclusion

With its city-manager form of government it is hardly surprising that the city of Dayton has developed a fairly sophisticated man-agerial style. There are important advantages which more political forms of city government would be unwise to reject. In particular, the monitoring of performance both in terms of internal efficiency and external impact on the community is highly developed. The striking feature of Dayton's approach is that this 'management effectiveness' style is coupled with a firm and long-standing com-mitment to citizen participation through neighbourhood priority boards. Again there are lessons to be learned. The board's formal role in annual budgeting is particularly interesting and could widen thinking about the future role of neighbourhood councils in Britain. The area offices and administrative councils are also interesting innovations which point the way towards area management although some would argue that this would be unnecessary in a city as small as Dayton. It is the emasculation of local politics which a British observer is likely to find most difficulty in coming to terms with.

Area management profile
Stockport – area organization

Introduction

The Metropolitan Borough of Stockport has a population of approximately 292 000 and is one of ten metropolitan districts in the Greater Manchester conurbation. The council consists of sixty members with three councillors being elected by each of the borough's twenty wards. Stockport was the first authority in Britain to experiment with an area committee system designed to move towards a corporate approach at the local level (in 1971) and was the first authority to introduce a formal area organization into its management structure at both the member and the officer level (in 1974). The area system covers the whole borough and involves area committees of elected members, area co-ordination of services, provision of local information offices, and the development of community councils to articulate neighbourhood views. It is not surprising that Stockport's area organization has attracted a good deal of interest in local government circles for it is probably the most comprehensive in the country.

Origins

In 1971, acting on the advice of the management consultants, Booz-Allen and Hamilton, the former County Borough of Stockport introduced a new system of corporate management.[1] This included three innovations in the way the council would relate to geographical areas within the the authority. The first was the creation of three area sub-committees of the Housing and Community Services Committee. This committee was responsible, *inter alia*, for housing, recreation, libraries, consumer protection and community development. The sub-committees, which included elected members drawn from the wards of their respective areas, exercised executive responsibility for the functions of the main committee. The stimulation of independent elected community councils each serving a neighbour-hood of 10 000–20 000 people had begun in 1968. The second in-novation was to encourage this work more positively and to establish links between the community councils and the area sub-committees. The third change was a restructuring of the internal organization of the council's field services so that field officers in different services covered areas having the same boundaries.

The area sub-committees were clearly seen as a success for in 1973 the council decided to extend their brief. Although continuing to exercise executive responsibility over certain functions, they were now able to advise on all aspects of local authority services affecting their areas. In addition, the sub-committees took up local issues with other public services as, for example, when one sub-committee and the local community council pressed successfully for a new railway station to be programmed for an existing council housing estate. The community councils were, at times, highly critical of the council and this made some of them unpopular in certain quarters. But the general feeling was that their criticisms were invariably constructive and the council promoted their development with some vigour.[2] Establishing coterminous service areas was seen as a step forward but it was still possible for different departments dealing with different aspects of the same problem to be working at cross-purposes. No officer was charged with developing inter-divisional co-operation at the local level and this was felt to be a weakness.

The reorganization of local government in England and Wales, which took effect on 1 April 1974, created the Metropolitan Borough of Stockport. The new authority has roughly twice the population of the former County Borough and embraces five previous local authorities. In 1972 a joint committee was established to bring together representatives of the constituent authorities to prepare proposals on how the new authority should be organized. *Inter alia*, the joint committee favoured a decentralized approach, partly because of concern over the possible remoteness of the new, larger authority, and partly because of the proven success of an area-based approach in the County Borough. The proposals of the joint committee on the management structure for the new authority appeared in 1973[3] and, in so far as the area organization is concerned, these were accepted and put into effect when the new council came into operation on 1 April 1974.

Aims

The area organization forms an integral part of the council's manage- ment structure and it is difficult, therefore, to attribute particular objectives to the area aspects. There are four main principles which underlie the overall management structure.[4] These concern: (1) realization of economies of scale; (2) organizational effective- ness; (3) responsiveness to local needs and aspirations and (4) satisfaction for both members and officers. It was not intended that the area organization should further the first, but it does play a role in achieving all the other three and particularly the aim of respon- siveness to local needs and aspirations. The more specific aims of Stockport's area organization presented in Table 12 have been distilled from a number of sources.[5] However, even this condensed list illustrates a considerable breadth of purpose.

Table 12 *Main aims of Stockport's area organization*

- To prevent the authority from becoming remote and inaccessible to the residents of the borough.

- To extend the corporate management approach being developed at the centre of the authority, down to the local level and so improve the effectiveness of services.

- To strengthen the elected member's representative role by providing an opportunity for members to become fully involved in all the council's activities within their wards.

- To provide a convenient channel of communication between the council and local community councils, and other residents' groups and indi- viduals.

- To make the best use of available office accommodation, inherited from the previous authorities, and to capitalize on the local knowledge built up by officers of the constituent authorities.

Geography

The new authority is divided into three areas (North, East and West) and service provision within each of these areas is co-ordinated by an area co-ordinator who operates from an area office. Housing, Environmental Health and Social Services are located in the same area office (with one or two exceptions) and their clerical and administrative support is provided by the area co-ordinator. In addition, most the council's other services operate in relation to areas which are coterminous with the three main areas. Town planning, building inspection, educational welfare, recreation (including libraries, parks and youth work), highway repairs and street cleansing all conform almost entirely to the three areas. The most notable exception is education which is linked in only an informal way with the area organization. Of course, schools have a major impact on the local community and education is therefore a significant omission. Even so the degree to which service area boundaries are coterminous is exceptionally high in Stockport.

However, political rather than management factors were the critical influence in deciding where the boundaries should be drawn. There are twenty wards in Stockport and the area boundaries always respect ward boundaries. The wards are grouped together in twos and threes to form eight area committees (three in North, three in East and two in West) which each cover an area with a population of less than 50 000. The geographical and size relationships between the three main areas and the eight area committees are clarified by Figure 22 and Table 13.

Table 13 *Populations of areas in Stockport*

Area Committee	Population	Operational Areas	Population
Tiviot Dale	32 900	North	114 000
Heath Bank	33 300		
Heaton Reddish	47 800		
Werneth	28 500	East	93 700
Marple	23 700		
Stepping Hill	41 500		
Cheadle	48 700	West	84 600
Bramhall	35 900		
Metropolitan Borough	292 300		292 300

Source: 1971 Census

The Local Government Act 1972 requires certain rules to be observed in the plotting of ward boundaries. The primary con-

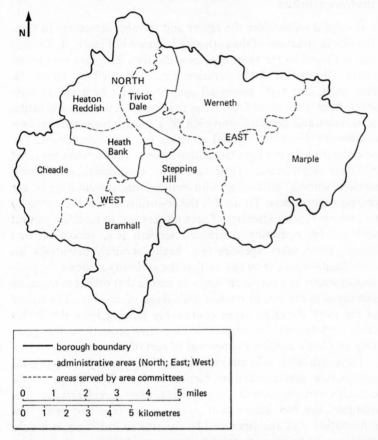

Figure 22   Metropolitan Borough of Stockport   Area organization

N

NORTH

Heaton
Reddish

Tiviot
Dale

Werneth

Heath
Bank

EAST

Cheadle

Marple

Stepping
Hill

WEST

Bramhall

——— borough boundary
——— administrative areas (North; East; West)
- - - - areas served by area committees

0   1   2   3   4   5 miles

0   1   2   3   4   5 kilometres

sideration is that the ratio of electors to councillors should, as far as possible, be the same in every ward. In addition, boundaries should be easily identifiable and should respect local ties but these requirements tend to be secondary. As a result ward boundaries, and thus area committee boundaries, sometimes do not reflect public perceptions of localities. There is, finally, a system of some twenty community (or neighbourhood) councils covering virtually the whole of the borough and these *are* related to neighbourhoods as defined by local residents.

Structure/activities

It is helpful to consider the officer and member structures in turn. The officer structure of the authority is shown in Figure 24. The key role is played by the three *area co-ordinators*. They are answerable to the Director of Administration but, as implied by Figure 24, their work cuts right across all council activity as it affects their areas. Each area co-ordinator has four main duties: co-ordination of services and projects, provision of a local information service. community development, and servicing the area committees. The co-ordinators do not have line authority over local services provided by other departments. Their task is to co-ordinate professional services without interfering with professional direction from the central departments. To do this the co-ordinator has the authority to convene regular meetings of area officers and to establish contact with officers operating centralized services (e.g. education) and officers from other agencies (e.g. health service). Essentially his co-ordination task is to ensure that the authority responds to community needs in a corporate way – to ensure that decisions taken by one division are not in conflict with those of another. The nature of the work therefore varies enormously ranging from day-to-day crisis work to close involvement in long-term projects, such as planning and implementing the renewal of part of the area.

There are nine information and advice centres which provide information and application forms for the whole range of the council's services as well as providing some direct services. For example, five can accept cash payments for rent and rates. The information staff are supervised by the area co-ordinator as are the community development staff who try to establish close relationships with local voluntary organizations and support and encourage the local community councils. The final aspect of the area co-ordinator's work is to service the area committees of councillors who look to him for the implementation of their decisions on locally based services.

It is difficult to isolate those costs specifically attributable to the area organization. For example, community development work and information centres exist in other authorities without an area organization. Also some of the cost of area administration (e.g. typing/clerical support for decentralized services) would be incurred regardless of the existence of an area organization. In 1976/77 community development cost £44 000, the information centres

Figure 23   Metropolitan Borough of Stockport. Simplified organization chart (officers)

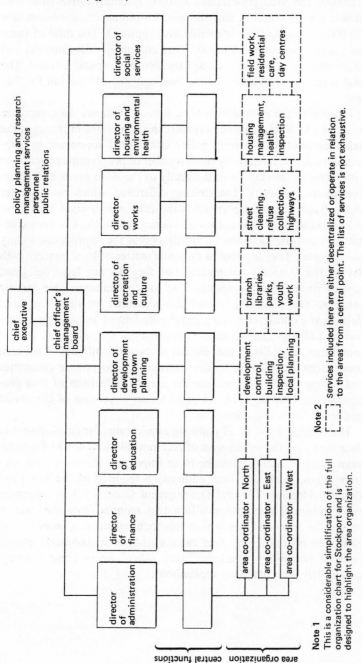

Note 1
This is a considerable simplification of the full organization chart for Stockport and is designed to highlight the area organization.

Note 2
Services included here are either decentralized or operate in relation to the areas from a central point. The list of services is not exhaustive.

£125 000, the area committees £20 000 (administrative time plus attendance allowances) and the area co-ordinators approximately £30 000 (including their administrative support). The total of these costs is approximately £220 000. When community development and information centres are excluded the figure is around £50 000. The total revenue expenditure for the borough was £45 million for that year.

Turning to the elected members, Figure 24 shows the committee structure. As with the officer structure this reveals the influence of the Bains Committee: a strong policy committee, supported by sub-committees, and a relatively small number of programme committees with terms of reference linked directly to the main needs and objectives of the authority. The striking difference, which runs counter to the Bains Committee view,[6] is the existence of eight area committees which cut right across all council activities. The area committees comprise local ward councillors plus the appropriate county councillor(s). They are free to raise any matter of local concern with any of the council's committees but they do not have delegated powers or budgets to spend. The area committees are strictly *advisory*. The general purposes sub-committee of the Policy and Resources Committee has a general oversight of the area organization and all the minutes of area committees are submitted to that committee. In addition, the relevant parts of the minutes of the area committees are referred to the appropriate programme committee and, if approved, they become the executive decision of that programme committee. Table 14 provides an indication of the varied business of area committees.

The consideration of all planning applications for development in their area and the submission of recommendations to the Development Control Sub-Committee is an important feature of the area committees' work. The local authority is required by the Town and Country Planning General Development Order 1973 to determine every planning application within two months from the date of receipt. In order to comply with this requirement it is necessary for each area committee to meet twice during each six-weekly council cycle of committee meetings. Every other one of these meetings deals solely with planning applications.[7]

*Figure 24   Metropolitan Borough of Stockport. Simplified committee
structure (elected members)*

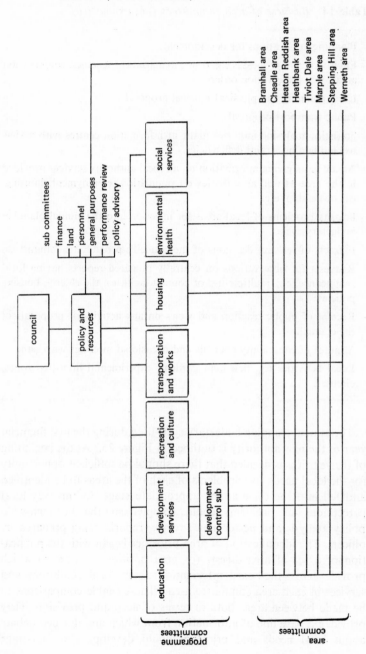

Table 14   *Business of area committees (not exhaustive)*

- Planning applications for development.
- Environmental proposals e.g. traffic management schemes, conservation areas, tree preservation orders.
- Local planning and physical renewal proposals.
- Public transport proposals.
- Statistics analysing inquiries made at information centres with a view to highlighting service deficiencies.
- Area digests giving information on all local authority services provided in the area as well as statistics on population, employment, housing, car ownership, etc.
- Priority problems of local areas for injection into the annual planning budgetary cycle.
- Extracts of relevant decisions of the council's programme committees.
- Requests for observations on centrally prepared reports having local significance, e.g. multiple use of council facilities, the elderly, housing policies.
- Receipt of public reaction and views on any activity or proposals of the council.
- Minutes of community councils and occasional meetings with same.
- Local activities e.g. best kept gardens, experimental litter-free zones, circuses.

The annual planning budgetary cycle used during the first financial year of the new authority is outlined in Figure 25.[8] At the beginning of the year it was decided that there should be sufficient opportunity for the local needs and problems of each of the areas to be identified and fed into the cycle at the appropriate stage. In this way local perceptions of problems could complement the borough-wide policy analysis and performance review reports being prepared by officers. The identification of area priorities began with the publication of a set of area digests (or area position statements) which provide across-the-board information about local conditions and services in each area committee area.[9] These enable comparisons to be made between areas both in terms of need and provision. They provided a base line of information from which an informed debate about local needs and priorities could develop. The four-stage

Figure 25 Outline of the Metropolitan Borough of Stockport annual planning budgetary cycle 1974/75

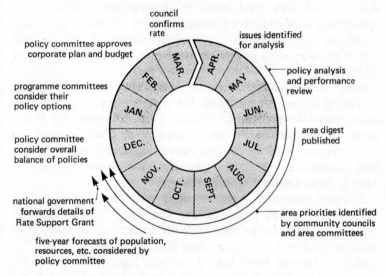

council confirms rate

issues identified for analysis

policy committee approves corporate plan and budget

policy analysis and performance review

programme committees consider their policy options

area digest published

policy committee consider overall balance of policies

national government forwards details of Rate Support Grant

area priorities identified by community councils and area committees

five-year forecasts of population, resources, etc. considered by policy committee

MAR. APR. MAY FEB. JUN. JAN. JUL. DEC. AUG. NOV. SEPT. OCT.

Note Fiscal year is April–March

process used to draw up community-based reports on local priorities is discussed more fully elsewhere.[10]

Planning and budgeting[11]

In terms of physical planning there can be little doubt that the area committees have provided a detailed and very valuable service. They have enabled the council to exploit the local knowledge of ward councillors and community councils *before* making decisions on environmental change. For example, the consultation system for development control has almost certainly resulted in a more sensitive use of planning powers. This is not to suggest that area committee recommendations are always accepted. There might quite reasonably be over-riding reasons why the Development Control Sub-Committee would disagree with an area, as for example when planning grounds for refusal of an application are extremely weak. When community feelings are running high locally rejection of area recommendations can naturally cause friction. But conflict of this kind should not be exaggerated. As a general rule the development control process has improved two-way communication between those responsible for planning policy and those affected. A useful side-effect of area involvement in development control is the opportunity it provides for younger planning officers to gain early experience in reporting to a council committee. In fact the area system provides early committee experience for officers from most divisions.

Some local planning work is undertaken by inter-divisional groups of officers for Stockport has tried to develop a corporate approach to the preparation of local plans. The plans for Heath Bank and Marple Town Centre are examples which involved the full participation of the relevant area co-ordinator, area staff and area committee. Indeed, the East area co-ordinator chaired the Marple Town Centre project group.

The area committees have no budgets but they have exerted an influence on overall policy making and budgeting and this was probably greatest during 1974/75. With the national curtailment of public expenditure in the years since then the budgeting process has tended to become more inward looking. Figure 25 outlines the process used in 1974/75. The area input involved several innovations: the values of officers were deliberately excluded; there was no constraint on the nature of the issues that could be raised; members, community councils and groups from each area were involved; an attempt was made to synthesize and rank priorities for action; and the process linked directly to the budgetary cycle. All of these were significant advances on much current practice in Britain, including most of the attempts to develop public participation under the Town and Country Planning Acts. The input of area priorities involved *all* councillors in a debate about *corporate*, as opposed to within-service, priorities and this was undoubtedly a significant breakthrough.

The chief weakness was the inadequate reporting back to area community councils on the impact of the area reports. Where local pressure for feedback was applied extensive reporting back did occur but this was on an *ad hoc* basis. Three other ways of improving the process were also revealed by experience. First, the process focussed on problems and needs and could be modified to give more emphasis on opportunities and ways of saving resources. Second, the lists of priorities tended to be very long and it would be useful to ask the areas to isolate their top priorities. Third, the process tended to have a bias towards physical problems possibly because of their visibility in the area. Care must be taken to ensure that attention is also given to social issues and less visible problems. In more recent years attempts have been made to rectify these weaknesses, but the area input to the annual cycle has diminished in importance, possibly because of changes in the financial climate.

So far the discussion of planning and budgeting has focussed on formal arrangements for area inputs, but there are undoubtedly more subtle channels of influence at work. It has to be remembered that each councillor, apart from serving on his area committee, will also serve on one, two, or perhaps three programme committees and may even be chairman of one of these. The insights gained from area committee work are bound to have at least some effect on the way councillors approach policy making in the programme committees. A further important feature is the relationships between the two tiers of local government. In the area committee the county and borough councillors are brought together sharing a similar purpose: tackling the problems of that particular neighbourhood. This contrasts with a much more common form of inter-tier exchange in which members find themselves representing their tier 'against' the other tier. There is some reason to believe that the area committees can bring the two tiers more closely together and this opens up additional possibilities for the influence of policy.

Service delivery

The public has enjoyed the benefit of a much wider range of locally based information than occurred prior to reorganization. During 1974/75 the information centres dealt with 198 000 inquiries. On the whole the staff are enthusiastic and this fact, coupled with the geographical spread of centres, suggests that public access to services was increased during 1974/75. However, in 1975/76 economies were required and the opening hours and level of staffing in the centres were reduced. Exact comparisons are difficult to make but, despite the reductions, there seems to have been a growth in the number of visitors to the centres during 1975/76, possibly because their work and locations have gradually become better known. The centres, and particularly those with a capacity to receive rent and rate payments, are undoubtedly more convenient for many members of the public and their general effect is to make the council a less impersonal organization.

The degree to which the area organization has improved the

effectiveness of the service delivery of the line departments is difficult to assess. The meetings of area officers convened by the area co-ordinators have provided a forum for the discussion of local issues which affect more than one department. The success of these meetings and their impact on service delivery depend on a number of factors including: the degree of delegation to area level within services, the attitudes of area officers, and the energy and drive of the area co-ordinators. All these factors are variable and it is, therefore, impossible to make sweeping conclusions. In some cases area officers have been reluctant to move beyond professional standpoints to think more broadly about local issues. In others, the area team has worked together productively on a local problem. For example, one team shared information about the problems of a particular housing estate and developed a range of low-level measures to ameliorate the situation involving administrative action by a number of departments.

In general terms the relationships between officers working for different divisions at the local level have improved. The co-location of housing, social services, and public health staff has increased contact and mutual understanding. At the same time, the central departments have not gone out of their way to encourage area staff to devote time to joint work with other departments. Reward systems and assessment of performance continue to be based on departmental criteria. It may be that some method of also measuring staff performance in relation to area needs will be necessary if significant co-operation at the area level is to be achieved. In a diluted form, the area committees have been used to assess the area performance of the council and they have developed a nuisance value acting as a check on the activities of the central departments. By exposing service deficiencies the area co-ordinator and area committee are not powerless to improve service performance not least by the use of informal networks. But there is no denying that, when the chips are down, they lack sufficient authority to develop a corporate approach at the local level.

Local accountability

Primary responsibility for the stimulation and arrangement of public participation rests with the area co-ordinator who co-operates with departmental directors and the public relations officer as appropriate. As mentioned earlier, a key feature of Stockport's approach to public involvement has been the formation of some twenty community councils covering virtually the whole of the borough. Their terms of reference are very broad. *Inter alia*, they set out to reflect and voice local feeling and opinion, identify community needs and consider ways of meeting them and, in some cases, attempt to foster community self-help. Apart from support from community development staff each council receives an annual financial contribution from the local authority of up to £200 to assist with essential running costs e.g. leaflets, posters, etc. The community councils are elected annually, usually at public meetings, and are non party-political. They have a 'special relationship' with the area committee(s) covering their area and they receive all area committee papers. In this way they are kept fairly well informed of council and other proposals relating to their area and can make their views known to the area committees at an early stage.

Chief doubts surround the degree to which the community councils are representative of local opinion. In some cases there is little doubt that they are genuine grass-roots organizations which are open and sensitive to local feelings. Others have, perhaps, become too involved in the bureaucratic administration of consultation. The Association for Neighbourhood Councils took the following view: 'There is a tremendous degree of activity on the [Stockport] councils, but since they tend to be part of the local authority and answerable to them it is possible that this lack of independence might make them, in some people's eyes, part of the "establishment".'[12] But it is too easy to blame the community councils themselves for any weaknesses in their local strength and support. One needs to ask why they do not attract more widespread community interest. Part of the problem is that they are relatively impotent. This is not to suggest that they are inconsequential. Indeed, on occasions, they have angered ward councillors very considerably! It is not surprising that this conflict between ward councillor and community council should arise from time to time. They both claim to represent local views and there are certain to be differences of opinion on some issues. If this leads to a lively debate then surely this is a healthy feature.

There is a danger, however, that these conflicts at the periphery of the organization will distract us from a more important insight. This is that both the community councils *and* the majority of ward councillors are relatively impotent despite the existence of the area organization. This is because, whilst there has been considerable geographical decentralization of services in Stockport, there has been little or no delegation or devolution of authority to the local level. Stockport is a more open authority than most and area influences do have some impact. But, paradoxically, the *control* of decision making in Stockport has probably become more centralized since reorganization. This applies within both the officer and the member structure.

Distributive effects

From the very beginning the area organization was applied to all areas of the borough and has not been used to focus resources on priority areas in any explicit way. The area digests did provide a systematic picture of community needs and council provision in each area and several of the council's major policy analysis reports have incorporated a geographical dimension highlighting the mal-distribution of services, e.g. the housing policies and elderly reports.[13] But there has been no attempt to analyse the allocation of resources between areas and no attempt to develop even modest area budgets which could be allocated to area committees in a way reflecting local needs.

The political complexion of the council is relevant here. During 1974/75 the Conservative Party had a very narrow majority but in the next two years it succeeded in increasing its number of seats considerably. Even so, two of the area committees in North Area (Tiviot Dale and Heath Bank) continue to have a majority of Labour councillors. Much of the business of area committees does not involve party political disagreement, but the existence of two area committees controlled by opposition members may partly explain the political reluctance to experiment with area budgets. This, of course, is not an argument against area resource analysis which could be conducted by central departments and reported to the Policy and Resources Committee who could re-direct resources through guidance to the programme committees.

Conclusion

Stockport has, arguably, the most developed area organization in Britain. The decentralized services have increased public access to council services and the co-ordination of activities at local level has improved service effectiveness, if only in minor ways. The system of community councils and area committees has opened up opportunities for the public to influence events and for elected members to strengthen their constituency role. But the area system is essentially advisory, some would say toothless. Much of its promise for developing a corporate and responsive approach to local problems and opportunities is thwarted by a lack of delegation within the officer structure and a lack of devolution within the political sphere. The nature of the area organization is under fairly continuous review and it is possible that Stockport will move to rectify these weaknesses and so sustain its record of innovation in this field.

Area management profile
Liverpool – Area Experiment

Introduction

The City of Liverpool has a population of approximately 550 000 and is one of five metropolitan districts in the Merseyside County. The council consists of ninety-nine members with three councillors being elected by each of the city's thirty-three wards. The communities living in Liverpool's inner residential areas have been the testing ground for a number of experiments designed to tackle urban deprivation. One of the most recent is the area management project sponsored jointly by the Department of the Environment and the City of Liverpool. It commenced in July 1974 and seeks to apply corporate management techniques, coupled with political responsiveness, to the urban problems of one inner city area containing 60 000 people.

Origins

The experiment has inter-connected local and national origins which are reflected in its joint sponsorship by local and central government. Since the mid-1960s the city has had a reputation for innovation and experiment. A bold example can be quoted from 1969 when the council invited the management consultants McKinsey and Co. Inc. to overhaul the city's management system and organization.[1] This resulted in a daring, if drastic, reduction of the number of committees and departments. Few would deny that the changes have created new problems[2] and, indeed, McKinsey soon modified their approach away from 'once-and-for-all' structural alterations to organizations. But it is easy to forget that Liverpool did venture bravely into unmapped territory and pushed forward contemporary thinking about management in local government. In so far as the area management project is concerned the McKinsey changes showed both the preparedness of the city to experiment and the need for some kind of action at a later date to knit together the working of the new 'super-departments' which tended to strengthen vertical, functional approaches at the expense of horizontal co-ordination.

Central government initiatives of the late 1960s focussed on the inner city of Liverpool included an action-research project on an educational priority area[3] and a national community development project in the Vauxhall area. However, an initiative which had more direct impact on the development of the area management project in Liverpool was backed by a voluntary organization: Shelter – the national campaign for the homeless. In 1969 Shelter expanded its concern from the literally homeless to those parts of the city where homelessness principally occurs. The Shelter Neighbourhood Action Project (SNAP) was a three-year experiment lasting from 1969 to 1972 in part of the deprived area of Granby, Liverpool 8. The final report of the project suggested that urban decline was a *total* problem and set out the case for a completely transformed urban programme. Considerable emphasis was placed on the development of a comprehensive corporate planning process at the local level.[4] 'The relevant planning process should combine all major programmes attacking the basic problems of the area . . . with the corporate planning of all resources . . . in a district budgeting cycle . . . which allowed the city to appeal for supplementary expenditures from government.'[5]

The project had an immediate effect on Peter Walker, then the Secretary of State at the Department of the Environment. In July 1972 Walker announced his intention to carry out studies 'to develop a total approach to the improvement of the urban environment'.[6] These developments are discussed further in Chapter 5. Suffice it to say that one of these studies was the Liverpool Inner Area Study. This was focussed on an area which included the SNAP project. From an early stage the consultants employed by the Department of the Environment to do the study[7] were anxious to develop the concept of area management. In November 1973 proposals for an experiment in area management were put forward and the project commenced, soon after local government reorganization, in July 1974.

Aims

The Liverpool Inner Area Study (IAS) proposal discusses the nature of area management as follows:

Area management as a concept is concerned with devolution, that is 'the delegation of portions or details of duties to subordinate officers or committees' (*Shorter English Dictionary*). It would involve bringing parts of the City's administration closer to the people it is designed to serve, through the actions of both elected members and officers. But it would go further than the decentralisation already being practised by individual programme departments, by fostering a corporate approach to the needs and problems of a particular area, and in particular the allocation of resources to that area.[8]

Reducing remoteness, developing an effective corporate approach, area resource allocation and improving the effectiveness of elected members were all seen as important questions. The general objectives of the experiment in exploring these issues are set out in Table 15 and are drawn from the IAS report.[9]

Table 15   *Objectives of the Liverpool area management experiment*

- To examine ways in which area management would better identify and meet the needs of people living in inner areas.
- To identify the possible roles, powers and duties of local elected members and community representation in area management.
- To consider the extent to which the local administration of other relevant agencies could effectively work with area management.
- To determine whether area management should be applied to other parts of the city.

Geography

The study is focussed on one inner area which has a population of 60 000 people (approximately 10 per cent of the city population). Three possible approaches to the definition of the area were investigated.[10] These were: (1) political, i.e. whether the area should be based on wards, or groups of wards; (2) technical, i.e. the administrative requirements of different departments; (3) communities, i.e. whether social groupings could be identified. None of the three approaches was acceptable on its own. Instead, an empirical approach was used in which practical requirements for the definition of the area were identified: the area should be large enough for local planning and decision making, small enough for area administration to be accessible to local people, should minimize unnecessary disturbance to social groupings and existing decentralized administration,

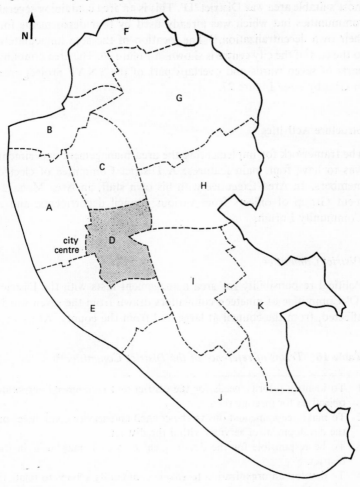

Figure 26   City of Liverpool   Planning disricts

N

F

G

B

C

H

A

D

city
centre

I

K

E

J

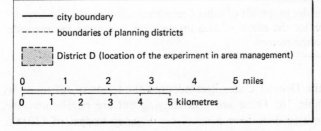

—— city boundary

------- boundaries of planning districts

District D (location of the experiment in area management)

| 0 | 1 | 2 | 3 | 4 | 5 miles |

| 0 | 1 | 2 | 3 | 4 | 5 kilometres |

and should, of course, be in the inner city. Given these criteria the most suitable area was District 'D'. This is an area containing several communities but which was already used by four departments for their own decentralization.[11] The location of the area immediately to the east of the city centre is shown in Figure 26. The area contains parts of seven wards and overlaps part of the SNAP project area in Granby – see Figure 27.

Structure/Activities

The framework for implementing the area management experiment was to have four main features: A District Committee of elected members, an Area Executive with his own staff, an Area Management Group of officers from various council departments, and a Community Forum.

District Committee

Political responsibility for area management rests with the District 'D' Committee of nineteen councillors drawn from the seven wards affected, from the council at large and from the county. At its first

Table 16   *Terms of reference of the District Committee*[12]

---

1 To identify priority needs for the district and recommend corporate objectives for meeting them.
2 To make recommendations to the council and service committees on the development of services within the district.
3 To be responsible for the development of area management in the district.
4 To develop an organization to enable community groups to relate to the committee.
5 To consider proposals of other committees affecting the district.
6 To monitor the effects of area management and make recommendations to the council.

---

meeting the District Committee adopted the terms of reference set out in Table 16. These are wide-ranging but are purely advisory. The committee does have a small contingency budget of £10 000, and special projects budget of £13 000 but these are of little sig-

Figure 27   City of Liverpool   The district 'D' area

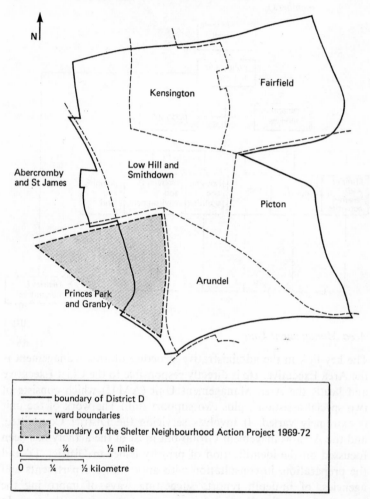

N

Fairfield

Kensington

Abercromby
and St James

Low Hill and
Smithdown

Picton

Arundel

Princes Park
and Granby

—————— boundary of District D
- - - - - - ward boundaries
▨ boundary of the Shelter Neighbourhood Action Project 1969-72

0   ¼   ½ mile
0   ¼   ½ kilometre

nificance. The membership of the District Committee is arranged
to reflect the political balance of the city council. All minutes of
the District Committee are submitted to the Policy and Finance
Committee and recommendations are submitted to the various
service committees as appropriate. Figure 28 provides a simplified
picture of Liverpool's committee structure.

Figure 28   City of Liverpool. Simplified committee structure (elected members)

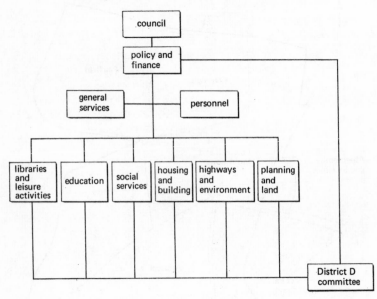

Area Management Unit

The key link in the administrative structure of area management is the Area Executive. He is directly responsible to the Chief Executive and heads the Area Management Unit (AMU) which consists of two special assistants, plus two support staff. The work of the unit is extremely varied. It involves servicing the District Committee, and the Area Management Group but most of the activity has been focussed on the identification of priority issues in District 'D' and the preparation, in consultation with appropriate departments and agencies, of in-depth reports suggesting ways of improving the impact of council policies and management practice on the area. In preparing an initial list of priority issues the AMU drew on a variety of sources ranging from statistical data, such as the revised 'social malaise' data prepared by the City Planning Officer,[13] through to the personal views of local councillors. Some of the issues investigated have important policy implications in relation to, for example, industrial development, pre-school provision and derelict property. Others have been focussed on ways of improving management practice with, for example, the development of a multi-purpose form for welfare benefits and an experiment in local housing management.

The AMU is located in an office in the city centre and not in District 'D'. The logic is that, given the lack of delegation in Liverpool, it is in the central municipal buildings where the majority of decisions about District 'D' are made. Location in the area would isolate the AMU without offering compensating advantages, for the AMU has no powers to provide advice or deliver services to the public. The annual cost of the Area Management Unit was £23 000 during 1974/75 which was shared between the Department of the Environment (75 per cent) and the city council (25 per cent). The city council's total revenue expenditure was around £100 million for that year.

Area Management Group

This brought together representatives from all relevant council departments, together with a representative from the Merseyside county. The Area Executive had administrative responsibility for the group, chaired its meetings and prepared its agenda, but he had no line authority over the representatives who remained wholly accountable to their own chief officers. As originally conceived, it was envisaged that the Area Management Group (AMG) would comprise those officers directly concerned with service delivery in District 'D'. In practice, attendance tended to be by more senior officers so that a more authoritative contribution of departmental views could be provided at the meetings. Much of the work on the priority issues mentioned earlier was executed by smaller teams of officers sometimes drawn from AMG members, but also from those more directly concerned with District 'D'. Figure 29 provides a simplified organization chart which should help to clarify the working relationships of the Area Management Unit and the Area Management Group. In 1975 the Area Management Group was discontinued in favour of a more flexible approach in which the Area Management Unit would form links with those officers most concerned with the issues being investigated.

Community Forum

It was originally envisaged that a community forum for District 'D' would provide a structure for public involvement in area

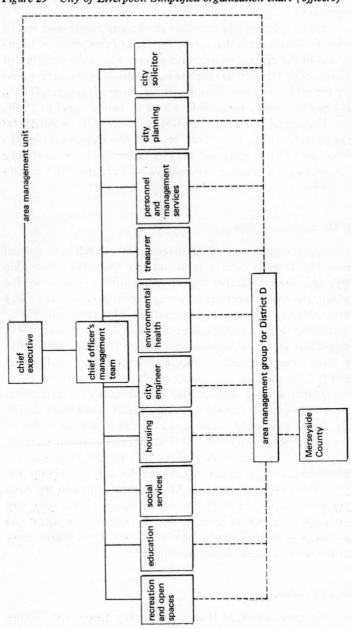

Figure 29   City of Liverpool. Simplified organization chart (officers)

Note The Area Management Group was discontinued in 1975.

management. The idea was to create a forum in which community groups, and others, could comment on council policies and put forward their own ideas and proposals for action. Council community development staff working with the Liverpool Council for Voluntary Service identified approximately twenty community organizations active in District 'D' and invited them to a meeting to consider whether a forum should be set up and, if so, what form it should take. A number of meetings were held which dealt with procedural matters, for example, voting rights and the relationship between the forum and the district committee. But the forum eventually collapsed after operating for little more than a year. The reasons were complex but a key problem was a conflict between the district committee and the forum as to the nature and degree of public involvement. As an alternative the Area Management Unit has worked with individual community groups on specific issues as appropriate.

Planning and budgeting

The area management project does have a small budget for the limited purpose of starting special projects, 'pump-priming' and meeting short-term contingencies, but the sum involved is small. The main impact of area management on policy planning and budgeting can be reviewed in two steps: first, the issue-based approach to policy analysis and, second, the development of area resource analysis.

The Area Management Unit chose to put much of its effort into the former and not without success. One or two examples will give an indication. As a response to the very serious unemployment situation in parts of District 'D' the AMU examined the council's policies and administrative procedures for providing opportunities for investment in industrial capital in the inner city. In conjunction with other constructive pressures in this field, the analysis was influential in bringing about a council decision to approve expenditure of £600 000 on small unit advance factory space in the inner city during 1976/77. A second example stemmed from the discovery of a group of sound houses in District 'D' which were blighted by a proposed school extension. A closer analysis of land use allocations of this kind, including proposals for public open space, revealed a major gap between desired expansion in the area of land to be used for community purposes and the resources being made available for their actual development. This led to a council decision to re-examine its policy on school site extensions in circumstances where there is no firm capital expenditure programme. This, in turn, has led to a complete review of land use policy for the inner city. Of course not all the area management policy initiatives were taken up. For example, pre-school provision is often an area where local authorities lack a corporate approach for Departments of Education and Social Services can find it difficult to agree on a clear and unified policy. An area management report on policy for the under-fives seems to have resulted in little managerial response. Perhaps the special projects budget will assist in bringing about change for the council has now agreed to a pre-school experiment using these funds. This is based on a school in District 'D' and involves joint working by Education and Social Services.

Area resource analysis involves the analysis of the allocation of resources to areas smaller than the local authority area. From an early stage it was recognized that Liverpool's framework for resource allocation was not designed for achieving area objectives. The consultants, in co-operation with all the council's spending departments, developed and applied a methodology designed to discover the amount of resources the council was devoting to District 'D'.[14] The analysis was carried out for the financial year 1973/74 and, quite apart from the detailed results, this showed that a high percentage of the council's budget *was* allocable to areas. The study was an *ad hoc* exercise and the departments found the analysis was time-consuming. However, this did not result from conceptual difficulties or lack of data, but because information is currently held in a way suitable for presenting an analysis for the city rather than for individual areas of the city.

The District 'D' tables provide a wealth of information which can be used to assess the degree to which council policy was directing resources into this inner city area.[15] Some of the results are striking. For example, Liverpool had adopted an education policy of position discrimination in favour of deprived groups some years earlier, and the tables show that this policy may need to be pursued with greater vigour. District 'D' contains 9·6 per cent of the population, but received only 7·2 per cent of that part of the overall education budget that could be allocated areally (which was 76 per cent of the total education budget). The district *does* receive a greater than average share of nursery school places, and is slightly favoured in the distribution of primary and secondary resources. But these advantages are more than cancelled out at the level of further education.

The consultants openly point to three important limitations of the study: first, no analysis of resource allocation to other areas; second, no attempt to assess the quality of output and, third, no rigorous analysis of local needs. But these drawbacks are not insurmountable. The area resource analysis for District 'D', apart from providing the Liverpool project with hard evidence on resource distribution, stands as an important contribution to wider understanding of the limits of conventional programme budgeting. It is possible that some form of areal analysis will be introduced into Liverpool's ongoing budgetary process.

Service delivery

As mentioned earlier, the area management project was not designed to improve public access to services by establishing a local presence in the area providing information and advice. Instead, as with the approach to policy analysis, attention was focussed on priority issues requiring practical management initiatives. Two examples are as follows. First, a key problem in District 'D' is family poverty caused by unemployment and low incomes. This problem is compounded by a low take-up of statutory welfare benefits. An analysis of existing procedures was undertaken and, following detailed discussions with the Department of Health and Social Security and experts in the field, it was decided to test the validity of producing and using a multi-purpose form for local authority welfare benefits. A form was designed and was tested in parts of District 'D' during 1976. A second example is provided by a housing management initiative which brings together a group of local officers concerned with the management of a particular estate. A locally based maintenance team has been established and this eradicated a long repairs backlog within two months. During 1976 experiments were in hand with new 'glazing' materials in order to improve security and ways of reducing rent arrears by, for example, the provision of a local rent office.

Whilst there are clear advantages in the centralized location of the Area Management Unit, this does limit its ability to bring about day-to-day innovation in service delivery. One wonders whether an area office involving the co-location of several departments could improve inter-departmental co-operation. But the problem probably runs deeper than the question of geographical decentralization for there has been little or no delegation of additional authority to the local level. Thus, middle managers, including those sympathetic to a corporate approach at the local level, often find it necessary to refer back to central departments before making even modest commitments to change. This involves procedural delays which have slowed down the flow of information and generally hampered initiatives designed to enhance service responsiveness.

Local accountability

The idea of a community forum failed despite lengthy discussion partly because of conflict between the district committee and the forum and partly because of the inability of the various community groups to find common purpose. One problem arose over the degree to which the forum should be independent of the District Committee. Some groups felt that councillors should not attend the forum for fear this would inhibit the expression of views. Others seemed to favour a closer working relationship with the District Committee.

A further problem was that some groups were sceptical of the District Committee, because it lacked executive power. This scepticism has also been felt by some of the members of the committee. This is not unnatural for they have realized the breadth of the committee's potential and have been frustrated with their inability to deal with the day-to-day decisions affecting the district. An internal report of the Area Executive made the following point: 'Members are not inclined to the "advisory role" which is predominantly the officer's domain, and seek the power to make effective decisions.' Though on occasions there has been substantial debate on issues outside its direct control, the need to defer constantly to service committees threatens the continued credibility of the (district) committee. This was the opinion of the consultants who also drew attention to the limits of a 'solo' approach:

It [area management] would need stronger powers, more specific responsibilities and a clearer place in the structure of corporate decision making. The key lies in the status of the district committee as, only if that is enhanced, can the staff of the Area Management Unit operate more effectively. It also would need to be extended to other disadvantaged parts of the city, where there is the greatest need for responsive local government.[16]

Distributive effects

Because the area management project is a 'solo' approach to one part of the city it can always be accused of seeking special treatment for one area. This is a problem for there are other parts of inner Liverpool which are probably just as deprived as District 'D'. By virtue of the additional attention it is receiving it is possible that there could be some re-distribution of effort in favour of District 'D'. At the same time, this is not an objective of the experiment and considerable care has been taken to avoid this. For example, several of the reports conclude with recommendations which relate to the whole of the inner city. But it would be quite wrong to assume that the area management project has ignored the distributive effects of policy. On the contrary, the area resource analysis discussed earlier in relation to planning and budgeting was a welcome breakthrough in distributive research. It remains to be seen whether Liverpool will take this approach forward.

Conclusion

The area experiment in Liverpool is an interesting attempt to take a deprived part of the inner city and, in the words of the Chief Executive, 'to look critically through the eyes of the consumer at the total range of services being provided'. The accent has been on ways of influencing the central decision-making machinery of the council to make it more sensitive to the priority problems found in areas like District 'D' and policy changes have resulted from this work. The chief drawback would seem to be the lack of delegation to area level both within the officer structure and within the political sphere. In these circumstances the project is more helpfully viewed as a centrally based attempt to improve responsiveness rather than as an experiment in area 'management'.

9 Comparative analysis of area management

The viable organization of the future will need to establish and integrate the work of organization units that can cope with even more varied sub-environments. The differentiation of these units will be more extreme. Concurrently, the problems of integration will be more complex. Great ingenuity will be needed to evolve new kinds of integrative methods. The viable organizations will be the ones that master the science and art of organization design to achieve both high differentiation and high integration.

P. Lawrence and J. Lorsch in *Organization and environment: managing differentiation and integration*, 1967

Introduction

The area management profiles presented in Chapter 8 illustrate five attempts by local government both to differentiate more adequately between different sub-areas of the authority and to improve the integration of government action. Information and appraisal were related to each area-based approach in turn: Boston, New York City, Dayton, Stockport and Liverpool. This chapter provides a *comparative* analysis which juxtaposes the different characteristics of the schemes in a systematic way. For consistency, and to enable ready cross-referencing to Chapter 8, the sections in this chapter follow those used in the profiles:

The cities
Origins
Aims
Geography
Structure and activities
Planning and budgeting
Service delivery
Local accountability
Distributive effects
Conclusion

This chapter tries to strike a balance between three themes: (1) comparative presentation of factual information about the schemes; (2) rudimentary assessment of the schemes; and (3) suggestions on how to improve area approaches in local government. No claim is made that what follows represents a rigorous evaluation based on detailed and extensive research. It is more a series of personal judgements and ideas which spring from the evidence presented in Chapter 8.

The cities

There are some striking differences between the five cities which need to be acknowledged at the outset. Table 17 shows the differences in size of population and size of council. The area-based unit for decentralization in New York City is the community planning district and some of these have a population size which is greater than the whole of Dayton! Clearly these differences in scale must be kept in mind when making comparisons.

Table 17 *Population and size of council*

	Population	Size of council	Number of people per councillor
Boston	638 000	9	70 000
New York	7 800 000	44	177 000
Dayton	205 000	5	41 000
Stockport	292 000	60	4900
Liverpool	550 000	99	6000

Figure 30 shows how the American cities have very high ratios of population to elected councillor when compared with the relatively low ratios in Britain. This makes it difficult for the American councils to encompass the divergent interests within each city. The problem is compounded in Boston and Dayton by the 'at large' system of elections which reduces the opportunity for the expression of neighbourhood interests. The problem is also present in New York City where the councilmanic districts are very large having an average population approaching 200 000. From the neighbourhood point of view the British system of relatively large councils coupled with ward-based elections is a major strength.

The system could, however, be improved if wards were made smaller and one councillor was elected to each ward. At present three councillors usually represent each ward. In relation to local issues and complaints this generates the need for a great deal of cross-checking between councillors serving the same ward. It also confuses accountability for it is possible for active ward members to be blamed for the poor performance of a colleague. One councillor to each ward would make the wards more local (they would have an average population of around 5000–6000), would remove possible duplication of effort by councillors and would give each a more visible, personal stake in neighbourhood affairs.

The form and politics of local government in the five cities differs enormously. Both New York City and Boston have a strong-mayor form and the mayors have had an important influence on the area-based approaches developed in these two cities. Stockport and Liverpool have the standard form of British local council but have a very different political make-up. Liverpool is Labour controlled although the Liberals held office in 1974 when area management was introduced. In Stockport the Conservatives have strengthened their control since 1974. By contrast local government in Dayton follows the city manager form and political conflict is muted.

Finally, New York City, Boston and Liverpool contain large inner city areas for they form the cores of much larger conurbations. Stockport and Dayton also contain inner areas which are threatened with decay but the scale and intensity of urban problems is considerably less than in the other three cities.

Origins

In New York City, Boston and Stockport the impetus for new forms of area approach came mainly from the cities themselves. The earliest developments were stimulated by the mayors in the 1960s. Mayor Lindsay was experimenting with various neighbourhood approaches in New York City as soon as he took office in 1966 and Mayor White was also quick to implement the idea of little city halls when he took office in Boston in 1968. Local political commitment was also an important stimulus to the development of area management in Stockport, which began in 1971 following the receipt of a report by the management consultants, Booz-Allen and Hamilton.

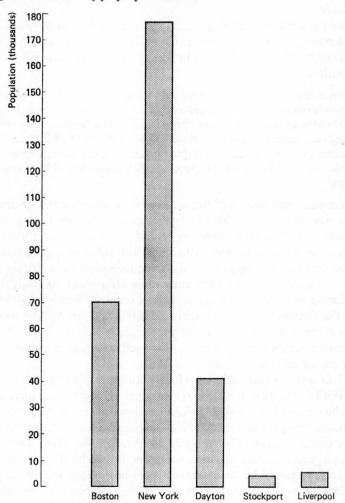

Figure 30   Number of people per councillor

In contrast, central government has played a key role in developments in Dayton and Liverpool. In 1967 Dayton was chosen to participate in the model cities programme. This federal area approach to one deprived part of the city was, through local initiative, extended to other neighbourhoods in 1969. The experiment with area management in Liverpool was suggested in 1973 by the consultants working

for the Department of the Environment on the Liverpool Inner
Area Study.

Should local or central government take the lead in developing
area management? Interestingly, Robert Yin and Douglas Yates in
their study of decentralization in American cities recommend local
initiative.

Given a choice between a federally initiated or a locally initiated policy,
we would opt for locally based policies reflecting the diversity of neighborhood characteristics and service characteristics. This is because we have
found that federal support was not a major condition of success on the
one hand, and, on the other hand, that the complexity of the neighborhood
service setting calls for a hand-tailoring of an innovation to its environment.[1]

From our small sample of five schemes we cannot confirm or deny
this view. However, we have uncovered examples of viable, ongoing
schemes which were promoted by central government and it would,
therefore, seem to be unwise to reject the value of initiatives by
Whitehall and Washington. At the same time there is, in Britain at
least, a great danger of local authorities sitting back to await the
outcome of the area management trials currently being sponsored
by the Department of the Environment (see Chapter 5). The trials
are of considerable interest and will certainly advance our understanding of area management. But they will not result in a blueprint
for use by other authorities.

This is partly because no two local authorities are identical. Each
is confronted with a unique set of socio-economic and physical
problems and has a unique political and managerial history. More
fundamentally the introduction and development of new approaches
like area management is a *learning process*. In Edgar Dunn's words
such a process involves an 'iterative exploratory series of experiments
in social action'.[2] In these circumstances no solution can be 'engi-
neered' outside the essentially evolutionary process of tentative
adjustments and changes to the established system of urban governance in a given area. This puts the ball firmly in the local government
court. There is a strong case for much more bold and genuine
innovation by individual local authorities who could be far more
adventurous in originating and testing new approaches such as area
management.

Aims

The aims of the various schemes set out in Chapter 8 are the formal statements of intent made by the authorities concerned. The precision with which these aims have been specified varies considerably. In addition, the objectives have been changed and modified in the light of experience and the relative significance attached to individual objectives has also altered over time. Further, the formal objectives may be inaccurate statements of actual practice. For example, in 1975 the Boston little city halls' formal objective of 'acting as the Mayor's representative in the neighborhoods' was dropped but one doubts whether this altered the nature of the work. For these reasons comparison of the aims of the schemes is particularly treacherous. Here the intention is only to consider the formal organizational aims, and to review these in the light of the three underlying objectives of area approaches – effectiveness, distribution and accountability – outlined in Chapter 3.

Table 18 provides a crude classification of the five schemes in terms of thirteen fairly specific objectives which are set out within the framework of underlying objectives. The table speaks for itself but one or two points are worth emphasizing. First, all five schemes seek to improve service delivery and the co-ordination of services. These are the only two specific objectives attracting unanimous support. Second, whilst all schemes seek to improve responsiveness in one way or another only one scheme – New York City – has the explicit aim of increasing delegation to the local level. Third, the aim of influencing the efforts of other actors, whether local residents or other agencies, is not highly subscribed to. Fourth, and strikingly, only one of the five schemes is explicitly committed to the idea of directing resources into deprived areas – from the outset the Liverpool scheme has been particularly concerned with the needs of people living in the inner city. Finally, in relation to accountability, all the schemes, except New York City, aspire to some form of local involvement but this conceals considerable variations.

In summary we can say that the aims of the Boston and New York City approaches are relatively restricted. They are primarily concerned to improve service delivery and responsiveness. The aims of the other three schemes are more disparate. Interestingly Dayton and Stockport have much in common – they share seven specific objectives. In general, however, the five schemes exhibit considerable diversity of intent.

Table 18 Classification of area scheme objectivee

Underlying objectives	Specific objectives	Boston	New York	Dayton	Stockport	Liverpool	Total
EFFECTIVENESS	1 Identify local problems	*		*	*	*	4
	2 Improve use of resources		*		*		2
Responsiveness	3 Increase delegation		*				1
	4 Feed into planning/budgetary process			*	*		2
	5 Test feasibility for extension		*			*	2
Service delivery	6 Improve complaints/information service to public	*		*	*		3
	7 Improve service delivery	*	*	*	*	*	5
	8 Improve co-ordination of services	*	*	*	*	*	5
Other actors	9 Encourage self-help			*	*		2
	10 Encourage involvement of other agencies			*		*	2
DISTRIBUTION	11 Direct extra resources to deprived areas					*	1
ACCOUNTABILITY	12 Develop the ward councillor role				*	*	2
	13 Develop public involvement	*		*	*	*	4
TOTALS		5	5	8	9	8	35

Geography

There are marked variations in the geographical size of the authorities. Figure 31 provides outline maps of the five cities drawn to the same scale. As with population, New York City is in a league of its own. Boston and Liverpool are compact urban areas and, like New York City, have a high density of population. As shown in Table 17 they both tower over Stockport and Dayton in terms of population and this contrasts sharply with the geographical comparison shown in Figure 31.

There is also considerable variation in the size of the sub-local authority units used for area management. These vary widely both within each city and between the cities. For example, in Dayton the areas served range from 11 000 to 79 000 population (excluding the central business district).

Two of the schemes were or are selective. In New York City the approach was first developed in relation to five experimental districts and has now been spread citywide in an amended form. Liverpool is the only one of the five schemes focussed on one area of the city. The schemes in Boston, Dayton and Stockport apply to the whole of the city. These three schemes have all developed a fairly extensive network of information centres or little city halls. For this reason they might be expected to have improved public access to services considerably.

There has been considerable respect for public opinion in defining area boundaries. In Dayton and Boston this has been the key factor and it was also taken into account in New York City and Liverpool. Stockport's system is based firmly on the wards. This strengthens member involvement but results in some areas being totally unrelated to public perceptions of neighbourhoods. The reverse tends to be true in Liverpool for the area served is poorly related to wards and this has probably worked against the development of ward councillor commitment.

To some extent there is a dilemma here, for there is a real tension between different requirements. As discussed in Chapter 5 these tensions should lead us away from the search for an 'ideal' size of area and, to a varying extent, the five schemes recognize the need for a multi-levelled approach. The Stockport system with its hierarchy of operational areas (three), area committee areas (eight), and community councils (twenty-three) is an explicit attempt to meet this problem. In the other four schemes the existence of smaller

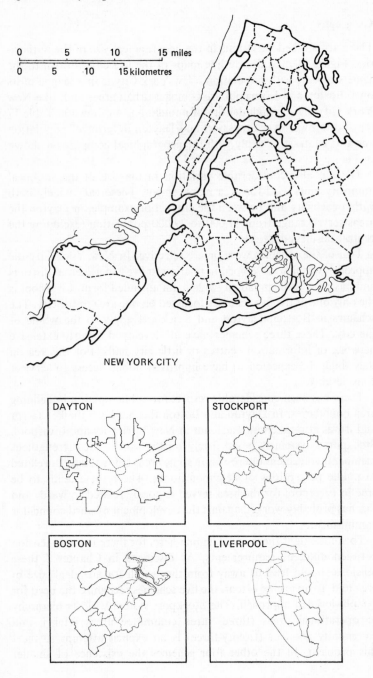

Figure 31   City maps drawn to the same scale

0   5   10   15 miles
0   5   10   15 kilometres

NEW YORK CITY

DAYTON

STOCKPORT

BOSTON

LIVERPOOL

neighbourhoods within the sub-areas is acknowledged but not given formal expression.

A final geographical question concerns the degree to which separate service districts are coterminous with each other. Service district boundaries in four of the five cities have relatively little in common and this works against an integrated approach at the local level. Stockport took the opportunity of local government re-organization in 1974 to re-align service boundaries and this has been a major asset of Stockport's area organization. Perhaps the grass is always greener! In recent times claims have been made by departments that the common boundaries in Stockport generate in-equalities in workloads for particular services.[3] My own view is that these difficulties are not insurmountable and that Stockport should not let slip its important advantage of coterminous areas for most services.

Structure and Activities

Half a dozen key characteristics of the structures of the area schemes are summarized in Table 19. All the schemes hinge, to a considerable extent, on the work of the *area managers or co-ordinators*. Generally speaking they are fairly well paid and bring considerable drive and enthusiasm to a difficult job. Since they lack authority over line department personnel serving their area much of their work is concerned with establishing good inter-personal relationships with local service officers. Whilst they lack delegated power they do have freedom to build links and networks as they feel fit and this gives them considerable scope to exert influence if not authority. These officers are particularly well placed to develop lateral communication links between departments as well as new links between the government and the community. Their role as contacts or reticulists is a relatively new one in local government.

Four of the schemes operate out of decentralized offices, the exception being Liverpool. Sometimes the area manager's office is linked with the area offices of line departments but this varies both within and between schemes. Sharing accommodation and services is probably given most emphasis in Stockport where the area co-ordinator provides typing and clerical services to some of the decentralized services (e.g. social services and housing).

None of the schemes has significantly increased the delegation of authority to area level, either to the area managers or to the line

Table 19   *Characteristics of area scheme structures*

Characteristic	Boston	New York	Dayton	Stockport	Liverpool
1 Area officer responsible for co-ordination, etc.	Little city hall manager	District manager	Community affairs co-ordinator	Area co-ordinator	Area executive
2 Decentralized offices	Yes	Yes	Yes	Yes	No
3 Increased delegation of authority to area level	No	Weak attempt	No	No	No
4 Formal officer group at area level	No	District service cabinets	Administrative councils	Area teams	Area management group*
5 Political arrangement	Link to mayor	Link to mayor	–	Area committees	District committee
6 Public involvement	Local advisory councils*	–	Neighbourhood priority boards	Community councils	Community forum*

*abandoned

department personnel. An attempt was, at least, made in New York City and this resulted in some increases in the control of local operations exercised by local line officials. But these were less far-reaching than had been hoped. In the other schemes the attempt has not even been made. This is an extremely important factor which accounts for much of the disappointment with the schemes. Without increased delegation or devolution[4] to area level it is difficult to see how the schemes can significantly increase the ability of the authority to respond swiftly and flexibly to the needs of different communities. In the absence of increased delegation or devolution the rhetoric about 'bringing government closer to the people' begins to have a hollow ring. The centralized and hierarchical power structure within all five city bureaucracies has hardly been touched by any of the area schemes.

With the exception of Boston, all the schemes involved the establishment of an inter-departmental group of officers at area level to discuss local problems and co-ordinate institutional action. No formal authority has been vested in these groups so that much has depended on the attitudes of the staff attending and on the personal qualities of the area managers. Not unexpectedly their success has been mixed. There is pride in small accomplishments but some of those involved have adopted a narrow departmental line. It may be that staff reward systems will need to be altered before we will see significant increases in local co-operation. At present, promotion depends exclusively on performance as measured by departmental criteria. Why not also reward staff for co-operative action on local issues? Job measurement is discussed again later in the chapter.

The political structures of the schemes are varied. In Boston and New York the situation is clear enough – the local managers are agents of the mayor. In Dayton the commissioners have no formal links with the neighbourhood priority boards. In Stockport and Liverpool the schemes draw in the local ward councillors through the mechanism of area committees. These provide opportunities for the local managers to key onto political networks of information and influence.

Four of the schemes started out with a formal structure for citizen involvement – the exception being New York City. In Boston and Liverpool the systems were abandoned in favour of more informal arrangements. Perhaps we can learn something here about the dangers of trying to impose participation from above. We return to the question of local accountability later in the chapter.

Finally, before moving on to look more closely at the activities of the various schemes, we should make some attempt to review costs. This is notoriously difficult for there are serious problems of definition – what to include and exclude – and of obtaining accurate figures for the same point in time. Table 20 is therefore put forward for the purpose of information rather than comparison. As the vast bulk of the costs are staff time the figures tend to reflect the amount of manpower devoted to each scheme and this ranges from five in Liverpool to 105 in Boston. There is a considerable variation in cost per head of population but this, again, merely reflects levels of activity – it tells us nothing about value for money. However, the variation does show that area innovation need not be expensive. Authorities can tailor area management to suit prevailing resource

Table 20   *Costs of the area management schemes*

	Boston[1]	New York[2]	Dayton[3]	Stockport[4]	Liverpool[5]
Annual cost	$1 220 000 (1976/77)	$846 000 (1972/73)	$700 000 (1976/77)	£220 000 (1976/77)	£23 000 (1974/75)
Population served	630 000	658 000 est	205 000	292 000	60 000
Cost per head of population	$1·90	$1·28	$3·40	£0·75	£0·38
Cost per head (£)	£1·10	£0·75	£1·97	£0·75	£0·38

Notes

1   Boston. This is the cost of the Office of Public Service, City of Boston Program Budget 1976/77, pp. 29–33.
2   New York City. This is the local and central costs of the Office of Neighborhood Government in the four experimental districts studied by Columbia University, Barton, A. *et al*, Decentralizing city government, 1977.
3   Dayton. This is the cost of the neighbourhood affairs activity within the Department of Housing and Neighborhood Affairs, City of Dayton, Program strategies 1976, p. 141.
4   Stockport. This is the cost of community development, information and advice as well as area committees and area co-ordination, Metropolitan Borough of Stockport, Corporate Plan and Budget 1976/77.
5   Liverpool. This is the estimated cost of the Area Management Unit, Department of the Environment (1973) proposals for area management, Liverpool Inner Area Study, p. 14.

situations. Information on costs as against benefits is only available for New York City. This research showed that the potential benefits were substantially greater than the costs but that, for various reasons related to the New York situation, the realized benefits were less than the costs.[5]

Planning and budgeting

All the schemes have involved some attempt to influence overall service planning and budgeting but the impact of area views seems to have been fairly limited. The most developed arrangements are found in Dayton and Stockport. Figures 21 and 25 illustrating the annual planning budgetary cycles in these two cities show a striking resemblance. Both attempt to feed area views directly into the council's policy-making and resource-allocating machinery. These authorities seem to be recognizing the opportunities provided by their area schemes for policy learning, i.e. for enabling local insights and priorities to influence overall policy making in a systematic way. But the gains have so far been limited and fragile. For example, Stockport's approach has been modified since 1974/75 and area inputs now have a less explicit role. In Boston and New York City the area input to annual budgeting is primarily related to assessing neighbourhood views on how the community development block grant should be spent. This, in itself, is an interesting policy process which attempts to take some account of neighbourhood priorities in the planning of expenditure and similar innovation in Britain is overdue. In Liverpool there is no formal area input into the annual cycle but the policy analysis reports of the Area Management Unit have influenced ongoing council policies.

Turning to physical planning, we find that links are sometimes tenuous. For example, in Boston the level of collaboration between the little city halls and the district planning staff of the Boston Redevelopment Authority is not yet highly developed. Perhaps Stockport has the most sophisticated arrangement. The area input into development control decision-making has almost certainly resulted in a more sensitive use of planning powers. Stockport has also attempted to broaden the scope of statutory local planning into an area corporate planning process involving all appropriate departments and the relevant area committee. This approach has important implications for central government which has been equivocal on the subject. On the one hand, as discussed in Chapter 5, the Department of the Environment has encouraged local authorities to develop a 'total' approach to area problems through devices like area management. On the other, the Department also takes the sectional view that local plans should be land use plans. It seems to frown on the idea of area corporate plans; presumably because central government finds difficulty in making a corporate response. The Town and Country Planning legislation is, as suggested in Chapter 1, one area where central government needs to reconsider whether its objectives are being achieved or whether procedures are hampering the development of creative approaches to local problem-solving.[6] To some extent this argument holds true for the American situation.

Two of the schemes – New York City and Liverpool – have toyed with the related ideas of area resource analysis and area budgets. Work in Liverpool on area resource analysis was particularly revealing. It showed that a high percentage of the council's budget *was* allocable to areas and that such area analysis provided a completely new insight on the distribution of resources. In particular it showed that Liverpool's policies of positive discrimination were far less radical than many had supposed. The New York City project also attempted to assess the geographical distribution of resources but there was insufficient commitment to modify the city accounting system on an ongoing basis. The Liverpool research was also a one-off study.

The lack of continuing progress with area resource analysis is disappointing, particularly as the limits of conventional programme budgeting are coming to be appreciated. There is an urgent need to add new dimensions to budgetary choice. Coding ongoing expenditure to geographical areas is one possibility that is not as difficult as many make out. For example, a gazetteer coding addresses to spatial units can be readily compiled and integrated into record keeping procedures.[7] The cost is minimal and the relevant information gain considerable.

In relation to area budgets, i.e. allocating sums of money to areas to be spent according to local priorities, there has also been little progress despite the considerable potential. The Liverpool scheme has a small area budget and this has been used as seed money to lever various departments into co-operative action. The New York City scheme involved allocation of a sizeable capital budget lump sum to the district cabinets and this also seems to have created opportunities for innovative action. At a time of economic recession it may seem misguided to recommend wider experiment with budget delegation. This runs counter to a prevailing view that funds need to be subject to even tighter central control. Certainly cost ceilings must be observed but this need not imply increases in centralized *detailed* control. On the contrary, during a period of no growth we desperately need a more creative use of resources. The allocation of limited sums to particular areas, preferably priority areas in terms of needs, is an approach with much potential which could be explored and developed by many authorities.

Service delivery

The idea of making service delivery more responsive to local needs is the lynchpin of all the schemes. More than that all the schemes seek to *integrate* service delivery. They challenge the view that 'urban decentralization can occur only within the context of a specific municipal service'[8] and strive actively to develop broader approaches which try to break down departmental barriers. The various ways in which the schemes have sought improvements in service delivery are summarized in Table 21.

Three of the schemes – Boston, Dayton and Stockport – have attempted to make public services more accessible in both the geographical and the psychological sense. To the average man in the street local government often appears remote and confusing – the town hall is a bus ride away and, even when you get there, you are passed from one department to another. Little city halls and local information centres therefore begin to fill a very real gap between the servers and the served and the arrangements in Boston and Stockport provide good pointers towards what can be done. Authorities considering similar approaches should bear in mind the need for supportive changes in departmental procedures and attitudes – merely opening a local office even if manned with sensitive and enthusiastic staff, is not enough.

From their area offices Boston, Dayton and Stockport provide 'across-the-board' information about services, a complaints service, as well as some direct services. These measures all improve public access particularly for those clients who are uncertain of the kind of help they need. But they also fulfil an important research function. Classifying the number and types of inquiries and providing regular statistics alerts higher organizational levels to emerging neighbourhood problems at an early stage.

The methods of improving service delivery listed in the bottom half of Table 21 are highly inter-related. There are serious limits to the amount of service co-ordination that can be achieved in the absence of a willingness on the part of departments to modify procedures and to increase delegation. In all the schemes individual managers and local line staff have managed to build links based on mutual understanding and trust. This *has* enabled them to work together to improve local services if only in modest ways. But all the schemes have their horror stories – of misunderstandings, downright hostility and soured relationships. In part this may well

Table 21 *Methods of improving service delivery*

Methods	Boston	New York	Dayton	Stockport	Liverpool
1 Improving public access to services	*		*	*	
2 Improving complaints/information service	*		*	*	
3 Providing services direct	*		*	*	
4 Improving the co-ordination of services		*	*	*	*
5 Changing line department procedures			*		*
6 Increasing delegation			*		

be the fault of particular individuals but some of the problems are more general. We need to recognize that it may not be easy to modify the attitudes and behaviour of line department personnel. Is it fair to expect an area manager or co-ordinator to generate commitment to an area approach more or less unaided?

Three aspects almost wholly neglected by the schemes would seem to be worth further consideration: training, measuring staff performance and delegation.

Training

First, organizational changes like area management should be accompanied by retraining of the officials involved. This does not necessarily mean sending them 'away on a course' but it does mean providing positive help and guidance in adjusting to new demands. There are many inexpensive ways of preparing staff for the stresses and strains of corporate working.[9] At a more general level, perhaps personnel officers need to place more emphasis on the evolution of a *corporate* approach to staff development to counter the over-reliance on professional training. The vast majority of local government officers still follow career paths within a single department –

often moving from authority to authority. Personnel officers could do much more to promote transfers or exchanges between departments to the benefit of both the individuals concerned and the authority.[10] Indeed, area management could be viewed as an ideal setting for the training and development of future senior and chief officers.

Job measurement

Second, there needs to be an explicit commitment to an integrated area approach from departments. This should involve a willingness not only to accept the legitimacy and value of inter-departmental work at the local level but also to encourage it positively. At root this is likely to involve adjustments to reward systems for staff. Job descriptions and methods of assessing staff performance would need to be reviewed to place a stronger emphasis on outputs, for example impact on local problems or improving client satisfaction with overall services. Of course, area staff would need to play a full part in reviews of this kind. Indeed they might even be the ones to press for such reviews to increase the relevance of their work and resultant job satisfactions. Management by objectives (MBO) is an approach which could be adapted to promote progress in this area. To simplify, MBO involves the continuous definition by an individual in consultation with his superiors of his/her key objectives (developed in the light of overall organizational objectives) and the measurement of performance against these objectives. It combines individual strength and responsibility with a common direction of vision and effort.[11] Various texts are available on MBO in local government[12] but these tend to advocate MBO in the context of programmes or departments. We need more experiment with management by *area* objectives (and other forms) which cut across programmes. This idea links with the concept of matrix management and is discussed further in Chapter 10.

Delegation

Third, there is a case for increasing delegation to the local level within many departments. In all the schemes delays were caused by the retention of detailed controls at too high a level within the departmental hierarchies. In Chapter 1 it was suggested that central government overloaded itself with an unnecessary concern for the details of local authority activity and that Whitehall could relax many aspects of detailed scrutiny without losing overall control. The same applies to a considerable extent within local authorities. The proof is in the remarkable variation in degree of delegation between departments. Thus, in Britain, area social services officers often enjoy far greater powers of discretion than their colleagues in, say, the housing or engineers' departments. Individual local authorities might usefully consider the variation in delegation between departments in relation to, for example, personnel decisions, budgeting, service delivery, planning, and relations with other departments and agencies. They will certainly find food for thought and there is a good chance they will find under-used human resources. They may even discover why some chief officers are more harassed than others!

Local accountability

Mention has already been made of the formal arrangements for involving ward councillors and/or 'community representatives' in the area management schemes (see Table 19). Strengthening local accountability was not an objective of the New York City scheme, and there was no structure for public involvement. In practice the district managers kept in contact with local community leaders but this was on an informal basis. In two of the remaining four schemes Boston and Liverpool, arrangements for formal public involvement collapsed at an early stage. The reasons in both cases are complicated. Eric Nordlinger suggests that in Boston the mayor and the Office of Public Service did not give a strong and enduring commitment to the idea of local advisory councils.[13] In Liverpool there was also some distrust and wariness between the district committee and the community forum and these fears were never overcome. Perhaps both Boston and Liverpool tried to go ahead too quickly with formal arrangements for public involvement and under-estimated the intricacies of building links with the community. In Dayton and Stockport neighbourhood priority boards and community councils have survived since the early 1970s. However, they continue to be strictly advisory and there is no devolution to local groups.

Turning to the role of the ward councillor there can be little doubt that area committees have been welcomed by many members in Stockport and Liverpool. Local councillors value the opportunity provided to monitor the impact of authority policies on their own constituency and the freedom to raise any matter of local importance. Interestingly the balance of knowledge between member and officer is tipped in favour of the member in area committees for he is able to draw on his personal knowledge of the neighbourhood. The chief problem with the area committees is that they remain strictly advisory and this frustrates many members who would like to see at least some powers devolved to the local level. In summary, then, none of the five schemes has taken significant steps to strengthen local accountability. Indeed some would argue that several of the schemes have merely created another administrative layer between the people and the centres of decision-making power. The lack of devolution is particularly disappointing when there is mounting evidence to suggest that the rift between 'them' and 'us', between the server and the served, is of critical importance not only to local government but society in general.

Robert Yin and Douglas Yates attach over-riding importance to the server–served relationship and their analysis of American experience holds, in many respects, for the British situation. They detect a series of forces – political, professional and technological – which, from the turn of the century, have centralized service delivery to the point where the earlier, intimate, street-level relationship between the servers and the served is all but destroyed.[14] Historically there was a kind of social symmetry in service delivery with servers and served sharing the same neighbourhood and living conditions. Personal relationships with clients were the norm and *trust* was a central ingredient in effective service delivery. These relationships were strengthened by ethnic ties in the immigrant city.

Some of the area schemes are trying to re-create this relationship. In Boston a little city hall leaflet asks:

Remember the good old days? It took all day to get to the beach. Hot dogs, beer and the trolley cost a nickel. The Sox always won. And Uncle Charley was the guy to talk to when you had a beef with City Hall . . . Little city hall is like having a dozen Uncle Charleys . . .

But Yin and Yates found that the status gap between servers and served was more likely to be closed where the relationship was based on some mutual influence over policy making. They found that this had occurred in a substantial number of decentralization schemes and concluded that: 'Whatever public programmes are designed in the future, there should by now be an automatic concern for considering the desires of those to be served as well as a some-what diminished arrogance by servers that they have all the answers.'[15] This may be progress but, in terms of local accountability, it does not take us very far. All our five schemes show a 'concern for considering the desires of those to be served' but power and control remain highly centralized. Without the introduction of measures to strengthen local accountability I fear the schemes will make very little progress in improving the server–served relationship. One idea would be to experiment more vigorously with new forms of partnership between local government and community groups. In Britain, tenant involvement with the running of council estates provides the germ of an approach and housing co-operatives further extend local control and responsibilities.[16] Another exciting possibility would be to develop 'across-the-board' partnerships and, perhaps, area committees could form the starting point. Whilst it is widely appreciated that section 101 of the Local Government Act 1972 expressly enables council committees to delegate their functions to sub-committees, it is not so well known that section 102 provides wide scope for co-option onto local authority committees and sub-committees.

In fact there are no restrictions on the number of people who may be co-opted onto council sub-committees provided such committees have no financial responsibility.[17] If financial control is involved two-thirds of the sub-committee have to be council members. Area committees therefore have a great deal of untapped potential for establishing new forms of partnership. If they remain advisory they could comprise a majority of co-opted-local residents. Even if they supervise area budgets up to a third of the members could still be co-opted. Area committees and indeed other forms of sub-committee are, then, fertile with possibilities for the development of new forms of relationship between the public and local government.[18]

A final and difficult question relating to local accountability asks: have the area management schemes reduced citizen alienation? The research for this book cannot provide a substantiated answer but others have addressed themselves to this question. Robert Yin and William Lucas conclude that, despite the rhetoric, there is no available evidence to justify decentralization on grounds of reducing alienation.[19] This is because the causes of alienation are complex. Decentralization of public services may only play a minor role in the totality of the individual's contacts with and information about his government. Even so, 'as part of a broad and consistent strategy to improve the linkage between the citizen and his government, decentralization may be one of many steps that together could decrease alienation'.[20] No doubt the advocates of increased neighbourhood control will immediately protest that, of course, there is no 'available evidence' for decentralization has never been on a bold enough scale to begin to have an impact on alienation. My own view is that if the area management schemes were modified in a way which strengthened local accountability then they could help to reduce alienation by diminishing feelings of political powerlessness. It is less clear whether such moves would increase public trust in government which is another crucial dimension to alienation.[21]

Distributive effects

All of the schemes have distributive effects just as virtually all local government activities do. But, as with practice in general, it proved very difficult to obtain retrospective information on these effects either because the data simply was not available or because the subject was politically sensitive. As shown in Table 18 only the Liverpool scheme had the explicit objective of directing extra resources into deprived areas. In practice the Liverpool arrangement has been ambiguous. On the one hand, it was deliberately located in the inner city with the express intent of helping an area with more than its fair share of deprivations. On the other hand, the area comprised only a part of the inner city and there are other areas in Liverpool with problems which are as acute if not worse. The project has, therefore, been concerned with directing more effort into the inner city in general rather than District 'D' in particular. At the outset the Dayton scheme was focussed on one inner city area but distributive aspects have been played down since the scheme went citywide. In the other three schemes considerable effort has been expended to ensure that resources and services were *not* re-distributed. Instead the accent has been on treating all neighbourhoods in the 'same' way and 'spreading the jam thinly'.

If positive discrimination in favour of deprived areas is an objective should an area approach be focussed on priority areas or would a blanket approach covering the whole authority be more successful? As discussed in Chapters 5 and 6 both British and American urban policies have favoured the selective approach. There are two reasons for this. First, groups suffering from *multiple* deprivation are *relatively* highly concentrated in particular areas.[22] Isolating priority areas and channelling funds into them should, therefore, result in a distribution of resources more closely related to needs. Second, and quite different, an approach focussed on one or two areas permits inexpensive experiment without requiring sub-stantial commitment either politically or administratively. It provides an opportunity to learn about the usefulness of an approach before applying it more widely. A danger is that experiment is used as an excuse for not undertaking more radical change – that the experi-ments are never followed up. Further problems are that areas not receiving special treatment are likely to complain and the priority areas themselves may suffer from labelling.[23]

Paradoxically, therefore, it may be preferable to use a blanket area approach to achieve significant progress with positive discrimination. First, it should be more easy to maintain political support in the local authority as a whole, both among members and residents. It would also avoid the stigma of labelling areas. Whilst it may be more expensive than a selective scheme this problem could be diminished by operating a 'skeleton' form of area management in areas with few problems. A blanket approach gets away from the idea that area initiatives are extra projects somehow separate from the ongoing functional programmes. It introduces an area dimension into all policy and expenditure decisions. This, in turn, enables comparisons between areas to be made in terms of needs and resources and this information is essential to sustain a powerful justification for re-distribution.

As mentioned in Chapter 7 national rather than local government is more able to withstand the political consequences of positive discrimination. Further, only central government can supply the necessary additional resources which are needed to supplement any re-direction of local authority expenditure. It follows that any strong form of positive discrimination will require the development of new forms of partnership between local and central government. Above all, however, such policies will always stand or fall by the strength of political commitment they enjoy.

Conclusion

Perhaps the over-riding characteristic of the schemes is their diversity. Throughout this chapter the uniqueness of each scheme has been plainly visible. Given the differences between cities and the origins and aims of the schemes this is hardly surprising. At the same time there are important similarities. A central aim of all five schemes is to improve service delivery and the co-ordination of services. All the schemes involve the appointment of a relatively new breed of officer –

an officer who is required to take an *area* viewpoint. Terms of reference differ but, essentially, the area officers in all the schemes attempt to thread together the activities of the various functional departments in a way which results in a more coherent and responsive service to the public. They have established important *lateral* communication networks between departments at local level and these have provided new opportunities for inter-departmental learning and action.

All the schemes are innovative and present a stimulating challenge to more conventional functional approaches, but a number of ways in which the schemes might be improved have been mentioned. In particular, more attention could be paid to the role of the schemes in planning and budgeting – in all cases the value of the schemes for policy learning is not fully appreciated. In terms of service delivery the schemes would be more productive if officers involved were given some retraining and if reward systems were modified. There is possibly most room for bold change in relation to delegation and devolution for, despite the rhetoric, none of the schemes has tackled the problem of over-centralized decision making both within the administrative and political spheres of local government. Without more delegation and devolution to area level there can be little hope of improving the deteriorating 'them' and 'us' relationship between those providing urban services and those receiving them. Finally, all the area schemes could explore more fully the distributional effects of urban policy in spatial terms and this would sharpen political interest in area approaches. Area resource analysis and area budgets are just two neglected methods which we could try out more widely. They could help us feel our way back towards a better balance between territorial and functional approaches to urban policy making.

Part Four
A learning local government

A number of theoretical shifts are taking place in various fields which, when taken together, could provide the basis for improved theories of public learning. Part Four consists of one longish chapter – Chapter 10 – which explores four particularly relevant theoretical perspectives.

First, planning theory and policy sciences are considered and the moves to redefine planning as less a means of determining the future and more a form of evolutionary experimentation are drawn out. Second, a review of organization theory points to new forms of management – such as matrix management – which have exciting possibilities for creating new forms of lateral relationship within urban government. Third, the application of cybernetic theory to local government provides powerful new insights on the operation of local government as an information processing network and on the importance of developing self-organizing systems within the government hierarchy. Fourth, recent writing in democratic theory has rediscovered the participatory theory of democracy and some of the implications for local learning and local accountability are considered.

Some of the theories which link these perspectives are considered before a final section stresses the importance of taking account of psychological and inter-personal aspects in developing theories of public learning.

10 Towards theories of public learning

Even the dogs may eat of the crumbs which fall from the rich man's table; and in these days when the rich in knowledge eat such specialised food at such separate tables, only the dogs have a chance of a balanced diet.

Sir Geoffrey Vickers in *The art of judgement*, 1965

Introduction

In this last chapter we will draw on a range of theoretical perspectives and our touch on many will inevitably be fleeting. No claim is made that what follows adds up to 'a balanced diet' in the sense used by Sir Geoffrey Vickers. But hopefully the mixture of approaches will stimulate the reader to develop new insights and fresh ideas on the nature of responsive policy making.

The idea of public learning has been the major underlying theme of this book. This involves public institutions actively seeking out problems and opportunities in the community and responding creatively to these challenges by continuously adapting ongoing institutional behaviour. The starting point in exploring this theme has been *practice*. All the previous chapters have been solidly grounded in experience. In Part One we looked at the way central and local government in Britain are edging towards new forms of public learning and identified area approaches as a promising avenue. In Part Two Anglo-American experiences with area approaches were examined in some detail. The empirical method was continued in Part Three with the analysis of the attempts by five particular cities to develop new area-based approaches to urban government. So far, then, the whole style of argument has been practice-oriented: lessons have been drawn more or less directly from experience and most of the suggestions put forward could be implemented in the short term.

This last chapter draws on all that has gone before but is more theoretical and more adventurous. It questions the current assumptions of practice more vigorously and aims to invoke new thinking rather than specific changes in the nature of urban government. The central theme of public learning is discussed in the light of four theoretical perspectives: planning theory and policy sciences, organization theory, cybernetics and democratic theory. Some of the attempts to link these theories are then considered. A final section reminds us that individual feelings and personal relationships are critical factors in any institutional setting and that this is particularly true when an institution adopts a positive attitude to public learning.

The theoretical perspectives

Before reviewing each theoretical perspective in turn it is important, first, to recognize a limitation of this approach and, second, to connect the perspectives to the key themes developed earlier in the book. The limitation of a review drawing on such a broad spectrum is that the treatment of individual fields may be superficial. This is unavoidable and not unacceptable for we are particularly interested in the *connections* (or absence of connections) between perspectives. Besides those interested in exploring more fully the contribution of each field can readily follow up the extensive literature cited.

The three key themes which illuminate different aspects of public learning were introduced in Chapter 3:

1 Effectiveness   – what gets done
2 Distribution   – who benefits
3 Accountability – who decides

These themes were used in Parts Two and Three to provide a framework for appraising area approaches. But they also provide a framework for assessing urban government as a whole. The four theoretical perspectives reviewed in this chapter cannot be pigeon-holed into one or other of these three themes. But individual perspectives do bear more on certain themes than on others. Figure 32 is a rough illustration of the relationships which should not, however, be taken too literally. It shows that planning theory and policy sciences span all three themes, that organization theory and cybernetics are more concerned with effectiveness and accountability than with distribution, and that democratic theory is less concerned with effectiveness than with who decides and who benefits. Accepting this as a very loose conceptual framework we can now consider each theoretical perspective in turn.

Figure 32   Main links between themes and four theoretical perspectives

themes \ theoretical perspectives	planning theory and policy sciences	organization theory	cybernetics	democratic theory
effectiveness	*	*	*	
distribution	*			*
accountability	*	*	*	*

* indicates a positive connection

Planning theory and policy sciences

By planning theory I refer to theory *of* planning rather than theory *in* planning. The former is concerned primarily with the *process* of planning: how plans are conceived and put into effect with the content of the plans taking a secondary role. In the latter, theory is mainly concerned to inform understanding of a particular area of concern. For example, location theory assists physical planners in their understanding of the urban system and economic theory is useful to economists preparing an economic plan. This distinction between procedural and substantive theory has been well made by Andreas Faludi[1] and has been drawn in relation to policy sciences by Harold Lasswell.[2] Yehezkel Dror also makes the distinction between 'policy-making knowledge' and 'policy-issue knowledge' but stresses that policy science must integrate them into a distinct study.[3] We shall return to policy science shortly but let us, for the moment, concentrate on the planning process.

In Chapter 2 a basic model of the planning (or policy making) process was put forward to illuminate the idea of planning as a form of rational, directed inquiry into the nature of community problems involving continuous review of the impact of public action upon these problems (see Figure 5). In that chapter I argued that the process should begin with down-to-earth problems and opportunities and not with abstract goals and the goals-versus-problems debate is not repeated here. Instead, the intention is to explore other models of the planning process. This presents some difficulty for the literature positively bulges with suggestions and some of these are highly sophisticated. For example, Yehezkel Dror's optimal model has eighteen phases starting with processing values, working through to policy execution and evaluation, and including communication and feedback channels interconnecting all phases.[4]

Fortunately, however, we can simplify our task by concentrating on the idea of *rationality*. Most models of the planning process fall somewhere along a continuum ranging from 'pure-rationality' to 'extra-rational' approaches. Dror, himself, provides a useful discussion of six models which rest at various points along this scale: (1) the pure-rationality model; (2) the economically rational model; (3) the sequential-decision model; (4) the incremental change model; (5) the satisfying model, and (6) the extra-rational model.[5] For our purpose it will suffice to consider briefly three models, two drawn from opposite sides of this spectrum and one which tries to combine the advantages of the other two. The three models are: rational-comprehensive, disjointed incrementalism and mixed-scanning.

The rational-comprehensive model

This model requires, *inter alia*, the specification of a comprehensive set of objectives, with relative weights, and a continuous supply of complete, accurate and timely information on needs, resources and priorities.[6] The model also requires a full set of valid predictions of the costs and benefits of each policy alternative, including the extent to which each will achieve the various objectives, consume resources, and realize or impair other values. Even without elaborating on further requirements of this model it is already evident that true rational-comprehensive planning is not a practical possibility for urban government. It is an ideal towards which much planning effort, including much corporate planning (see Chapter 2), has aspired but few now labour under the illusion that such a rigorous, all-encompassing process can be perfected in practice.

Some of the drawbacks are that such a synoptic attempt at problem solving is beyond man's limited intellectual capacities, fails to recognize that information is either not available or available only at prohibitive cost, ignores the high costs of analysis and is ill-suited to the diverse forms in which policy problems actually arise.[7] More fundamentally the process ignores the political realities of urban government for it assumes that agreement can be reached on the objectives to be pursued when these are the subject of continuing social conflict.[8]

Disjointed incrementalism

Charles Lindblom has challenged the validity of rational-comprehensive planning even as an ideal. He puts up a strong argument for 'muddling through' – an approach which is explicitly non-comprehensive and which he has described as 'disjointed incrementalism'.[9] Essentially this process is: incremental, usually involving only small changes; means oriented, in that ends are chosen that are appropriate to available or nearly available means; serial, in that problems are not solved at one stroke but are successively attacked; remedial, in that decisions are made to move away from ills rather than towards objectives. The decision process is seen as disjointed for a large number of individuals and groups have access to it at different points. Important consequences of alternative policies can be ignored at particular points for what is ignored at one is likely to become central at another.

There can be no doubt that disjointed incrementalism is highly descriptive of the public planning process in many cities, but this does not necessarily mean that it is a desirable model. The approach has been attacked for its inherent conservatism. For example, Yehezkel Dror has argued that 'the earmark of enlightened leadership is it can overcome the incremental-change predisposition, and initiate innovative policies to achieve a significantly better society.[10] Tony Eddison has also argued that to advocate incrementalism is to 'unwittingly buttress complacency'.[11] Amitai Etzioni notes that such a process works to the advantage of the most powerful since partisans in the process invariably differ in their respective power positions. He argues further that the approach neglects basic societal innovations as it is focussed too much on the short run.[12]

Mixed-scanning

The mixed-scanning model, advanced by Amitai Etzioni, combines elements of the previous two models but is neither as Utopian in its assumptions as the rational-comprehensive model nor as conservative as disjointed incrementalism.[13] Etzioni argues that societal decision-making requires two sets of mechanisms: (a) high-order, fundamental policy making processes which set basic directions, and (b) incremental processes which prepare for fundamental decisions and work them out after they have been reached. Mixed-scanning provides both by, first, scanning the whole subject area but not in great detail and, second, homing in on those aspects revealed as needing more in-depth examination. Mixed-scanning might miss areas in which only detailed study would reveal trouble but, by omitting the detail required by rational-comprehensive planning, it makes overview feasible. It is superior to incrementalism for it explores longer-run alternatives and is less likely to miss trouble spots developing in unfamiliar areas.

Mixed-scanning has grown in popularity during the 1970s and, in 1975, was recommended as the preferred approach by a research study into structure planning in Britain.[14] Its flexibility would seem to be a major attraction for the balance between scanning and probing can be easily adjusted to suit changing circumstances. Perhaps a danger is that 'mixed-scanning' sounds highly technical. It would be a pity if local politicians were put off this elegantly simple approach by its name. Local government officers might usefully consider how to introduce the approach without the jargon.

I now want to pick up three aspects of planning which should receive increased attention if planning theory is to make a more positive contribution to the development of public learning: politics, social research and implementation.

Planning and politics

As Melvin Webber put it back in 1969: 'Planning is unavoidably and inherently a political activity . . . Insofar as the outcomes of planned actions effect a reallocation of benefits and costs (and they almost always do), the problems they address can have no technical solutions – only political ones.'[15] There is no need to labour this point here. The importance of strengthening the role of politicians in the public planning process has been argued in both Chapters 2 and 4. However, at the level of theory, there seems to be a reluctance on the part of many academics to tackle the political dimensions of planning. Even some 'progressive' academics seem to be more concerned with strengthening the planner's role *vis-à-vis* that of the politician than with developing forms of planning which positively strengthen the political process.[16] Those who still believe that the search for scientific bases for confronting problems of social policy may yet succeed are referred to a paper by Horst Rittel and Melvin Webber.[17] This presents a closely argued catalogue of some ten reasons why planning problems are political problems.

From the point of view of public learning the main conclusion we can draw is that there is no one 'best answer' to urban policy problems. In a plural society different sub-groups of the population will pursue different and often conflicting objectives. Planning theory therefore needs to develop an improved capacity for recognizing the differences within society. Further, it needs to renew the search for more effective ways of learning about the views and aspirations of minority groups who tend to lose out in a political process which favours the influential and articulate.

Social research

Since the late 1960s there has been a major expansion in social research by the institutions of urban government. On the whole this research has sought mainly to gather *facts* about the city to supplement the census and other nationally prepared statistics. Examples are the many house condition surveys and transport studies executed in various cities. But there has also been a fair amount of research designed to explore *values*. For example, many of the first wave of structure plans involved attitude surveys of the affected population.

This research activity is, of course, directly concerned with public learning and much of it has enlightened local policy making. But much of it has not. The reasons are complex but two weaknesses stand out. First, there are countless occasions on which data is gathered in advance of any penetrating thought as to precisely how it is to be used to improve decision making. The cry so often goes up that 'we lack adequate information' that it is tempting to believe that well-researched findings will inevitably be useful. A learning approach rejects this hit-and-miss method of research for learning requires not that data is gathered but that information *changes* institutional behaviour. In public learning research begins with a clear definition of the political and managerial choices the research is designed to inform.

A second major weakness concerns the usefulness of the traditional social survey as a means of eliciting public preferences. The traditional questionnaire clearly has a continuing value as a tool for discovering basic facts, but as a means of revealing 'what people want' or 'what they are prepared to do without' it has serious limitations. The problems stem from the difficulty of obtaining information through a finite series of questions which shows how a respondent rates many variables *vis-à-vis* each other. During a period of no growth in public services it becomes even more important to discover the *comparative* importance different sub-groups of the population attach to different services and issues. This is because improvements in institutional performance will depend, more so than in the past, on switching resources and effort from low priority to high priority problems.

Trade-off gaming is a relatively undeveloped technique which confronts this problem.[18] The respondent is involved in a hypothetical situation in which he allocates units to various elements whose relative importance the researcher is attempting to judge. The game is structured so that respondents cannot declare themselves in favour of everything: they are forced to demonstrate their priorities. This approach would seem to have considerable potential for public learning particularly during an era of no growth. But there are other avenues, notably the whole area of social indicators, which should also be more fully explored if we are to improve the policy relevance of social research.

Planning and implementation

It is astonishing how little attention has been paid to the connection between planning and implementation. Library shelves are weighed down with books about planning and policy making which pay little or no attention to the problems of actually getting things done. Planning practice is no better for large amounts of energy are spent preparing plans of all kinds with little or no thought to the complex chains of reciprocal interaction required to implement public policy. There is lip service in planning theory and planning education to the importance of policy execution and review but there is little or no understanding of what this involves.

Worse than that, the idea that implementation is a separate activity which happens after plans are formulated still seems to be widely accepted. In one of the few available books on implementation Jeffrey Pressman and Aaron Wildavsky don't beat about the bush:

The separation of policy design from implementation is fatal. It is no better than mindless implementation without a sense of direction. Though we can isolate policy and implementation for separate discussion, the purpose of our analysis is to bring them into closer correspondence with one another.[19]

In my view the present most urgent problem for planning theory, education and practice concerns the relationship between planning and implementation. The remarkable study by a group of leading planners on education for planning published in 1973 lifted the debate on 'knowledge and capability for urban governance' well above the terrain of professional squabbles[20] but even this excellent report says virtually nothing about implementation. There is still little appreciation, even in many planning schools, that building support for policies is an integral part of designing them.

In relation to implementation we find all the models of the planning process so far discussed as wanting in some respects. The basic model in Chapter 2, rational-comprehensive planning and mixed-scanning all divorce planning from implementation to some extent. Disjointed incrementalism accepts the problems of implementation but too willingly succumbs to the dynamic conservatism of existing bureaucracies.

Planning and learning

Perhaps we need to re-define planning in a way which knits its meaning inextricably to action and to the idea of continuous learning from experience. John Friedmann has made important advances in this direction by articulating a novel form of planning which he calls 'innovative planning'.

In innovative planning, different kinds of technical experts apply their skills directly to the development of new organizational responses to the needs perceived. Rather than preparing elaborate proposals that are preliminaries to action, *they achieve a fusion of plan-making with plan-implementing activities during the course of the action itself.* In innovative planning, plan and action become coterminous.[21]

This represents a radical departure from past conceptions of the meaning of planning. In a more recent paper Friedmann has taken these ideas further. I quote at some length for his ideas are of direct relevance to the notion of public learning.

As I have used the term until now, and in accord with custom, planning stands for advance decision-making. From this I am able to deduce such related terms as order, control, predictability, blueprint, command, guidance, monitoring, goal achievement, rationality.

I shall now propose that we discard this usage and substitute for it the *linkage of knowledge to action.* In this formulation, planning is concerned neither with knowledge nor with action by itself, but with the mediation between them.

This new, still unfamiliar definition, has the advantage not only of broadening the scope of planning but of rescuing us from the impossible and indeed repugnant task of rendering the future more predictable. For as the linkage of knowledge to action, planning can be instituted only in those social systems that remain in a deep and fundamental sense *open to the future and the world*.[22]

Such a view of planning places relatively *little* importance on forecasting and prediction and puts much more emphasis on developing our capacity to deal with the future in the very process of happening. The central problem is not to design the future but to 'design new institutional arrangements capable of responding flexibly, withstanding strain, and initiating wholly new sets of activity in response to always new, unprecedented situations'.[23]

Edgar Dunn supports this argument by spelling out the fundamental limitations of conventional modes of prediction and planning.[24] In his view planning should be less a means of determining the future and more a form of evolutionary experimentation:

Social learning involves more than the engineering of prophecy or the playing out of an optimum strategy in a stochastic game with fixed rules and objectives. Social learning is much involved with changing the 'name of the game'. At root, the learning process is manifest as an iterative exploratory series of experiments in social action.[25]

We shall return to these exciting ideas on innovative social learning for we will discover that they find support in the other theoretical perspectives we consider below.

Policy sciences

So far our discussion has been couched in terms of planning theory but it all also falls within the ambit of a new interdisciplinary field called 'policy sciences'. In describing the various models of the planning process the words 'planning' and 'policy making' have been used interchangeably. Both have been applied to the process whereby government arrives at a course of action which is ' "bigger" than particular decisions, but "smaller" than general social movements'.[26]

This respects common usage but it is important to attempt to throw more light on the relatively new term *'policy analysis'*. We can distinguish two meanings. First, as discussed in Chapter 2, policy analysis is commonly used in practice to refer to a systematic investigation of a particular policy area. Second, policy analysis is also used to refer to a much wider set of academic approaches to the study of public policy. These draw on a range of disciplines including political science and systems analysis. This broader scientific orientation to public policy has given birth to the new interdisciplinary field called '*policy sciences*'. It is impossible to do justice to such a broad subject in the space available. The following thumb-nail sketch just tries to highlight the awareness within the policy sciences of learning and adaptation.

The origins of the policy sciences can be traced to the pioneering work of Harold Lasswell in the 1950s.[27] Yehezkel Dror has done much to popularize the concept since the mid-1960s. He views it as an overarching meta-science embracing many aspects of planning and decision-making including rationality, the role of values, learning and creativity:[28]

Policy sciences is concerned with the contribution of systematic knowledge, structured rationality and organized creativity to better policy making. It constitutes a main effort to reassert the role of intellectualism and rationalism in guiding human destiny.[29]

In recent years the policy sciences have flourished. In 1970 a new journal, *Policy Sciences*, was founded, graduate programmes in public policy have emerged on both sides of the Atlantic and a rising volume of articles and books are now appearing. Hugh Heclo has provided a valuable review of the field.[30] He discerns two basic approaches: case studies and programmatic analysis. The former is the most well-established and frequently used mode of academic policy analysis. It links well with reality but lacks an agreed framework in which to compare the variety of case study findings. The latter tries to identify policy with a set of programme choices, among which is sought the most efficient means of employing scarce resources. This is an increasingly influential mode of academic policy analysis which has the potential for getting to grips with the distributive effects of policy. However, Heclo feels that, in direct contrast to the case studies, the programmatic approach still resembles an analytic framework in search of realism. He argues for a mood combining both: an analytic realism.

This approach stresses relationships and dynamic behaviour for 'the phenomena at issue are moving events, routines, strategies and adaptations.'[31] He points unmistakably to the need for a learning approach to policy studies:

The challenge is not to decompose process or content but to find relationships which link the two, not to reify collectivities into individual deciders but to understand the networks of interaction by which policy results. A perspective which views policy in terms of learning and adaptation offers, I believe, the greatest promise for advances in policy studies which will be both analytic and realistic.[32]

Of course, governments have always been learning mechanisms to a certain extent. The message of policy sciences is that learning from experience has usually been accidental and sporadic. Those working in local and central government should find little difficulty in agreeing with Dror:

One of the amazing weaknesses in much contemporary public policymaking is that there is no systematic learning from experience. Very few evaluations of the real outcome of complex policies are made, and there are even fewer on which improvements of future policymaking can be based.[33]

Dror argues that this weakness can be rectified relatively easily and at low cost by requiring an explicit audit of a policy's results after a definite period of time has elapsed. To do this he believes it will often be necessary to establish 'special analytical units in charge of learning feedback in larger organizations'.[34] In Chapter 2 I suggested that such units (often called corporate planning units in British local government) *can* play an important role in developing public learning. But I also warned of the dangers of believing that learning can be centralized.

In closing this cursory review we can say that the policy sciences have advanced the idea of public learning considerably and that they hold out considerable promise for the future. However, in concentrating on the process and content of policy they may have paid insufficient attention to the organizational dimensions of public policy making. The making and execution of policy are inextricably linked to a particular organizational setting. As stressed earlier planning and implementation cannot be viewed as separate processes. Or, as Aaron Wildavsky puts it, 'organizational design and policy analysis are part of the same governmental process'.[35] In the next section we therefore turn to organization theory.

Organization theory

The tendency of organizations to fight to remain the same – the 'dynamic conservatism' so vividly described by Donald Schon[36] – has been a key question addressed by this book. In Chapter 7 it was suggested that a major failing of both British and American approaches to urban problems has been the absence of any real awareness of the need to transform the behaviour of existing institutions. And the discussions of area management in Chapters 8 and 9, whilst they were also concerned with political change, were primarily concerned with organizational change and development. In this final chapter we have seen how improvements in planning theory and policy sciences are unlikely to have a significant impact if they neglect the organizational setting. So what do we mean by organization theory and what insights does it provide on the notion of public learning?

Following Warren Bennis we can distinguish two sets of tasks which organizations must undertake if they are to survive: 'they must maintain the internal system and co-ordinate the "human side", and they must adapt to and shape the external environment.'[37] R. J. S. Baker divides his review of general theories of organization into three sections.[38] First, classical organization theory which is basically concerned with order and authority, rationality and legality, and with mechanisms. Second, human relations and related theories which are employee-centred and are concerned with psychology and inter-personal relations, behaviour and motivation, the individual and the group. Third, organic and systems theories which recognize the complexity of the organizational task and stress organizational variety, lateral and informal communication, feedback and self-adjusting control mechanisms. All three varieties of organization theory provide important insights on how to organize the institutions of urban government to further public learning. Here I want to concentrate on the question of *uncertainty*. Local government operates in an uncertain environment and this is one of the most important reasons why learning approaches are so vital.

There is a mounting body of evidence which suggests that the best way to organize is contingent upon the uncertainty of the task being performed by the organizational unit. For example, Burns and Stalker identified two types of organization – mechanistic and organic.[39] The mechanistic form was effective in stable markets but the organic form was more effective where the technological and market conditions were changing. Another important study by Lawrence and Lorsch stressed two aspects of organization design.[40] First, each subtask should be organized in a way which facilitates the effective performance of that subtask. Second, design must provide for the integration of the differentiated subtasks so as to achieve successful completion of the whole task. Successful organizations were found to have differentiated internal structures when the subtasks varied in predictability.

The reason why task uncertainty is the key variable in organization design is because *alternative organization forms represent alternative capacities for processing information.* This is clearly explained by Jay Galbraith:

If the task is well understood prior to performing it, much of the activity can be preplanned. If it is not understood, then during the actual execution of the task more knowledge is acquired which leads to changes in resource allocations, schedules, and priorities. All these changes require information processing *during* task performance. Therefore, *the greater the task uncertainty, the greater the amount of information that must be processed among decision makers during task execution in order to achieve a given level of performance.*[41]

Organization design strategies

It is useful, then, to conceive of organizations as information-processing networks. Organizations use a range of strategies for handling greater complexity and I now draw directly on Jay Galbraith to outline seven main approaches.[42] These are set out in Figure 33.

1 Rules and procedures This involves specifying the necessary behaviours in advance of their execution in the form of rules or procedures. Employees are taught the job-related situations with which they will be faced and the behaviours appropriate to those situations. If everyone adopts the appropriate behaviour the resultant aggregate response is an integrated or co-ordinated pattern of behaviour. The chief limitation is that rules and procedures can only be applied to those job-related situations which can be anticipated in advance. By way of example many local government services are administered efficiently and equitably by the use of rules and procedures. But we all know of situations, often unexpected or unusual ones, where the application of rules and procedures breaks down.

Figure 33   Organization design strategies

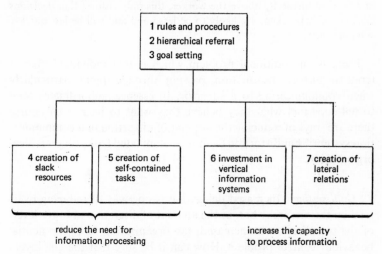

Source: Galbraith, J. *Designing complex organizations* 1973, p. 15.

2   Hierarchy   A hierarchical structure is useful for two reasons. First, the introduction of managerial roles improves the capacity of the organization to deal with uncertainty. This is because, as un-anticipated events arise, new problems can be referred upwards to the manager who has the information to make a new decision. This is sometimes referred to as exception reporting. Second, the hierarchy is also a hierarchy of authority and reward power and in this way the managers can determine the behaviour of the task performers. Galbraith stresses that the hierarchy is employed in addition to, not instead of, the use of rules. He goes on to describe the weakness of hierarchy in a way which will be all too familiar to those who work in local and central government.

The weakness of hierarchical communication systems is that each link has a finite capacity for handling information. As the organization's subtasks increase in uncertainty, more exceptions arise which must be referred upward in the hierarchy. As more exceptions are referred upward, the hierarchy becomes overloaded. Serious delays develop between the upward transmission of information about new situations and a response to that information downward.[43]

W. W. Daniel has described the problem more bluntly:

If decision-making power rests solely at a level one or two steps removed in a vertical hierarchy above the worker, this only ensures that decisions are more slowly taken, are likely to be less good and will be less quickly acted upon.[44]

There is an additional problem which is that individual officers tend to distort information passing through them particularly when communicating to a superior. In essence, subordinates tend to tell superiors what they believe they want to hear.[45] Of course there are ways of reducing the amount of distortion in a communication system[46] but distortion cannot be eliminated from a hierarchical organization.

3 Goal setting   Increased delegation is one way of reducing overload on the hierarchy but, as the amount of discretion at lower levels of the organization is increased, the organization faces a potential behaviour control problem. How can it be sure that the employees will consistently choose the appropriate response to the job-related situations which they will face? Organizations can make two responses. First, they can substitute professional training of the work force for detailed supervision. That is, shift from control based on surveillance to control based on selection of responsible, trained workers. A limitation, however, is that in the presence of interdependence, an alternative which is best by professional standards may not be best for the whole organization. A second response, therefore, is to specify goals or targets to be achieved in a way which allows employees to select behaviours appropriate to the target. Goal setting helps co-ordinate interdependent subtasks and still allows discretion at the local subtask level. Traditionally local government has relied heavily on the professional approach with its attendant strengths and weaknesses. In Chapter 9 the case for wider experiment with new forms of management by objectives (a form of goal setting) was put forward as a means of better harnessing the creative potential of individual officers and teams.

The three strategies outlined so far have been presented in a mechanical fashion. As the complexity of organizational tasks increases the volume of information processing can overwhelm an organization operating in this way. The organization must also adopt a strategy *either* to reduce the information necessary to co-ordinate its activities *or* to increase its capacity to process more information. Galbraith identifies two ways to reduce the amount of information that is processed and two ways of increasing capacity – see Figure 33.

4 Creation of slack resources An organization can reduce the number of exceptions that occur by simply reducing the required level of performance. For example, a deadline for the production of a piece of work could be relaxed or the man-hours devoted to the task increased. The longer the scheduled time available, the lower the likelihood of a target being missed, the fewer the exceptions, the less the load on the hierarchy. Slack resources do, of course, involve a cost to the organization which needs to be compared with the relative costs of the other three strategies for handling the overload.

5 Creation of self-contained tasks This involves a change from the functional task design to one in which each group has all the resources it needs to perform its task. In local government this could involve creating full-time groups around projects, geographical areas, client groups etc. The amount of information processing is reduced in three ways. First, there is no longer a need to schedule and re-schedule the demands for shared resources. Second, there is usually a reduction in the division of labour and therefore fewer distinctly different resources whose work needs to be co-ordinated and scheduled. Third, the point of decision is moved closer to the source of information. However, no group is completely self-contained, or else it would not be part of the same organization. There is certainly room for experiment with this kind of approach in local government. But the inter-relationships between urban problems discussed in Chapter 2 would imply some difficulty in isolating particular tasks. We can now turn to the two strategies which increase the capacity to process information.

6 Investment in vertical information systems This strategy increases the capacity of existing channels of communication, creates new channels, and introduces new decision mechanisms. It makes fuller use of information acquired during task execution and often uses computers and the new information technology. At its most advanced it provides on-line, real-time information, that is a continuous flow of formalized data to and from all decision points. A good example is an airline reservation system which allows rapid updating of a constantly changing situation and makes the information instantly available everywhere. Galbraith summarizes this strategy as follows:

The investment strategy is to collect information at the points of origin and direct it, at appropriate times, to the appropriate places in the hierarchy. The strategy increases the information processing at planning time while reducing the number of exceptions which have overloaded the hierarchy.[47]

7   Creation of lateral relations   The last strategy is to employ lateral decision processes which cut across lines of authority. The level of decision making is moved down the hierarchy to where the information exists rather than bringing up information to the points of decision. It decentralizes decisions but without creating self-contained groups. There are several forms of lateral relations and Galbraith identifies seven which range from obvious to fairly sophisticated arrangements. These seven forms are listed in Table 22 together with examples drawn from British local government.

The ingrained departmental approach of traditional local (and central) government was discussed in Chapters 1 and 2. Functional arrangements can lead to the development of greater expertise in certain areas and this can result in a 'learning effect' by a build-up of specialist knowledge. However, the overwhelming drift of this book has shown that narrow departmentalism has tended to blinker local analysis and action – the functional approach has constrained local learning. Innovation with lateral relations is therefore of particular interest to those concerned to develop public learning.

Several of the forms shown in Table 22 will be familiar. Direct contact and liaison roles are commonplace and task forces, or working groups as they are sometimes called, are also widely used. None of these approaches challenges functional management. As Galbraith observes:

The task force is a temporary patchwork on the functional structure, used to short-circuit communication lines in a time of high uncertainty. When the uncertainty decreases, the functional hierarchy resumes its guiding influence.[48]

In Chapters 8 and 9 we have seen how the various area management schemes have helped to push forward local government experiment with lateral relations. In several of the schemes we have seen how permanent teams have been established and how new integrating roles, such as area co-ordinators, have been introduced. However we have *not* seen any evidence of bold forms of lateral relationship, that is, managerial linking roles or matrix management – see Table 22. The former increases the power and influence of the integrator by, for example, giving him approval authority over certain aspects of the work or by giving him some budgetary control. Matrix management further extends the power of the integrator by establishing dual reporting relationships. That is, an individual within the matrix reports to two bosses who jointly determine performance goals with him and determine his chances for promotion.

Table 22 *Forms of lateral relationship*

Form of relationship*	Examples from British local government
1 Utilize *direct contact* between managers who share a problem	Commonplace
2 Establish *liaison roles* to link two departments which have substantial contact	Officer to link the work of the social service department and the area health authority
3 Create temporary groups called *task forces* to solve problems affecting several departments	Inter-departmental groups preparing a policy report, e.g. on the elderly
4 Employ groups or *teams* on permanent basis for constantly recurring inter-departmental problems	Teams bringing together those officers working in a particular geographical area
5 Create a new role, an *integrating role*, when leadership of lateral processes becomes a problem	Area co-ordinator
6 Shift from an integrating role to a *linking-managerial* role when faced with substantial differentiation	Some policy planners fulfill this role
7 Establish dual authority relations at critical points to create *matrix management*	No examples although some authorities use secondment

*Source: Galbraith, J, *Designing complex organizations,* 1973, p. 48.

Matrix management

There is considerable misunderstanding about matrix management in local government. The term has been used loosely, by for example the Bains Committee,[49] to refer to the task force and team approaches shown in Table 22. The result is that some authorities may already feel they have developed a form of matrix organization. However, the crucial feature of matrix management is that there is *dual authority*: each individual within the matrix reports to two managers. The non-functional manager may be concerned with an area, a project, a client group or some other issue cutting across functional perspectives and his task may be temporary or permanent. Matrix management can therefore take many forms but, to deserve the name, the non-functional manager must share authority in rewarding and penalizing members of his team. Simplified diagrams of functional and matrix forms of organization are shown in Figures 34 and 35.

There has been a good deal of experiment with matrix management by progressive business firms[50] but, so far as I am aware, no attempt has yet been made to apply the approach to urban government. Yet it has immense potential as an instrument for public learning as well as a tool for staff development. It does not involve reorganization into new authorities or the establishment of separate teams or similar upheavals. Instead it can concentrate the attention of existing agencies on new dimensions and issues, redirect human resources into creative problem-solving and provide a form of management which can more readily respond to political priorities. It can do all of this *whilst preserving the advantages of the functional divisions of urban government*. I am *not* suggesting matrix management is a panacea, nor even that it is desirable or workable in all authorities. But I am saying that it holds out exciting possibilities which are within the reach of any adventurous authority prepared to exercise a little imagination.

Cybernetics

We now turn to a subject with a rather forbidding name and it is helpful to begin with one or two definitions. The concept of 'system' – any entity, conceptual or physical, which consists of interdependent parts – underpins much of modern management science. Indeed, it also underlies much recent thinking in urban planning[51] and,

Figure 34   Traditional functional management

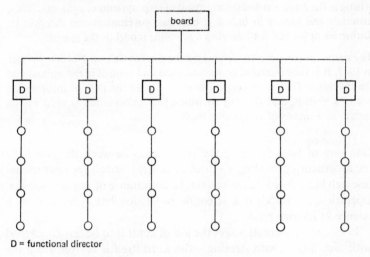

D = functional director

Figure 35   Example of matrix management

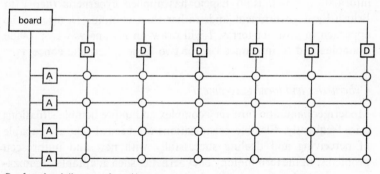

D = functional director   A = area manager

through the techniques of systems analysis, has influenced the development of corporate planning. More important, as a powerful instrument of human thought in the decades since the war, systems theory has enlightened our understanding of the human individual, of society and of our ecosystem.[52]

Two related cousins of general systems theory are operational research and cybernetics. Stafford Beer provides definitions of both:

Operational research is the attack of modern science on complex problems arising in the direction and management of large systems of men, machines, materials and money in industry, business, government and defence. Its distinctive approach is to develop a scientific model of the system . . .[53]

The name *cybernetics* was defined by the mathematician Norbert Wiener in 1947. It is the science of communication and control in the animal and the machine. That is to say, cybernetics studies the flow of information round a system, and the way in which that information is used by the system as a means of controlling itself.[54]

One way of understanding the relationship between the two is to see cybernetics providing a source of control models for operational research but this would understate the importance of this new science. Operational research is a scientific profession but cybernetics is a science in its own right.

In essence, cybernetics sees the job of control to be less concerned with dictating as with steering – the word itself is derived from the Greek for steersman. As with the organization theories discussed above, cybernetics attaches central importance to information processing for control and steersmanship are closely related to information flows. Raul Espejo has applied cybernetic theory to British local government and, rather than continue to discuss the approach in abstract terms, I will draw on his analysis to provide examples and to introduce one or two basic cybernetic concepts.[55]

Cybernetics and local government

Modern communities are very complex and unpredictable situations arise frequently. Flexible organizations are needed that are capable of perceiving and dealing successfully with new and unforeseen problems. In the terminology of cybernetics such adaptable organizations are viable systems. That is they are systems which can change as rapidly as the environment in which they operate while remaining internally stable. The local authority is an organization seeking to handle the immense complexity of the real world. Variety is a measure of complexity, that is the number of possible states of the system. Ashby's law of requisite variety says that only variety can absorb variety.[56] In other words, the more complex the system being controlled the more complex the channels of information that are needed by the controlling system. The local authority can achieve requisite variety in two ways: by filtering the variety (information) that comes from the community and by amplifying its own variety by improving the information network. These strategies are, essentially, the same as the two broad approaches to organization design advanced by Jay Galbraith and illustrated in Figure 33.

However, cybernetics takes us further by outlining the basic structure of any viable system. A main source of cybernetic insights is the study of biological organization and control methods. Evolutionary processes have resulted in the emergence of extremely sophisticated and successful organisms, man being perhaps the most obvious example. Espejo's work uses Stafford Beer's model which is based on the human nervous system.[57] There is insufficient space to elaborate on the model here but Beer identifies five physiological (or neurological) control levels in the body's nervous system. And Espejo's work searches local government information systems and decision processes to see how well the local authority performs on each of these levels.

Before springing to conclusions we should note the three main characteristics of viable systems. First, they are contained within, and are comprised of other viable systems – they are recursive. Second, the whole is more than the sum of the parts – they have synergy. Third, they have internal equilibrium and stability – they exhibit internal variety balance.

Espejo concluded, first, that local authorities are kept at an artificially low level of viability by central government. They lack a capacity for real corporate policy making for local authority departments are more subsystems of the departments of state than of their own authority. This ties in with Chapter 1 which showed that central government controls were both sectional and too restrictive. Second, the research showed that the structural capacity of the local authority to map the complexity of its environment was inadequate. In particular, a solely functional arrangement of departments reduces local authority variety too drastically as perception is focussed on too narrow a subject. Espejo recommends areal subdivisions of functional departments and more work on area analysis and area management to amplify local authority variety. Third, procedures for collecting and relaying information about community needs and opportunities were found to be lacking. Espejo recommends the use of a range of synchronized, social indicators operating in as near real time as possible, that is being transmitted instantly to policy makers. Finally, he concludes that authorities were ill-equipped to modify their behaviour even when they perceived community problems. For example, the research showed that management boards and policy committees were swamped with detail which stymied attempts to develop policy guidance. This could be rectified by designing powerful filters of departmental variety or, in the language of organization theory, a more refined system of exception reporting.

This cursory review of the cybernetic approach represents a drastic simplification but the texts are there for the interested reader to follow up.[58] Perhaps most interesting from the point of view of public learning is the idea of the self-organizing system.[59] This is located within a hierarchy of systems but is capable of improving its own organization and performance. Stafford Beer again:

It becomes more and more apparent as the argument proceeds that the features of living organisms which we most admire and seek to understand are properties of self-organizing systems. Learning and adaptation, growth and evolution, occur through entropic processes which do not demand 'control centres' but utilise pervasive natural laws.[60]

Interestingly, Aaron Wildavsky in his study of evaluation in organizations arrives at a strikingly similar conclusion independent of cybernetic principles:

The idea of the self-evaluating organization must mean more than this: a few men trying to force evaluation on an organization hundreds or thousands of times larger than they are. The spirit of the self-evaluating organization suggests that, in some meaningful way, the entire organization is infused with the evaluative ethic.[61]

Here we have emphasized the role of cybernetics in developing theories of *public* learning. But it is interesting to note that some psychologists see cybernetics making an increasingly important contribution to theories of *individual* learning. The idea of progressive modification of behaviour as a result of interaction with the environment moves beyond stimulus and response theories which, since they lack feedback, are ill equipped to explain *changing* behaviour:

The science of cybernetics, which is concerned explicitly with problems of control in animals and machines, seems likely to provide a language which is more suitable for the analysis of human and animal behaviour, than the terminology of stimulus-response theories of learning.[62]

To close our discussion of cybernetics it is worth emphasizing a point brought out in Chapter 7. This is that cybernetics helps us to get away from sterile models of institutions as being either centralized or decentralized since any viable system is both at once.[63]

Democratic theory

It is not an unacceptable wrench to move from the idea of self-organizing systems to the idea of democracy and self-government. Indeed, we shall see shortly how several writers have attempted to weld together cybernetic thinking and social and political theory. However, it is useful to concentrate first on the basic theories of democracy and the degree to which they encompass the notion of participation.

Carole Pateman points out that the widely accepted theory of democracy is one in which the concept of participation has only the most minimal role.[64] She reviews five well-known examples of recent work on democratic theory to support this view: Schumpeter, Berelson, Dahl, Sartori and Eckstein. The emerging 'contemporary theory of democracy' sees democracy as a political *method* – as a form of representative government. It involves the competition of leaders (elites) for the votes of the people at periodic, free elections. Responsiveness of leaders to non-elite demands is ensured primarily through the sanction of loss of office at elections but decisions can also be influenced by pressure group activity. Participation, so far as the majority is concerned, is participation in the choice of decision makers. Sartori goes so far as to argue for a minimization of active public participation in the political process for he fears this would lead straight to totalitarianism.[65]

Pateman challenges this contemporary view by arguing that the theory of representative government is not the whole of democratic theory. She draws on Rousseau, John Stuart Mill and G. D. H. Cole to advance a participatory theory of democracy which emphasizes the educational value of participation in sustaining democracy:

The theory of participatory democracy is built around the central assertion that individuals and their institutions cannot be considered in isolation from one another. The existence of representative institutions at national level is not sufficient for democracy; for maximum participation by all the people at that level socialisation, or 'social training', for democracy must take place in other spheres in order that the necessary individual attitudes and psychological qualities can be developed ... The major function of participation in the theory of participatory democracy is therefore an educative one, educative in the very widest sense, including both the psychological aspect and the gaining of practice in democratic skills and procedures.[66]

Thus defenders of the participatory theory argue that it is *more* than a method. 'It is based on a moral purpose – how men live together to achieve the good society. Its paramount values – equality, participation and local control – are paramount and *a priori*, not deduced from men's imperfect behaviour in an imperfect society.'[67]

The theory of participatory democracy underlies the idea of strengthening local accountability which has been a recurring theme of this book. Part Two discussed the growing pressures for increased devolution of government decision making in both British and American cities and also noted the opposing centralizing forces. The review of particular area management schemes in Part Three showed that these cities had made attempts to increase public involvement but that, consistent with Pateman, there is a need for stronger forms of participation if the relationships between the servers and the served are to be significantly improved. Participatory democracy also overlaps with the ideas on planning and learning discussed earlier in this chapter. John Friedmann, for example, sees planning as a transactive process involving mutual learning – a process by which scientifically schooled intelligence joins with the personal knowledge of the affected population.[68]

Community power studies

The consideration of ways of strengthening public involvement in local government cannot be divorced from study of the nature of power and influence in cities. Beginning with Floyd Hunter's study of power in Atlanta in 1953[69] a substantial body of American literature on community politics and decision making has now been built up. Kenneth Newton identifies three broad approaches.[70] First, the *reputational* approach developed by Hunter basically involved finding well-informed respondents who could draw up lists of influential people. Hunter found an elitist power structure in Atlanta in which about forty leaders, mostly businessmen, set the framework and content of public policy. The main criticism of the reputational method is that it never gets beyond reputational or perceived power to real or actual power.

A second school of community power studies, known as the

pluralist approach, rejects the elitist view and attempts to reach a picture of real power by analysing actual decisions.[71] The pluralists contend that power does not rest with a single elite but is distributed between different groups and individuals depending on the issue, the time and the place. The main problem with this approach is how to select the issues for analysis. Further, the approach is ill-equipped to explain the non-emergence of issues.

This led to a third approach pioneered by Bachrach and Baratz who drew attention to the *non-decision* as a second face of power, that is the power to prevent issues from ever reaching the public arena in the first place.[72] The whole non-decision-making argument implies that a community may contain groups which are powerful enough to manipulate public opinion and create a false consensus among some sections of the public. These arguments are contested by the pluralists who maintain that non-decisions cannot be investigated in any direct fashion and that there are serious difficulties in defining whether consensus is false or genuine.

The debate between the three schools continues but this conflict tends to obscure the fact that their empirical conclusions are not so dissimilar:

Most studies find relatively low levels of public participation in community politics and most find that a fairly small number of people are continuously active, most find a high proportion of middle- and upper-class people among the activists, and most find that decision-makers are generally unencumbered by any direct influence exerted by the mass of citizens, although indirect influence may be exerted by different groups in different ways.[73]

The community power studies remind us forcefully that *participatory approaches have to be introduced into a situation in which power and influence are already unevenly distributed.*

In these circumstances it is not sufficient to argue for neighbourhood government and increased local control. In David Harvey's words this 'will simply result in the poor controlling their own poverty while the rich grow more affluent from the fruits of their riches'.[74] This potential conflict between local accountability and re-distribution was brought out in Chapters 1, 3 and 7. To reconcile the tension between these two objectives it is imperative to escape the centralization–decentralization dichotomy. Local accountability can and should be strengthened but *it must be coupled with policies of*

*redistribution decided by higher levels within the government hier-
archy*.[75] These distributive policies are political policies and will
tend to reflect the balance of power and influence within the city.
This returns us to the importance of understanding community
power structures. We should never lose sight of Herbert Gans's
cardinal question: 'Who plans with what ends and means for which
interest groups?'[76]

Some linking theories

We have now reviewed four theoretical perspectives on urban
governance: planning theory and policy sciences, organization
theory, cybernetics and democratic theory. To some extent they
overlap. For example, organization theory and cybernetics share a
concern for the development of effective organizations. We have
already referred to some efforts to bring together some of these
perspectives – for example, John Friedmann[77] and Andreas Faludi[78]
link planning and democracy. We now turn briefly to one or two
other attempts at synthesis.

Cybernetics and societal guidance

Karl Deutsch has linked cybernetic concepts with government in a
book with the revealing title *The nerves of government*.[79] The 'nerves'
are the channels of communication and decision. His approach views
government less as a problem of power and somewhat more as a
problem of steering and he tries to show that steering is decisively a
matter of communication. Information flows and learning are
central to this thesis.

Amitai Etzioni, in his book *The Active Society*[80] uses cybernetic
concepts to develop a theory of societal guidance. Essentially,
Etzioni wants to replace the apathy/stability model of society with
its antithesis, a model of activity/stability. This means that new ways
must be found to introduce consensus-building into the process of
government. Active participation is therefore central and Etzioni
argues that extensive changes in the organization of societal decision-
making are essential.

John D. McEwan has also pointed to links between self-organizing
systems and participatory democracy.[81] In particular he draws
political conclusions from two contrasting models of decision
making and control. The first is the rigid pyramidal hierarchy with

lines of communication and command flowing from top to bottom. There is a fixed delineation of roles and the 'brain' of the system is at the top. The second is a cybernetic model which 'is characterized by a changing structure that modifies itself under continual feedback from the environment . . . and involves complex interlocking control structures. Learning and decision-making – the "brain" – are distributed throughout the system, denser perhaps in some areas than in others'.[82] In this second model the higher levels do not control the lower by coercive sanctions; rather they exert influence by feeding information to bias the autonomous activity of the sub-groups.

It is fair to say that the links between cybernetics and politics are very much the subject of continuing debate. The definition of 'control' would seem to be a stumbling block. The cybernetician can happily talk of value-free control methods whereas the politician and political scientist find difficulty in separating this concept from power and authority – who is to decide what?[83]

Organization, participation and planning

Writers on participation in planning have rarely explored the implications of a participatory approach for existing organizations. One attempt to study this connection by Richard Warren Smith argues that: '. . . we need participatory input to plan and manage complex environments; that participatory inputs are incompatible with hierarchical planning processes; that participatory planning requires *reticular* planning-decision structures.'[84]

Smith points out that hierarchical systems are particularly effective in executing the directives issuing from a central control point. Elsewhere, I have described this as a top–down process.[85] In contrast adaptive systems are oriented outwards and their performance should be measured not only in terms of effective compliance with central direction but also in terms of adaptations to conditions outside the system. Directives flow down but 'directives' must also come from the lower units which are in contact with the environment. This may be described as a bottom–up process.[86] In addition the adaptive system must reorganize itself to accommodate the changing needs of the lower units. As with centralization and decentralization the issue is not *either* 'top–down' *or* 'bottom–up' – it is how to combine the best of both.

Drawing on Likert,[87] Smith argues that an adaptive organization must have horizontal as well as vertical co-ordination – there must be a high level of co-operative behaviour between superiors and subordinates, *and especially among peers*. In other words, the co-ordinative function in behavioural systems must have a *reticular* organization in order to be adaptive, stable and enduring. The importance of strengthening lateral relationships by, for example, matrix management, was discussed earlier in relation to organization theory.

Smith emphasizes that the fundamental property of learning, self-organizing systems is that their structure is a function of their environmental experience. A change in experience includes a change in structure. He closes by trying to throw new light on community protest: 'The resistance of a community to upper level intervention should signal to the upper levels that changes may be occurring, that new adaptations are being made, rather than signalling insubordination in the community.'[88]

Public learning

One of the most valuable attempts at a synthesis of different perspectives, which centres on the whole notion of public learning, has been provided by Donald Schon.[89] His remarkable book, *Beyond the stable state*, has been referred to frequently in earlier chapters. Here I want to draw particular attention to his views on implementation and the idea of networks and network roles.

Schon insists that the formation of policy cannot be separated from its implementation for implementation is itself a process of local public learning.

Every alleged example of local implementation of central policy, if it results in a significant social transformation, is in fact a process of local social discovery. After-the-fact there may be a way to state the new social policy to which all the local discoveries conform. But before the fact, there is no single policy statement which can be used to induce them.[90]

He goes on to argue that the centre of the organization therefore needs to be less concerned with specifying courses of action than with developing a role as an initiator, facilitator and goad to local learning:

The opportunity for learning is primarily in discovered systems at the periphery, not in the nexus of official policies at the centre. Central's role is to detect significant shifts at the periphery, to pay explicit attention to the emergence of ideas in good currency, and to derive themes of policy by induction. The movement of learning is as much from periphery to periphery, or from periphery to centre, as from centre to periphery.[91]

It is for this fundamental reason that Schon argues for new networks within and between organizations and stresses the importance of developing new network roles.

Network roles vary in character but make common demands on their practitioners, each of whom attempts to make of himself a node connecting strands of a network which would otherwise exist as disconnected elements:

The risks of the roles are many, since the broker may often be squeezed between the elements he is trying to connect. The need for personal credibility is high, since each role demands that the person be acceptable and believable to different organizations and persons, each of whom tends to hold different criteria for acceptance.[92]

Schon rightly observes that no one learns to play network roles through formal education or training and perhaps much of the skill cannot be 'taught' in the conventional sense. Even so there are clearly important implications for professional education which have hardly begun to be considered. Gaming simulation[93] is one approach to individual and group learning which holds out some promise. At least it addresses the question of interpersonal networks and can provide simulated experience of the interplay of various interests and commitments. But it is only one approach and it is relatively under-developed. The requirements of public learning continue to lay down a provocative challenge to the institutions concerned with education for urban governance.

Psychology and relationships

There is a final crucial area which we have touched on continuously but never specifically. This is people: how we think and how we relate. In one sense urban government is only as capable of innovative learning as the people involved. As discussed at some length in this chapter, procedures, structures, information flows and so on do constrain local learning and need to be changed. But none of these ideas are of any practical value unless we, as individuals involved in urban governance, are prepared to modify the way we think and behave.

My basic premise is that there is a great deal of room for developing the individual potential of staff working in local government –

the latent talent described by Tony Eddison.[94] At a time of no growth the case for using staff to the best advantage is strengthened. There is, of course, an extensive literature on employee motivation and the role of the individual personality in the work situation.[95] The advice ranges over a broad spectrum from more sensitive and supportive behaviour by individual managers through to organizational re-design. Here I want to touch on just two aspects of personal behaviour which need attention if we are to develop practical approaches to public learning: inertia and communication.

Inertia

Resistance to change can be for good as well as bad reasons. As Sir Geoffrey Vickers argues:

Stability is not the enemy of change. It is the condition of any change which can hope to be welcome and enduring. The inertia of institutions and of concepts does indeed resist change sometimes usefully, sometimes mischievously. But stability, in the sense which I am giving it, is a condition of future development, as well as of conservation.[96]

Our first step must be to recognize that 'stout-hearted defenders' are just as valuable as 'fluid-minded innovators'.[97] It is the *reasons* why change is resisted rather than the resistance itself which should receive attention.

Often resistance is linked to vested interest. As Tony Eddison observes, the individual in his working situation devotes energy to buttressing his status and security and some to his actual job.[98] Part of the problem is that reward systems tend to be related to inputs rather than outputs – to the number of staff supervised rather than to what they actually achieve. A learning local government would place much more emphasis on systematic follow-up to discover, for example, what happens to clients after a service has been provided. It would try to modify reward systems so that pay, status and security were linked to evidence of impact on community problems and needs. This contrasts with a common current situation where rewards encourage bureaucratic growth and empire building. Revising reward systems is one way of stimulating a more relevant approach to the task and increasing job satisfaction, but there may be deeper psychological factors working against innovation.

Edward de Bono has provided a most elegant analysis of the way the mind organizes and patterns incoming information.[99] This remarkable capacity is both its greatest strength and greatest weakness. The danger is that firm patterns, once established, may be difficult to change. In a separate book de Bono discusses the use of lateral thinking which emerges as a means of escaping from past patterns of thinking and generating fresh ideas.[100]

In my view local government needs to give much more explicit attention to creativity. A range of techniques – lateral thinking, brainstorming, synectics – are used in the business world but are practically unheard of in local government.[101] I am not suggesting these techniques should replace existing approaches but, provided they are related carefully to particular organizational settings, they do have considerable potential for overcoming the inertia of past practice and stimulating imaginative approaches to problem-solving.

Communication

The reasons why staff may be frustrated and not give their best are complex and no two situations will be the same. A root problem, however, is likely to be the lack of genuine communication or empathy between tiers in the organizational hierarchy. This problem has been labelled the 'opaqueness of organizations' by R. W. Evans who set out to answer the question: How many people believe that they understand the problems of those who work beneath them, or that those for whom they work understand theirs?[102] Evans found that people at the top believed they understood lower level problems whereas junior ranks felt management were out of touch. It matters little which, if either, of these two views is right but it speaks volumes about the lack of mutual understanding which can develop in any organization.

Tony Eddison suggests that, rather than turning to the extensive literature on inter-personal behaviour, we might learn more by thinking about our own encounters, thinking about how we react, asking why we react in particular ways, assessing our real impact on others and their real impact on us: 'Again there are no precise answers and certainly no prescribed patterns of behaviour, but this phenomenon of people not reading people is a kind of "organizational blindness" which serves as an obstacle to the development of the potential of the whole department.'[103] In particular, we can say that it serves as an obstacle to the development of learning approaches by local government.

The business of people needing to 'read' each other more sensitively has been eloquently discussed by Sir Geoffrey Vickers.[104] He reminds us that the *way* change is brought about is as important as the change itself. In his view the first step required to bring about change is to achieve in the minds of all concerned an appreciation of the situation – an appreciation vivid enough to elicit a commanding mis-match signal. This signal could be regarded as a threat (i.e. to the continuance of present practice) or as an opportunity (i.e. for creative innovation). Vickers points out that the 'appreciative setting' of an individual will differ depending on his location within the organization. There has to be time for the appreciation to sink in before the second stage of change which will involve a response to the mis-match signal by a series of instrumental judgements.

Vickers argues convincingly that the critical change is at the point of acceptance. It is not enough to understand and obey, it is a question of identifying with the change. It is the development of commitment – what Vickers calls a shift from a potential fact to a potential act – which is fundamental. This is a psychological change which is theoretically obscure but is one of the most familiar facts of experience.[105]

The importance of overcoming unjustified inertia and of improving genuine communication are vital to any organization. Increased attention to these inter-personal aspects is, however, an imperative for local government at present. This is because fuller use of staff resources offers the greatest potential for the continued development of local government during an era of no growth in public services.

Conclusion

We have seen that each of the four theoretical perspectives reviewed – planning and policy sciences, organization theory, cybernetics and democratic theory – has a contribution to make to the development of improved theories of public learning. Some of the limitations of individual perspectives have been touched on. For example, planning theory has tended to separate planning from implementation and has thus reduced the possibilities of learning directly from experience. Opportunities for different perspectives to learn from each other have also been hinted at. For example, greater exchange between policy sciences and organization theory would probably be fruitful. Some suggestions have been made regarding approaches deserving more attention by those concerned to improve urban government. Again, examples are the idea of matrix management and the idea of strengthening local democratic accountability provided it is coupled with policies of redistribution decided by higher levels within the government hierarchy.

This final chapter has, however, been less concerned with setting out specific recommendations than with trying to create settings – landscapes of ideas – which could stimulate others to develop further the notion of public learning. Such developments will have a lot to do with making connections between hitherto relatively isolated theoretical perspectives and reconciling these with the important psychological and inter-personal aspects of bringing about change in the institutions of urban government.

Postscript: relationships between central and local government

This page draws attention to a few significant developments in central–local relationships which occurred in the short time between the writing of the book and its printing in January 1978. The page numbers in brackets refer to this book.

A useful review of *central–local relationships* (pp. 24–35) by the Central Policy Review Staff appeared in September 1977 titled *Relations between Central Government and Local Authorities*, HMSO, London.

In relation to *structure and local plans* (p. 29) a circular has appeared suggesting little movement in Department of the Environment thinking on the statutory planning system since 1974. See 'Town and Country Planning Act 1971: memorandum on structure and local plans', DoE Circular 55/77, July 1977.

In relation to *social service plans* (p. 31) the Department of Health and Social Security has improved its approach considerably. See 'Forward planning of local authority social services', DHSS Circular LASSL (77)13, June 1977.

In relation to *finance* (pp. 32–5) reference should be made to the development of cash limits which tighten central control of local authority capital expenditure. See 'Cash limits 1977–78', Cmnd 6767, HMSO, London, March 1977.

Government policy for the *inner cities* continues to develop. The *urban programme* (pp. 125–6) was transferred from the Home Office to the Department of the Environment in June 1977, was widened in scope and, from 1979/80, will run at £125 million per year. Responsibility for *Comprehensive Community Programmes* (pp. 129–30) was also transferred from the Home Office to the DoE in June 1977. Finally the government has entered into *special partnerships* (pp. 133–4) in seven inner-city areas to unify action for their regeneration. See statements by Peter Shore, Secretary of State for the Environment, to the House of Commons on 6 April and 8 November 1977.

Notes and References

Preface (pp. 9–13)

1 Schon, D. A., *Beyond the stable state*, Temple Smith, London, 1971, p. 116.
2 Cooper, D., *The grammar of living*, Pelican, Harmondsworth, 1976, p. 1.

Chapter 1 Central government and local autonomy

1 On national government see Hanson, A. H. and Walles, M., *Governing Britain*, Fontana, Glasgow, revised edition, 1975. On local government see Richards, P. G., *The reformed local government system*, George Allen and Unwin, London, 1973.
2 Jackson, W. E., *Local government in England and Wales*, Pelican, Harmondsworth, 1969. First published 1945, p. 36.
3 Ibid. pp. 37–38.
4 This draws on Buxton, R., *Local Government*, Penguin Education, second edition, Harmondsworth, 1973, pp. 57–60. The loss of local government functions is catalogued more fully by Robson, W. A., *Local government in crisis*, George Allen and Unwin, London, 1966.
5 National Health Service Act 1946.
6 Trunk Roads Act 1946. Note that the definition of 'trunk road' has been greatly extended since that date. Part of the bitterness at recent motorway public inquiries seems to have been caused by the remoteness of the staff working for central government's Road Construction Units. See Morris, T., 'The highway men', *New Society*, 9 September 1976, pp. 549–550.
7 Gas Act 1948.
8 Electricity Act 1947.
9 Water Act 1945.
10 Water Act 1973.
11 Local Government Act 1972 and National Health Service Reorganization Act 1973.

12   Layfield Committee, *Report of the Committee of Enquiry into Local Government Finance*, Cmnd 6453, HMSO, London, May 1976, p. 13.

13   *Capital* expenditure is incurred on objects of lasting value (even though that value may diminish in the course of time). *Revenue* expenditure (sometimes referred to as running costs or current expenditure) is usually constantly recurring and does not produce a permanent asset. The cost of erecting a school by a local authority is an example of capital expenditure whilst the expenditure on the general maintenance of the school – the teachers' salaries, cleaning, heating, lighting and repayments on the money borrowed to build the school – are revenue. This is a simplification of the difference between capital and revenue but will suffice for this book. More details on this and the whole labyrinthine world of local government finance are provided by Hepworth, N. P., *The finance of local government*, third edition, George Allen and Unwin, London, 1976.

14   This distinction draws on Dunn, E. S., *Economic and social development. A process of social learning*, Johns Hopkins University Press, Baltimore and London, 1971, pp. 8–10.

15   *Democracy and Devolution Proposals for Scotland and Wales,* Cmnd 5732, HMSO, London, September 1974, p. 1.

16   Minns, R. and Thornley, J., 'The case for Municipal Enterprise Boards, *New Society*, 2 September 1976, p. 499.

17   Griffith, J. A. G., *Central departments and local authorities*, George Allen and Unwin, London, 1966. See page 316.

18   This problem is explored more fully in Hambleton, R., 'A guideline is a trap', *New Society*, 24 March 1977, pp. 601–602.

19   Examples are the consultation papers on: Neighbourhood councils in England issued by the Department of the Environment in June 1974; Transport policy issued by the Department of the Environment in April 1976; Priorities for health and personal social services in England issued by the Department of Health and Social Security in March 1976; Housing policy issued by the Department of the Environment in June 1977.

20   Griffith, op. cit., p. 375.

21   Co-ordination of local authority services for children under five. A joint letter of the Department of Health and Social Security and the Department of Education and Science, March 1976. Circulars relating to the rate support grant are, of course, prepared by relevant central departments working together.

22 See minutes 5.13, 5.14 and 5.24 of the preliminary consultation meeting on rate support grant held at the Department of the Environment on 28 October 1974.

23 An attempt to explain why the statutory planning system is out of step with current realities is provided in *Planning and the future*, a discussion paper published by the Royal Town Planning Institute, November 1976, pp. 5–12. Details of Scotland's regional reports are provided in Scottish Development Circulars 4/75 and 51/75 and financial plans are described in Scottish Office Finance Circular 47/76. See page 316.

24 School for Advanced Urban Studies, Community land training programme, 1975, Elements 2 and 3.

25 *Transport Supplementary Grant: submissions for 1976/77*, Department of the Environment Circular 43/75, April 1975.

26 *Housing Strategies and Investment Programmes: Arrangements for 1978/79*, Department of the Environment Circular 63/77, June 1977.

27 *Local authority social services: 10 year development plans 1973–1983*, Department of Health and Social Security Circular 35/72, August 1972. See page 316.

28 Hambleton, R. and Scerri, V., 'Three views of need', *New Society*, 18 October 1973, pp. 146–147.

29 Hepworth, op. cit., pp. 270–271. See page 316.

30 A full discussion of this and the two other forms of grants (specific grants and supplementary grants) is provided in Layfield Committee, op. cit, Chapter 12. See also Hepworth, op. cit., Chapter 3.

31 Layfield Committee, op. cit., pp. 93–99.

32 The system was modified a little on local government reorganization by, for example, the introduction of a 'subsidiary sector' which is mainly concerned with the purchase of land for corresponding key sector programmes. See *Capital programmes*, Department of the Environment Circular 86/74, June 1974.

33 *Reform of Local Government in England*, Cmnd 4276, February 1970, p. 28.

34 *Local government in England*, Cmnd 4584, February 1971, p. 6.

35 Layfield Committee, op. cit., p. 65.

36 Ibid., p. xxv.

37 See particularly Chapter 5. My own view is that the report stands up well to scrutiny but two provocative appraisals are: Davies, B., 'Layfield's split vision', *New Society*, 27 May 1976,

pp. 473–474; Cripps, F. and Godley, W., *Local government finance and its reform – A critique of the Layfield Committee's Report*, October 1976, Department of Applied Economics, University of Cambridge.

38 *Local Government Finance*, Green Paper, Cmnd 6813, May 1977.
39 Ibid., p. 5. See page 316.
40 See, for example, Central Policy Review Staff, *A joint framework for social policies*, HMSO, London, 1975.
41 Jackson, B., 'A minister for children?', *New Society*, 15 January 1976, pp. 94–96.
42 Boaden, N. T., *Urban policy-making*, Cambridge University Press, Cambridge, 1971; Davies, B., *Social needs and resources in local services*, Michael Joseph, London, 1968.
43 Redcliffe-Maud Committee, *Local government reform*. Short version of the *Report of the Royal Commission on Local Government in England*, Cmnd 4039, HMSO, London, June 1969, p. 17.
44 *Joint care planning: health and local authorities*, Department of Health and Social Security Circular, March 1976, and also May 1977.
45 *Devolution: the English dimension – A consultative document*, HMSO, London, December 1976.

Chapter 2 The purposeful local authority

1 A useful discussion of the traditional and other views is provided in Stewart, J. D., *Management in local government – a viewpoint*, Charles Knight, London, 1971, Chapter 1.
2 Fuller accounts of the nature of corporate planning in local government are provided in Stewart, op. cit.; Eddison, T., *Local government – management and corporate planning*, Leonard Hill, London, 1973; Stewart, J. D., 'Corporate planning' in Bruton, M. J. (ed.), *The spirit and purpose of planning*, Hutchinson, London, 1974, pp. 205–227.
3 Friend, J. K. and Jessop, W. N., *Local government and strategic choice*, Tavistock, London, 1969; Friend, J. K., Power, J. M. and Yewlett, C. J., *Public planning – the inter-corporate dimension*, Tavistock, London, 1974.
4 See McLoughlin, J. B., *Urban and regional planning. A systems approach*, Faber, London, 1969. The mood of contemporary thinking is well conveyed in Wilson, A. G., 'Models in urban

planning – a synoptic review of recent literature, *Urban Studies*, Vol. 5 No. 3, 1968, pp. 249–276.

5 See Faludi, A., *Planning theory*, Pergamon, Oxford, 1973, Chapter 1.

6 To some extent this was acknowledged in Department of the Environment, Structure Plans, Circular 98/74, 1974, which told authorities to avoid 'unnecessary expense and time' and to concentrate on what is essential.

7 Schon, D. A., *Beyond the stable state*, Temple Smith, London, 1971, Chapter 2.

8 See Needham, B., 'Concrete problems not abstract goals', *Journal of the Royal Town Planning Institute*, Vol. 57 No. 7, 1971, pp. 317–319; Faludi, A., 'Problems with "problem-solving"', *Journal of the Royal Town Planning Institute*, Vol. 57 No. 9, 1971, p. 415; Needham, B. and Faludi, A., 'Planning and the public interest', *Journal of the Royal Town Planning Institute*, Vol. 59 No. 4, 1973, pp. 164–166.

9 Chadwick, G., *A systems view of planning*, Pergamon, Oxford, 1971. The debate is not over. See Drake, M., *et al*, *Aspects of structure planning in Britain*, CES RP 20, Centre for Environmental Studies, London, 1975, pp. 142–144.

10 Goals have been defined as 'statements of directions in which planning or action is aimed . . . They are ideals over a horizon which will never be attained, since progress towards them over time implies their reformulation in yet higher ideals.' See Lichfield, N., 'Goals in planning', paper presented to the Town and Country Planning Summer School, Town Planning Institute, London, 1968.

11 There is no shortage of literature on the use of corporate planning in the business world. For a straightforward guide see Argenti, J., *Corporate planning*, George Allen and Unwin, London, 1968. For a more abstract treatment see Ansoff, H. I., *Corporate strategy*, McGraw-Hill, New York, 1965, and Ackoff, R. L., *A concept of corporate planning*, Wiley, New York, 1970. Theories underlying corporate planning, such as operational research and cybernetics, are discussed later in Chapter 10.

12 Novick, D., *Program budgeting*, Harvard University Press, Cambridge, Mass., 1965.

13 See, for example, Stewart, J. D., 'Programme budgeting in British local government,' *Local Government Finance*, August

1969, pp. 313–319; Armstrong, R. H. R., 'The approach to PPBS in local government,' November 1969, pp. 454–466; Eddison, op. cit., Chapter 4.

14   See, for example, Wildavsky, A., 'Rescuing policy analysis from PPBS', *Public Administration Review*, March/April 1969.

15   Ways, M., 'The road to 1977', *Fortune*, January 1967, reprinted in Emery, F. E. (ed.), *Systems thinking*, Penguin, Harmondsworth, 1969, pp. 372–388.

16   Buchanan Report, *Traffic in towns*, HMSO, London, 1963.

17   Planning Advisory Group, *The future of development plans*, HMSO, London, 1965.

18   Denington Report, *Our older homes. A call for action*, HMSO, London, 1966.

19   Plowden Report, *Children in their primary schools*, HMSO, London, 1967.

20   Seebohm Report, *Report of the Committee on Local Authority and Allied Personal Social Services*, HMSO, London, 1968.

21   Herbert Report, *Report of the Royal Commission on Government in Greater London*, HMSO, London, 1960.

22   Maud Report, *Report of the Committee on the management of local government*, HMSO, London, 1967.

23   Mallaby Report, *Report of the Committee on the staffing of local government*, HMSO, London, 1967.

24   Bains Report, *The new local authorities – management and structure*, HMSO, London, 1972.

25   Stewart, 'Corporate planning', op. cit., p. 209.

26   Redcliffe-Maud Report, *Report of the Royal Commission on Local Government in England*, HMSO, London, 1969.

27   A straightforward discussion of the Redcliffe-Maud analysis and the new two-tier system is provided in Buxton, R., *Local government*, Penguin Education, Harmondsworth, 1973, Chapters 9 and 10. Reorganization in Scotland also introduced a two-tier system but the structure is a more radical break with the past, see Wheatley Report, *Scotland: local government reform, Report of the Royal Commission on Local Government in Scotland*, HMSO, Edinburgh, 1969.

28   Plowden Committee, *Committee on the control of public expenditure*, HMSO, London, 1961.

29   *Public expenditure – a new presentation*, Green Paper, April 1969.

30   A very readable account of the central government public expenditure process is provided in Heclo, H. and Wildavsky, A.,

The private government of public money, Macmillan, London, 1974. See Chapter 5 for a detailed discussion of PESC.

31 *The reorganisation of central government*, White Paper, October 1970, p. 13.

32 Central Policy Review Staff, *A joint framework for social policies*, HMSO, London, 1975.

33 For further details see Heclo and Wildavsky, op. cit., Chapter 6.

34 Stewart, 'Corporate planning', op. cit., p. 208.

35 Skitt, J. (ed.), *Practical corporate planning in local government*, Leonard Hill, London, 1975, p. 4.

36 Approaches to corporate planning in Gloucestershire, Newcastle, Greater London, Ealing, East Suffolk, Grimsby, Sheffield and Coventry are discussed. See *Municipal Journal*, 3 September to 12 November 1971. For a wide-ranging discussion of corporate planning at this time see Greenwood, G. and Stewart, J. D., *Corporate planning in English local government: an analysis with readings 1967–72*, Charles Knight, London, 1974.

37 Bains Report, op. cit.

38 The 'Grey Book', *Management arrangements for the reorganised National Health Service*, HMSO, London, 1972.

39 Ogden Report, *The new water industry – management and structure*, HMSO, London, 1973.

40 Ibid., p. 25.

41 Paterson Report, *The new Scottish local authorities – management and structure*, HMSO, London, 1973.

42 Department of the Environment, *The Sunderland Study*, HMSO, London, 1973.

43 Four articles on position statements appear in *Corporate Planning*, Vol. 2 No. 1, February 1975, Institute of Local Government Studies.

44 The term also has a wider meaning as the foundation block of the new inter-discipline of policy sciences. For an excellent discussion of this wider scene see Heclo, H., Review article, 'Policy analysis', *British Journal of Political Science*, No. 2, 1972, pp. 83–108. This and other theoretical underpinnings of corporate planning are discussed further in Chapter 10.

45 Several contributors discuss the role of the elected member in policy making in *Corporate Planning*, Vol. 2 No. 2, June 1975, Institute of Local Government Studies.

46 Bains Report, op. cit., p. 25.

47   Rogers, S., 'Performance Review Sub-Committees', *Corporate Planning*, Vol. 2 No. 3, November 1975, p. 1.

48   *Rate fund expenditure and rate calls in 1975–76,* Department of the Environment Circular 171/74, December 1974, para 4.

49   A particularly revealing attack on corporate management is provided by the Director of Education for Oldham who specifically rejects the idea of setting corporate priorities in favour of a return to departmentalism, at least in so far as the education service is concerned. See Pritchett, G. R., 'Municipal malaise', *Times Education Supplement*, 12 November 1976, p. 21.

50   P A Management Consultants, *Introducing policy or corporate planning into local government*, undertaken for the Lothian Regional Council, May 1975, two volumes totalling nearly 300 pages.

51   Stewart, J. D., 'The responsive local authority', *Municipal Journal*, 21 July 1972, reprinted in Stewart, J. D., *The responsive local authority*, Charles Knight, London, 1974, p. 96.

52   Eddison, T., 'A question of attitudes', *Municipal Journal*, 6 December 1974, pp. 1545–1548.

53   Planning and the 'reticulation' of knowledge are discussed further in Power, J. M., 'Planning – magic and technique' in 'Beyond local government reform – some prospects for evolution in public policy networks', Institute for Operational Research Conference Paper, December 1971. The importance of mediators whose part it is to act across the boundaries of institutions and systems is also stressed in Marris, P., 'New forms of government' in Hatch, S. (ed.), *Towards participation in local services*, Fabian Tract 419, February 1973.

54   Guthrie, R., 'How to work together', *New Society*, April 1976, pp. 74–75.

55   The idea of community planning is discussed in Stewart, *Management in local government*, op. cit., Chapter 6 and in Stewart, *The responsive local authority*, op. cit., Chapter 4. Several articles on inter-agency planning appear in *Corporate Planning*, Vol. 3 No. 3, December 1976, Institute of Local Government Studies.

56   Metropolitan Borough of Stockport, *The elderly. A policy report*. From Chief Executive's Department, March 1976.

57   *Joint care planning – health and local authorities*, Department of Health and Social Security Circular, March 1976. See also follow-up circular dated May 1977.

58 Stewart, J. D., 'The government of cities and the politics of opportunity', *Local Government Studies*, January 1975, pp. 16–17.

59 See, for example, Blaydon, S., 'Corporate planning – can the councillor take control?', *Municipal Review*, July 1974, pp. 90–92. Members would do well to be on their guard for there are books which advocate a manipulative approach by policy 'experts'. See Benveniste, G., *The politics of expertise*, Croom Helm, London, 1972.

60 I draw heavily on an outstanding paper – Benington, J. and Skelton, P., 'Public participation in decision-making by governments' in *Government and programme budgeting*, papers of a seminar published by the, then, Institute of Municipal Treasurers and Accountants, March 1973.

61 See Bradshaw, J., 'The concept of social need', *New Society*, 30 March 1972, pp. 640–643. A considerable amount of work has been carried out using various forms of social indicator. Unfortunately much of this work has been more concerned with technical artistry than with deriving policy guidance. It is not enough to map where problems are. We need to understand what the processes are which bring them about. Only a few of the many indicator studies have attempted to do this. For one small step in this direction see Barrowclough, R., *A social atlas of Kirklees*, for Batley Community Development Project by Department of Geography, Huddersfield Polytechnic, 1975.

62 Stewart, J. D., 'Corporate planning – the councillor must take control', *Municipal Review*, March 1974, pp. 444–446.

63 See Tabb, W. K., 'Alternative futures and distributional planning', *American Institute of Planners Journal*, January 1972, pp. 25–32; Levy, F. S., Meltsner, A. J. and Wildavsky, A., *Urban outcomes*, University of California Press, Berkeley, 1974. Area resource analysis, which is one approach to distributional effects, is discussed further in relation to Liverpool in Chapter 8. A report which looks at the distribution of resources between dependency groups within the elderly and argues for transfers is Metropolitan Borough of Stockport, op. cit.

64 See, Bachrach, P. and Baratz, M. S., *Power and poverty*, Oxford University Press, London, 1970, particularly Chapter 3 on non-decisions; Levin, P., 'Opening up the planning process' in Hatch, S., op. cit.; Corina, L., *Local government decision*

making, Paper No. 2 from Department of Social Administration and Social Work, University of York, 1975.

65   See particularly Levin, op. cit.
66   See Schon, op. cit., pp. 48–50.
67   Ibid., p. 15.
68   Talk on BBC Radio 3, 17 October 1976.
69   Schon, op. cit., p. 30. See also Wildavsky, A., *Evaluation as an organizational problem*, Centre for Environmental Studies, University Working Paper 13, 1972, and Michael, D. N., *On learning to plan and planning to learn*, Jossey-Bass, San Francisco, 1973.

Chapter 3   Area approaches

1   These initiatives are reviewed in some detail in Chapters 5, 6 and 7.
2   Harvey, D., *Social justice and the city*, Edward Arnold, London, 1973, p. 11.
3   Pressman, J. L. and Wildavsky, A., *Implementation*, University of California Press, Berkeley, 1973, p. 143.
4   I am grateful to Barbara Webster and John Stewart of the Institute of Local Government Studies, Birmingham for help in clarifying these concepts at an Inlogov seminar in October 1976.
5   The bi-monthly national magazine *Community Action* first published in February 1972 provides an indication of the extent and sophistication of public action group activity.
6   Clark, G., 'Neighbourhood self-management', in Hain, P. (ed.), *Community politics*, John Calder, London, 1976, pp. 114–115.
7   See for example, Hindess, B., *The decline of working class politics*, Paladin, London, 1971.
8   For example, in the Metropolitan Borough of Stockport the average population served by one councillor was 2182 before reorganization and 4805 after reorganization.
9   There are, of course, still relatively few councillors with first-hand experience of those forms of area approach which directly affect their role, such as area committees. These observations are based mainly on my experience at Stockport although they are borne out with the discussions I have had with councillors serving on area committees in other authorities.
10   See announcement by Peter Walker, then Secretary of State for

the Environment, *Hansard* (House of Commons), 23 March 1972 (cols. 1698–99).

11 *Housing Act, 1974: Renewal Strategies,* Department of the Environment Circular 13/75, January 1975.

12 *Area Management,* paper circulated by the Department of the Environment, September 1974.

13 Yates, D., *Neighborhood democracy,* Lexington Books, Lexington, Mass., 1973, p. 23. Note that Yates's use of decentralization encompasses delegation and devolution.

14 Arnstein, S., 'A ladder of citizen participation in the USA', *Journal of the American Institute of Planners,* July 1969.

15 Altshuler, A. A., *Community Control,* Pegasus, New York, 1970, p. 44.

16 Yin, R. K. and Lucas, W. A., 'Decentralization and alienation', *Policy Sciences,* Vol. 4, 1973, pp. 327–336.

Chapter 4   Local government in Britain and America

1 Finer, S. E., *Comparative government,* Pelican, Harmondsworth, 1975, p. 588. First published in 1970. This work contains, *inter alia,* useful introductory chapters on the governments of Britain and the USA together with a selected bibliography. However, attention is focussed almost exclusively on central governments.

2 Sharpe, L. J., 'American democracy reconsidered', Parts 1 and 2, *British Journal of Political Science,* Vol. 3, 1973, p. 3. This two-part article (pp. 1–28 and 129–167) is a fascinating study which suggests that American city government may be less democratic than its British counterpart.

3 See, for example, Banfield, E. C. and Wilson, J. Q., *City Politics,* Vintage Books, New York, 1966, Chapter 6, and Yin, R. K. and Yates, D., *Street-level governments,* Lexington Books, Lexington, Mass., 1975.

4 Grodzins, M., 'Centralization and decentralization in the American Federal System' in Goldwin, R. A. (ed.), *A Nation of States,* Rand McNally, Chicago, 1963.

5 This discussion is deliberately drastically condensed to facilitate ready comparison with the American forms. A readable introduction to British local government is provided by Buxton, R., *Local Government,* Penguin Education, second edition, Harmondsworth, 1973.

6   A useful lead in to the literature on community power structures in America and its relevance for Britain is provided by Newton, K. 'Community politics and decision-making: the American experience and its lessons' in Young, K. (ed.), *Essays on the study of urban politics*, Macmillan, London, 1975.

7   See Banfield and Wilson, op. cit., Chapter 9.

8   See Yates, D., *Neighborhood democracy*, Lexington Books, Lexington, Mass., 1973, pp. 15–19, and Merton, R. K., 'The latent functions of the machine' in Merton, R. K., *Social Theory and Social Structure*, The Free Press, New York, 1957.

9   Fainstein, S., and Fainstein, N. I., *Political representation and the urban district*, Paper to the annual meeting of the American Sociological Association, San Francisco, August 1975.

10 Hindess, B., *The decline of working class politics*, Paladin, London, 1971.

11 This picture is confirmed by other work. See Sharpe, op. cit., pp. 19–21.

12 Sharpe, op. cit., p. 162 and Banfield and Wilson, op. cit., p. 94.

13 For a recent account see Gyford, J., *Local politics in Britain*, Croom Helm, London, 1976.

14 Stewart, J. D., 'Towards new studies of urban policymaking', in Stewart, J. D., *The responsive local authority*, Charles Knight, London, 1974, pp. 141–142.

15 Perlman, J. E., 'Grassrooting the system', *Social Policy*, September–October 1976 (available from Suite 500, 184 Fifth Avenue, New York, NY 10010).

16 Donnison, D., 'Micro-politics of the city' in Donnison, D. (ed.), *London: urban patterns, problems and policies*, Heinemann, London, 1973, pp. 383–404; Green, G., 'Politics, local government and the community', *Local Government Studies*, June 1974, pp. 5–16; Hambleton, R., *Community preferences – a local authority viewpoint*, Paper to the Institute of British Geographers Urban Study Group, Portsmouth, September 1974.

17 The bi-monthly national magazine *Community Action* provides an ongoing account of public action group activity of this kind, available from P.O. Box 665, London SW1X 8DZ. For a series of essays on community action see Hain, P. (ed.), *Community politics*, John Calder, London, 1976.

18 Prewitt, K. and Verba, S., *An introduction to American government*, Harper and Row, New York, second edition, 1976.

19 This is the figure for government grants in 1973/74. The other sources were rates 28 per cent and other income 27 per cent. Notice that these figures relate to *total* local authority income and not just 'relevant expenditure' which is illustrated in Figure 4. Source for these proportions is Layfield Committee, *Report of the Committee of Enquiry into Local Government Finance*, H M S O, London, May 1976, p. 384.

20 This is a drastic simplification of an extremely complex subject. In particular I have left out any discussion of 'special revenue sharing' which is a term used widely in the early 1970s. Some argue that special revenue sharing was a less restrictive form of block grant. Others say that Nixon's White House staff just wanted another name for block grants. In practice block grants vary in the degree of federal intrusiveness and it is helpful to think in terms of a continuum from general revenue sharing to categorical grants. The Advisory Commission on Intergovernmental Relations (ACIR) have published many useful reports on federal aid. See A C I R, *Special Revenue Sharing: an analysis of the administration's grant consolidation proposals,* 1971; A C I R, *General Revenue Sharing: an A C I R evaluation,* 1974; A C I R, *Block grants: a roundtable discussion,* 1976, and Walker, D. B., *The changing pattern of federal assistance to state and local governments,* A C I R internal paper, July 1976. For more information on general revenue sharing see Caputo, D. A. and Cole, R. L., *Urban politics and decentralization,* Lexington Books, Lexington, Mass., 1974 and Scheffer, W. F., *General revenue sharing and decentralization,* University of Oklahoma Press, Norman, 1976.

21 An interesting theme feature on planning in the U S A appears in *Built Environment,* April 1974, pp. 169–186. The focus is on physical planning but there is also some discussion of regional planning and revenue sharing.

22 Moynihan, D. P., 'Policy vs. programme in the 1970's', *The Public Interest,* Summer 1970, pp. 90–100. This theme is developed by Solesbury, W., 'Programmes into policies', *Built Environment,* December 1975, pp. 190–193.

23 Sharpe, op. cit., p. 5.

24 This is a simplification for there is little or no agreement on the definition of federal structure. See Rufus Davis, S., *The Federal Principle: A journey through time in search of a meaning,* University of California Press, Berkeley, 1976. Also note that

the current interpretation of the Constitution by the Supreme Court is that national laws (that is, laws of the US Congress) are 'the supreme law of the land' and override any state laws that interfere. In theory, therefore, the federal government could deprive the states of almost all their functions. In this way the United States resembles a unitary form of government.

25　Wildavsky, A., *A bias towards federalism: a review essay on planning, organization theory and governmental structure*, Working Paper No. 40, Graduate School of Public Policy, University of California, Berkeley, 1975.

26　Several references are provided by Sharpe, op. cit., p. 4.

27　Wildavsky, op. cit., p. 2.

28　This draws heavily on the format developed by Sharpe, op. cit.

29　For a concise summary see Redcliffe-Maud Committee, *Local government reform*. Short version of the *Report of the Royal Commission on Local Government in England*, Cmnd 4039, HMSO, London, June 1969.

30　Advisory Commission on Intergovernmental Relations, *Metropolitan America: Challenge to Federalism*, Washington DC, 1966; quoted in Prewitt and Verba, op. cit., p. 448.

31　Both these points can be illuminated by evidence from the case study cities discussed in Chapter 8. In Dayton strong feelings about rights were made quite explicit at the public meeting of the City Commission on 14 July 1976. A white resident from Oakwood (one of the suburbs) addressed the commission to complain about 'adult' bookstores in downtown Dayton. The black Chairman of the Commission was brusque in reply saying that he didn't like 'gratuitous insults from neighbors': only when Oakwood was part of the city could the residents expect to influence Dayton's policies. On the question of taxation the Task Force on the New York City Crisis identified equalization of personal income tax rates for city residents and commuters as the single largest saving/revenue gain. It would bring in an additional $113 million and would 'represent an important step toward . . . metropolitan area financing which clearly holds much promise as one lasting remedy to the City's fiscal ills'. See *Statement of the Task Force on the New York City Crisis*, 9 June 1976, p. 30.

32　It is worth noting that bussing is a major political issue which impacts considerably on day-to-day local government administration in the cities. Chapter 8 touches on the role of the little city halls in relation to bussing in Boston.

33 Wildavsky, op. cit., p. 1.
34 Ibid., p. 31.
35 Lindblom, C. E., *The intelligence of democracy: decision-making through mutual adjustment*, The Free Press, New York, 1965.
36 See, for example, Dahl, R. A., *Who governs?*, Yale University Press, New Haven, 1961 and Dahl, R. A., *Democracy in the United States: promise and performance*, Rand McNally, Chicago, 1972, Chapter 17.
37 Sharpe, op. cit., p. 135.
38 Banfield and Wilson, op. cit., pp. 84–85.
39 Fainstein and Fainstein, op. cit., p. 6.
40 Niskanen, W. and Levy, M., *Cities and schools: a case for community government in California*, p. 22, Working Paper No. 14, Graduate School of Public Policy, University of California, Berkeley, 1974, quoted in Wildavsky, op. cit., p. 33.
41 Richardson, H. W., *The economies of urban size*, Saxon House, London, 1973, Chapter 7; Long, J., 'The impact of scale on management structures and processes', *Local Government Studies*, April 1975, pp. 45–59. For a wide-ranging review essay see Stewart, M., 'Review essay on city size and urban policy', *Policy and Politics*, Vol. 3 No. 3, March 1975, pp. 89–103.
42 Keith-Lucas, B., 'What price local democracy?', *New Society*, 12 August 1976, p. 341.
43 Sharpe, op. cit., p. 7.
44 Banfield and Wilson, op. cit., pp. 3–4.
45 Schattschneider, E., *The semi-sovereign people*, Holt Reinhart, New York, 1960, pp. 34–35, quoted in Sharpe, L. J., op. cit., p. 19.
46 Newton, K., *City politics in Britain and America*, Birmingham University, Birmingham, 1968, p. 7, quoted in Sharpe, L. J., op. cit., p. 21.
47 Sharpe, op. cit., p. 22.
48 Ibid., p. 24.
49 Ibid., p. 25.
50 Ibid., p. 26. See also Fainstein and Fainstein, op. cit., pp. 1–6 for a useful discussion of political disorganization and the dominance of corporate forms.
51 See, for example, Community Development Project, *The costs of industrial change*, London, January 1977. For a particularly

good neo-marxist analysis of local government see Cockburn, C., *The Local State*, Pluto, London, 1977.

52 Levy, F., Meltsner, A. J. and Wildavsky, A., *Urban outcomes*, University of California Press, Berkeley, 1974; Yin, R. K., *On the equality of municipal service outcomes: street cleanliness*, April 1974, WN-8625-OEO, Rand Corporation; Randall, G. W., Lomas, K. W. and Newton, T., 'Area distribution of resources in Coventry', *Local Government Finance*, No. 11, November 1973; Webster, B. and Stewart, J. D., 'The area analysis of resources', *Policy and Politics*, September 1974; Liverpool Inner Area Study, *Area resource analysis: methodology*, IAS/LI/5, 1974 and Liverpool Inner Area Study, *Area resource analysis: District D Tables 1973–74*, IAS/LI/9, 1976, both available from Department of the Environment, London.

53 See, for example, Gyford, J. and Baker, R., *Labour and local politics*, Fabian Tract 446, January 1977.

54 See a useful collection of essays by Rein, M., *Social science and public policy*, Penguin Education, Harmondsworth, 1976. The roots of these ideas can be traced to the work of the German sociologist Karl Mannheim. See Mannheim, K., *Ideology and Utopia*, Harcourt Brace (Harvest Books), New York, 1936.

55 Weiss, R. S. and Rein, M., 'The evaluation of broad aim programs: experimental design, its difficulties and an alternative', *Administrative Science Quarterly*, March 1970, pp. 97–109; Friedmann, J., *Retracking America: a theory of transactive planning*, Anchor Press/Doubleday, New York, 1973, Chapters 6 and 7; Yin, R. K. and Yates, D., 'Street-level governments', Lexington Books, Massachusetts, 1975, pp. 180–186; Friedmann, J. and Abonyi, G., 'Social learning: a model for policy research', *Environment and Planning*, Vol. 8 No. 8, December 1976, pp. 927–940.

56 Yates, op. cit., pp. 13–14. At a later point Yates seems to move his ground when he states that 'decentralization obviously does fragment urban government' (p. 160). My point is that if decentralization brings services together it could reduce fragmentation.

Chapter 5   Neighbourhood policies in Britain

1 This chapter draws on Hambleton, R., 'Policies for areas', *Local Government Studies*, Vol. 3 No. 2, April 1977, pp. 13–29.

2   See, for example, Holterman, S., 'Areas of urban deprivation in Great Britain: an analysis of 1971 Census data', *Social Trends*, Vol. 6, 1975, pp. 33–47; Hatch, S. and Sherrott, R., 'Positive discrimination and the distribution of deprivations', *Policy and Politics*, Vol. 1 No. 3, 1973, pp. 223–240.

3   Several of the national community development projects have argued that the root causes of deprivation lie in structural determinants of income inequality. See Coventry Community Development Project, Final report. *Coventry and Hillsfields: prosperity and the persistence of inequality*, March 1975.

4   Meacher, M., 'The politics of positive discrimination' in Glennerster, H. and Hatch, S. (eds.), *Positive discrimination and inequality*, Fabian Research Series 314, March 1974; Community Development Project, *Gilding the ghetto. The state and the poverty experiments*, February 1977.

5   See, for example, West, R. R., and Lowe, C. R., 'Regional variations in need for and provision and use of child health services in England and Wales', *British Medical Journal*, 9 October 1976, pp. 843–846. This includes references to several other studies showing territorial injustice in the allocation of health service resources.

6   *Priorities for health and personal social services in England. A consultative document*, Department of Health and Social Security, HMSO, London, March 1976.

7   *Sharing resources for health in England. Report of the Resource Allocation Working Party*, Department of Health and Social Security, HMSO, London, 1976.

8   Layfield Committee, *Report of the Committee of Enquiry into Local Government Finance*, Cmnd, 6453, HMSO, London, May, 1976.

9   North West Economic Planning Council, *Supplementary evidence to the Committee of Enquiry into Local Government Finance,* August 1975.

10 A useful analysis of the balance of responsibility among tiers of government is provided by Maas, A. (ed.), *Area and power. A theory of local government*, The Free Press, New York, 1959.

11 In recent years this opposition has been documented by those directly affected in the voluntary magazine *Community Action*, first issue February 1972.

12 Buchanan Report, *Traffic in towns*, HMSO, London, 1963.

13 Stewart, J. D., 'The government of cities and the politics of

opportunity, *Local Government Studies*, January 1975, p. 10.

14   Planning Advisory Group, *The future of development plans*, HMSO, London, 1975.

15   Skeffington Report, *People and planning*, HMSO, London, 1969.

16   *Neighbourhood councils in England*, consultation paper from the Department of the Environment, June 1974. Neighbourhood councils in Stockport are discussed further in Chapter 8.

17   Kay, A., 'Planning, participation and planners', in Jones, D. and Mayo, M. (eds.), *Community work one*, Routledge and Kegan Paul, London, 1974, pp. 199–213.

18   Miller, S. M. and Rein, M., 'Community participation: past and future', in Jones, D. and Mayo, M. (eds.), *Community work two*, Routledge and Kegan Paul, London, 1975, pp. 3–24.

19   There is a burgeoning literature in this subject area. For a recent review see Mercer, C., *Living in cities. Psychology and the urban environment*, Penguin, Harmondsworth, 1975. For an earlier excellent analysis see Alexander, C., 'A city is not a tree', *Design*, February 1966, pp. 47–55.

20   Lee, T., 'The urban neighbourhood as a socio spatio schema', *Human Relations*, Vol. 21 No. 3, 1968.

21   Baker, J. and Young, M., *The Hornsey Plan. A role for neighbourhood councils in the new local government*, Association for Neighbourhood Councils, 1971.

22   Plowden Report, *Children and their primary schools*, HMSO, London, 1967.

23   Halsey Report, *Educational priority, Volume 1: EPA problems and policies*, Department of Education and Science, HMSO, London, 1972.

24   Barnes, J. (ed.), *Educational priority, Volume 3: Curriculum innovation in London's EPAs*, Department of Education and Science, HMSO, London, 1975.

25   Smith, G., *Educational priority, Volume 4: The West Riding Project*, Department of Education and Science, HMSO, London, 1975. There is other work which is positive about the role of schooling. See Reynolds, D. *et al*, 'Schools do make a difference', *New Society*, 29 July 1976, pp. 223–225.

26   Field, F. (ed.), *Education and the urban crisis*, Routledge and Kegan Paul, London, 1977.

27   *Tenth Report of the House of Commons Expenditure Committee: Policy making in the Department of Education and Science*, HMSO, London, 1976.

28 Auld, R., *The William Tyndale Junior and Infant Schools: a report*, Greater London Council, 1976. See Mack, J., 'Tyndale measured', *New Society*, 29 January, 1976, pp. 221–222 and 'A school that failed', *New Society*, 22 July 1976, pp. 178–179.

29 Seebohm Report, *Local authority and allied personal social services*, HMSO, London, 1968.

30 See Kogan, M. and Terry, J., *The organization of a social service department: a blue-print*, Bookstall Publications, London, 1971; Brunel University, *Social Services departments, Developing patterns of work and organization,* Heinemann, London, 1974.

31 Schaffer, B. B. *Northwest Onestop Welfare Centre: the experiment and its lessons so far.* Report to the Royal Commission on Australian Government Administration, December 1975.

32 Benington, J., 'Strategies for change at the local level: some reflections', in Jones and Mayo, *Community work one*, op. cit., p. 260. The source for the ninety-four meanings of 'community' is Hillery, G. A., 'Definitions of community: areas of agreement', *Rural Sociology*, Vol. 20 No. 2, 1955, pp. 111–123.

33 A different interpretation of these three strands is provided by Cockburn, C., *Local state*, Pluto, London, 1977, pp. 112–20.

34 See Leissner, A., and Joslin, J., 'Area team community work: achievement and crisis', in Jones and Mayo, *Community work one*, op. cit., pp. 118–147.

35 Calouste Gulbenkian Foundation, *Community work and social change*, Longman, London, 1968.

36 For example we shall see in Chapter 8 that community workers in Stockport are employed by the Director of Administration and spend much of their time assisting neighbourhood councils.

37 See Hambleton, R., 'Corporate and responsive', *Municipal Journal*, 6 September 1974, pp. 1063–1066 and Else, R., 'Corporate planning and community work', *Community Development Journal*, January 1975, pp. 30–37.

38 Calouste Gulbenkian Foundation, *Current issues in community work,* Routledge and Kegan Paul, London, 1973.

39 Batley, R. and Edwards, J., 'CDP and the urban programme' in Lees, R. and Smith, G. (eds.), *Action research and community development*, Routledge and Kegan Paul, London, 1975.

40 Demuth, C., *Government initiatives on urban deprivation,* Briefing paper 1/77, The Runnymede Trust, 1977, p. 4. See p. 316.

41 *CDP – A general outline,* Home Office, 1969.

42 Ibid., p. 3.

43 *The national community development project*, Inter-project report to the Home Secretary, 1973.

44 Ibid., p. 35.

45 Milner Holland Report, *Report of the Committee on Housing in Greater London*, HMSO, London, 1965, p. 228.

46 Denington Report, *Our older homes: a call for action*, HMSO, London, 1966.

47 *Housing Act 1969. Area Improvement*. Ministry of Housing and Local Government Circular 65/69, para 37.

48 A review of this policy is provided by Roberts, T. J., *General Improvement Areas*, Saxon House, London, 1976.

49 Graham, P., 'Are action areas a mistake?', *Municipal Journal*, 5 July 1974, pp. 809–811; Paris, C., 'Housing action areas', *Roof*, January 1977, pp. 9–14.

50 *Housing Act 1974: Housing Action Areas, Priority Neighbourhoods and General Improvement Areas*, Department of the Environment Circular 14/75, para 15.

51 This has led at least one authority to try to develop a zonal approach to housing renewal. See Leicester City Council, *Renewal strategy*, July 1976.

52 *Housing Act 1974: Renewal Strategies*, Department of the Environment Circular 13/75.

53 Shelter Neighbourhood Action Project, *Another chance for cities*, Shelter, London, 1972. The SNAP experiment is discussed further in the Liverpool section of Chapter 8.

54 Statement by Secretary of State for the Environment, House of Commons, 26 July 1972.

55 Department of the Environment, *Making towns better. Reports on Sunderland, Rotherham and Oldham*, HMSO, London, 1973.

56 Department of the Environment, *Inner Area Studies. Liverpool, Birmingham and Lambeth. Summaries of consultants' final reports*, HMSO, London, 1977.

57 Statement by Home Secretary, House of Commons, 18 July 1974.

58 A useful background paper on urban deprivation and the idea of urban deprivation strategies has been produced by Inlogov at the request of the Home Office. See Stewart, J. D., Spencer, K. and Webster, B., *Local government: approaches to urban deprivation*, Home Office Urban Deprivation Unit Occasional Paper No. 1, 1976. See p. 316.

59 Booz-Allen and Hamilton, *Report to the West Norfolk District*

Council, June 1973, and Simkins, A., 'Towards area management', *Municipal Journal,* 21 March 1975, pp. 390–392.

60 Department of the Environment, *Proposals for area management, Liverpool Inner Area Study,* November 1973.

61 Department of the Environment, *Area Management. Consultation paper,* November 1974.

62 Horn, C. J., Mason, T., Spencer, K. M., Vielba, C. A. and Webster, B. A., *Area management: objectives and structures.* Area management monitoring project, first interim report, Institute of Local Government Studies, February 1977.

63 City of Newcastle upon Tyne, *Top priority. Newcastle's approach to priority areas,* A Council Green Paper, 1976.

64 Hambleton, R., 'Local planning and area management', *The Planner,* September 1976, pp. 176–179.

65 Seebohm Report, op. cit., para 590.

66 Freeson, R., Speech to the 'Save our Cities' conference, Bristol, 10 February 1977. See p. 316.

67 *Policy for the inner cities,* White Paper, Cmnd 6845, June 1977.

68 This tension between comprehensive policy making and local responsiveness is discussed further in Hambleton, 'Corporate and responsive', op. cit.

69 Randall, G. W., Lomas, K. W. and Newton, T., 'Area distribution of resources in Coventry', *Local Government Finance,* No. 11, November 1973; Webster, B. and Stewart, J. D., 'The area analysis of resources', *Policy and Politics,* September 1974; Department of the Environment, *Area resource analysis: District D tables 1973–74,* Liverpool Inner Area Study, July 1976.

70 Townsend, P., 'Area deprivation policies', *New Statesman,* 6 August 1976, pp. 168–171.

Chapter 6 American approaches to neighbourhoods

1 Scaduto, A., *Bob Dylan,* Abacus, London, 1972, p. 160.

2 Kerner Commission, *Report of the National Advisory Commission on Civil Disorders,* US Government Printing Office, Bantam Books, New York, 1968, p. 203.

3 Carmichael, S. and Hamilton, C. V., *Black Power. The politics of liberation in America,* Pelican, Harmondsworth, 1969, first published in the USA in 1967.

4 A useful collection of essays offering a range of perspectives

on American urban problems is provided in Frieden, B. J. and Morris, R. (eds.), *Urban planning and social policy*, Basic Books, New York, 1968.

5   Lupsha, P., 'On theories of urban violence', *Urban Affairs Quarterly*, Vol. 4, 1969, pp. 273–96, reprinted in Stewart, M. (ed.), *The City: problems of planning*, Penguin, Harmondsworth, 1972, pp. 453–477.

6   Marris, P. and Rein, M., *Dilemmas of social reform. Poverty and Community Action in the United States*, Pelican, Harmondsworth, 1974, p. 336. First published in 1967.

7   For a concise appraisal see Gans, H. J., 'The failure of urban renewal: a critique and some proposals', *Commentary*, Vol. 39 No. 4, April 1965, pp. 29–37 reprinted in Gans, H. J., *People and plans. Essays on urban problems and solutions*, Pelican, Harmondsworth, 1972, pp. 239–261. For a brief review and references to a dozen further sources see Frieden, B. J. and Kaplan, M., *The politics of neglect: urban aid from model cities to revenue sharing*, MIT Press, Cambridge, Mass., 1975, pp. 22–27.

8   Lewis, G., 'Citizen participation in urban renewal surveyed', *Journal of Housing*, No. 81, 1959.

9   Arnstein, S., 'A ladder of participation in the USA', *Journal of the American Institute of Planners*, July 1969.

10   Personal communication from Charles Kirchner who was City Co-ordinator with Springfield at this time.

11   See Marris and Rein, op. cit., pp. 37–44.

12   Cloward, R. and Ohlin, L., *Delinquency and opportunity: a theory of delinquent gangs*, The Free Press, Glencoe, 1960.

13   Hallman, H. W., 'Neighborhood Power: a ten year perspective', *Neighborhood Decentralization*, November–December 1974.

14   Mogulof, M., 'Coalition to adversary: citizen participation in three federal programs', *Journal of the American Institute of Planners*, July 1969, pp. 225–244.

15   A useful collection of essays on the American poverty programme is provided by Sundquist, J. L. (ed.), *On fighting poverty. Perspectives from experience*, Basic Books, New York, 1969.

16   Marris and Rein, op. cit., p. 328.

17   Frieden and Kaplan, op. cit., p. 32.

18   Marris and Rein, op. cit., p. 328.

19   Moynihan, D. P., *Maximum feasible misunderstanding*, The Free Press, New York, 1970, p. 87.

20 Boone, R., 'Reflections on citizen participation and the Economic Opportunity Act', *Public Administration Review* 32, 1972.
21 Moynihan, op. cit., p. 145.
22 Hallman, op. cit., p. 3.
23 Yin, R. and Yates, D., *Street-level governments*, Lexington Books, Lexington, Mass. 1975, p. 22.
24 Cole, R. L., *Citizen participation and the urban policy process*, Lexington Books, Lexington, Mass. 1974, p. 14.
25 Kramer, R., *Participation of the poor*, Prentice-Hall, Englewood Cliffs, N.J. 1969, pp. 260–261.
26 Marris and Rein, op. cit., pp. 304–336.
27 Moynihan, op. cit., p. 4.
28 Marris and Rein, op. cit., p. 316.
29 Hallman, H. W., *Neighborhood government in a metropolitan setting*, Sage Library of Social Research, 1974, p. 286.
30 For a comprehensive review of this programme see Frieden and Kaplan, op. cit.
31 Yin and Yates, op. cit., p. 23.
32 Frieden and Kaplan, op. cit., pp. 47–49.
33 Ibid., p. 271.
34 Marris and Rein, op. cit., p. 328.
35 US Department of Housing and Urban Development, *Improving the quality of urban life*, Washington, HUD, 1967, p. 20.
36 Warren, R. L., 'Model cities first round: politics, planning and participation', *Journal of the American Institute of Planners*, July 1969, p. 246.
37 Mogulof, op. cit., p. 230.
38 Frieden and Kaplan, op. cit., p. 189.
39 Center for Community Change, *General revenue sharing: influencing local budgets. A citizen's action guide*, September 1975. This is a very useful and well-presented report.
40 Gilmer, J., Guest, J. W. and Kirchner, C., 'The impact of federal programs and policies on state–local relations', *Public Administration Review*, December 1975, pp. 774–779.
41 Community development has many meanings. Here it will be clear that the community development block grant programme is primarily, but by no means wholly, concerned with physical change. Full details of the programme including a progress report on the first year are provided in US Department of Housing and Urban Development, *Community development block grant program, first Annual Report*, December 1975. See

also Center for Community Change, *Citizen involvement in community development: an opportunity and a challenge. A citizen's action guide*, November 1976.

42   See Frieden and Kaplan, op. cit., pp. 240–242.

43   Davidoff, P., 'Advocacy and pluralism in planning', *Journal of the American Institute of Planners*, Vol. 31 No. 4, November 1965; Peattie, L. R., 'Reflections on advocacy planning', *Journal of the American Institute of Planners*, Vol. 34 No. 2, March 1968.

44   See Schuttler, B. L. and Shannon, K. 'The charrette process. A citizen based process for planning institutions and communities', Grimmets Chance, Clarkesville, Maryland, 1974. Riddick, W. L., *Charrette processes. A tool in urban planning*, George Shumway, York, Pennsylvania, 1971; Scriven, B., 'Charrettes – an approach to design participation', *Architect's Journal*, 23 February 1972, pp. 411–412.

45   See Jowell, R., 'A review of public involvement in planning', *Social and Community Planning Research*, Research Publications, London, October 1975. This discusses a range of forms of citizen involvement based on a brief United States study tour.

46   One example is provided by Lawrence Halprin Associates. See Goldstein, B., 'Participation workshops', *Architectural Design*, April 1974, pp. 207–212.

47   Video and a range of other approaches are discussed in a refreshing way in Nicholson, S., and Schreiner, B. K., *Community participation in decision making*, Open University, Social Sciences: a second level course, Urban Development Unit 22, The Open University Press, Milton Keynes, 1973.

48   See Berube, M. and Gittell, M. (eds.), *Confrontation at Ocean Hill-Brownsville*, Praeger, New York, 1969, and Gittell, M., *et al, School boards and school policy*, Praeger, New York, 1973. For a brief synopsis see Ravitch, D., 'School decentralization in New York City, 1975', *Neighborhood Decentralization*, May–June 1975. Much of the material in Yin and Yates, op. cit., concerns within-service decentralization and provides references to over 250 further sources.

49   See Yin and Yates, op. cit. An appraisal of selected cities is provided by Washnis, G. J., *Municipal decentralization and neighborhood resources*, Praeger, New York, 1972. An early analysis of little city halls is provided by Nordlinger, E. A., *Decentralizing the city: a study of Boston's Little City Halls*, MIT Press, Cambridge, Mass., 1972. A special issue of *Public*

Administration Review in October 1972 provides ten articles on various aspects of decentralization. One of these provides a useful overview with references to a further 160 sources: Schmandt, H. J., 'Municipal decentralization: an overview', *Public Administration Review*, Vol. 30, October 1972, pp. 571–588.

50 Kotler, M., *'Neighborhood government*, Bobbs-Merrill, New York, 1969; Kotler, M., 'The ethics of neighborhood government', *Social Research*, Summer 1975, pp. 314–330; Hallman, H. W. 'Neighborhood government in a metropolitan setting', op. cit.; Morris, D. and Hess, K., *Neighborhood power: the new localism*, Beacon Press, Boston, 1975.

51 See, for example, Silberman, C. E., 'Up from apathy: the Woodlawn experiment' in Frieden and Morris, op. cit., pp. 183–197. For a full exposition of Alinsky's approach to building people's organizations see Alinsky, S. D., *Reveille for radicals*, Vintage Books, New York, 1969. First published 1946.

52 For more information on these various strands see Hallman, 'Neighborhood Power', op. cit., pp. 6–7; Kotler, M., 'Rise of Neighborhood power', *Focus*, December 1975, monthly newsletter of the Joint Center for Political Studies, Washington DC; Hamer, J., 'Neighborhood control', *Editorial Research Reports*, Vol. 11 No. 16, October 1975.

53 See Hallman, H. W., 'Neighborhood councils: their status in 1976', *Neighborhood Decentralization*, May–June 1976, and Hallman, H. W., 'City charter provisions for neighborhoods', *Neighborhood Decentralization*, January 1974.

54 Hallman, 'Neighborhood Power', op. cit., p. 13.

55 Perlman, J. E., 'Grassrooting the system', *Social Policy*, September–October 1976 (available from Suite 500, 184 Fifth Avenue, New York, NY 10010).

56 The housing systems of Britain and America are very different and comparisons should be made with care. Direct government intervention, including the provision of public housing and, more recently, the stimulation of voluntary housing associations, is far greater in Britain than in America. Nevertheless, Britain has been considerably slower than America to recognize the crucial role of building society lending policies in aggravating urban decay. In recent times some efforts have been made to rectify this: see Weir, S., 'Red line districts', *Roof*, July 1976, pp. 109–114; Lambert, C., *Building societies, surveyors and the*

---

older areas of Birmingham, Working Paper 38, Centre for Urban and Regional Studies, University of Birmingham, 1976; Williams, P., *The role of financial institutions and estate agents in the private housing market*, Working Paper 39, Centre for Urban and Regional Studies, University of Birmingham, 1976.

57 *Home Mortgage Disclosure Act 1975,* Public Law 94–200, Title III, 94th Congress, S.1281, 31 December 1975.

58 Naparstek, A. J. and Cincotta, G., *Urban disinvestment: new implications for community organization, research and public policy*, a joint publication of the National Center for Urban Ethnic Affairs and the National Training and Information Center, 1976.

59 Further details are provided in the *Federal Register*, Vol. 40 No. 208, 28 October 1975.

60 Ahlbrandt, R. S. and Brophy, P. C., 'Neighborhood Housing Services: a unique formula proves itself in turning around declining neighborhoods', *Journal of Housing*, Vol. 33 No. 1, January 1976; Cassidy, R., 'Neighborhood Housing Services: everybody's getting something out of it', *Planning*, the Magazine of the American Society of Planning Officials, 18 November 1975.

61 *National Neighborhood Policy Bill,* 94th Congress, S.3554, introduced in the Senate on 11 June 1976.

62 Statement by Senator Proxmire when introducing the Bill, Congressional Record – Senate, S.3554, 11 June 1976.

63 Hamer, op. cit., pp. 802–803.

64 Note that in America *proposed* legislation is often referred to as an Act. This can be confusing to readers from Britain where the practice is to always refer to proposed legislation as bills until formally approved by Parliament.

65 *The Neighborhood Government Act 1975,* Congressional Record, 94th Congress, Vol. 121 No. 146, S.2192, 1 October 1975.

66 *The Neighborhood Government Act 1975,* Congressional Record, 94th Congress, Vol. 121 No. 122, S.2192, 28 July 1975.

67 Speech by Jimmy Carter at Brooklyn College, New York, on 7 September 1976.

68 Levy, F., Meltsner, A. J. and Wildavsky, A, *Urban outcomes,* University of California Press, Berkeley, 1974; Yin, R. K., *On the equality of municipal service outcomes: street cleanliness,* WN-8625-OEO, Rand Corporation, April 1974. Both of these

sources refer to other American studies on the unequal distribution of government services.

69 Wood, R., 'Housing and environmental escapism', *Journal of the American Institute of Planners*, Vol. 36, November 1970, p. 422.

70 Frieden and Kaplan, op. cit., p. 257.

Chapter 7 Lessons from experience and an analytical framework

1 Marris, P., 'Images of Progress 2: America', *New Society*, 6 January 1977, pp. 9–10.

2 Ibid., p. 9.

3 Max Weber lived from 1864 to 1920. A concise statement of his analysis of bureaucracy is provided in 'The Essentials of Bureaucratic Organization: an ideal-type construction' in Merton, R. K. *et al* (eds.), *Reader in bureaucracy*, The Free Press, Glencoe, Illinois, 1952, pp. 18–27.

4 Beer, S., *Designing freedom*, Garden City Press, Letchworth, 1974, pp. 75–76.

5 Beveridge Report, *Social insurance and allied services*, Cmnd 6404, HMSO, London, 1942.

6 Marris, op. cit., p. 10.

7 See, for example, Townsend, P., 'Area deprivation policies', *New Statesman*, 1976, pp. 168–171.

8 See Stewart, J. D., 'The government of cities and the politics of opportunity', *Local Government Studies*, January 1975, pp. 3–20.

9 See Rein, M., *Social science and public policy*, Penguin Education, Harmondsworth, 1976, particularly Chapter 3.

10 Friedmann, J. and Abonyi, G., 'Social learning: a model for policy research,' *Environment and planning*, Vol. 8 No. 8, December 1976, pp. 927–940.

11 Marris, op. cit., p. 10.

12 Arnstein, S., 'A ladder of citizen participation in the USA', *Journal of the American Institute of Planners*, July 1969.

13 The seven elements are listed in Chapter 3. The source is Yates, D., *Neighborhood democracy*, Lexington Books, Lexington, Mass., 1973, p. 23.

14 Cole, R. L., *Citizen participation and the urban policy proeess*, Lexington Books, Lexington, Mass. 1974, Chapter 1.

15 Yin, R. K. and Yates, D., *Street-level governments,* Lexington Books, Lexington, Mass. 1975, Chapter 2.

16 Barton, A., *et al*, *Decentralizing city government*, Lexington Books, Lexington, Mass. 1977, Chapter 1.
17 This is still a comparatively rare feature of local government practice but one example, which involves analysis of the distribution of resources between different dependency groups, is Metropolitan Borough of Stockport, *The elderly. A policy report*, from Chief Executive's Department, March 1976.
18 Schumacher, E. F., *Small is beautiful*, Abacus, London, 1974, p. 202, author's emphasis. This same conclusion is a central message of cybernetics and is discussed further in Chapter 10.

Boston

1 The mayor receives an annual salary of $40 000 and the councillors receive $20 000 each. For purposes of comparison heads of city departments are generally paid between $20 000 and $35 000 a year.
2 Kerner Commission, *Report of the National Advisory Commission on Civil Disorders*, 1968.
3 The renewal of Boston's West End involving the total clearance of a vibrant neighbourhood to make way for luxury apartments is a particularly infamous project. See Gans, H. J., 'The human implications of slum clearance and relocation', *American Institute of Planners Journal*, February 1959, pp. 15–25, reprinted in Gans, H. J., *People and plans*, Pelican Books, Harmondsworth, 1972, pp. 188–216.
4 Although some of the personalities have changed there is a useful summary of the kinds of allegation made in Nordlinger, E. A., *Decentralizing the city: a study of Boston's little city halls*, MIT Press, Cambridge, Mass., 1972, pp. 292–298.
5 A more detailed analysis of the failure of local advisory councils is provided in Nordlinger, op. cit., pp. 254–265.
6 Ibid., p. 285.

Other sources

The primary source material for this profile is a series of interviews conducted with staff of Boston City Hall in June 1976 including: Director of OPS, two little city hall managers, a field representative and a trainee; Director of Community Development; a principal planner with the Boston Redevelopment Authority; a principal budget analyst plus a series of more informal conversations.

Published documents
Hallman, H. W., 'Little city halls in Boston', *Neighborhood Decentralization*, November 1973, pp. 1–3.
Nordlinger, E. A., *Decentralizing the city: a study of Boston's little city halls*, MIT Press, Cambridge, Mass., 1972.

City Hall documents
Little city hall fact sheets 1973 to 1976.
City of Boston Municipal Register for 1974/75.
City of Boston Program Budget 1976/77.
The Neighborhood Improvement Program, a civic newspaper, 1 July 1975.
Neighborhood improvement program for the City of Boston, Program Summary, 15 January 1976.
Application for federal assistance under the community development block grant program, 1975.
Dorchester background information and planning issues, Boston Redevelopment Authority, June 1975.

New York City

1 A drastically simplified sketch of the governmental structure is as follows: New York government has features of the mayor-council form, for it does have a strong elective mayor and a legislative body which enacts its local laws. However it has another body, the Board of Estimate, which has important policy and decision-making powers. The City Council consists of one member elected from each of the thirty-three councilmanic districts plus two Councilmen-at-large from each of the five boroughs giving a total of forty-three members. The Council President, elected from the City at large, presides over the Council. The Board of Estimate consists of the three officials elected citywide – the Mayor, the Council President and the Comptroller (or financial watchdog) – and the five Borough Presidents. The three citywide board members have four votes each, the Borough Presidents two, so that the members elected to represent the whole City have more votes (twelve to ten). The Board has a key role in zoning and city planning and, together with the City Council, participates in the budget-adoption procedure. The mayor is the chief executive officer of the City. He initiates policy and programmes, appoints and

supervises the heads of most city agencies, and may remove them. He prepares and submits the City budgets and acts for the City in relationships with the state and federal governments.

2   Barton, A. H. *et al, Decentralizing city government, An evaluation of the New York City district manager experiment*, Lexington Books, Lexington, Mass. 1977.

3   There is an extensive literature on these and other innovations which can only be touched on here. A concise summary including leads into this literature is provided by Hallman, H. W., 'Decentralization in New York City: eight years under Mayor Lindsay', *Neighborhood Decentralization*, January 1974, pp.6–8.

4   Firth Murray, A., *Neighborhood government in New York City*, Office of Neighborhood Government, City of New York, March 1974, p. 14.

5   The schools in each district are governed by a locally elected school board which is answerable to the central board for its conduct of the schools. For more information see Berube, M. and Gittell, M. (eds.), *Confrontation at Ocean Hill–Brownsville*, Praeger, New York, 1969; Gittell, M. *et al, School boards and school policy*, Praeger, New York, 1973, and Ravitch, D., 'School decentralization in New York City: 1975', *Neighborhood Decentralization*, May–June, 1975.

6   Each board consisted of the councilmen-at-large from the borough in which the district was located, the councilman from the district, and between five and nine members (later expanded to fifty) who were residents of the district appointed by the Borough President.

7   Office of Neighborhood Government, *Plan for neighborhood government in New York City*, June 1970.

8   A useful synopsis of the evolution of the district manager experiment appears as Chapter 3 in Barton *et al*, op. cit.

9   Lindsay, J. V., Mayor, *Program for the decentralized administration of municipal services in New York City communities*, December 1971.

10   One study draws explicit parallels between three London boroughs and four New York district management experiments. See Savitch, H. V., 'Leadership and decision-making in New York City and London', *Policy and Politics*, Vol. 2 No. 2, 1973, pp. 113–133.

11   Three other districts were added early in the life of the programme and, in a substantially modified form, sixteen 'expan-

sion districts' were added in 1973. This was when it became apparent that Mayor Lindsay was not going to run again and this move was designed to build support for continuation of the programme. The expansion districts did not have a full-time manager and were chaired by a high-level city official such as a Commissioner. With the inauguration of Mayor Beame in January 1974 the approach was again modified and applied citywide.

12 Lindsay, op. cit., p. 10.
13 See Brumback, R., 'Selected projects of the district manager experiment', *New York City Neighborhood Project*, Bureau of Applied Social Research, Columbia University, January, 1975, pp. 8–11.
14 Ibid., pp. 43–45.
15 The following findings are from the Columbia University study. See Barton, *et al*, op. cit.
16 Yin, R. K., Hearn, R. W. and Shapiro, P. M., 'Administrative decentralization of municipal services: assessing the New York experience', *Policy Sciences*, Vol. 5, 1974, pp. 57–70.

Other sources

Discussions were held with the Director, Bureau of Applied Social Research, Columbia University and several of the research staff who worked on the New York City Neighborhood Study. Interviews were conducted with City Hall officials including the Director, Office of Neighborhood Services and senior officials of the City Planning Commission for New York City were also consulted. However, most of the material is drawn from the extensive literature on urban decentralization in New York City.

Publications

Barton, A. H., 'Research report on New York experiment', *Neighborhood Decentralization*, January–February 1976, pp. 5–8.
Fainstein, S. S. and Fainstein, N., 'Local control as social reform: planning for big cities in the seventies', *American Institute of Planners Journal*, 1976, pp. 275–285.
Hallman, H. W., 'Decentralization in New York City: eight years under Mayor Lindsay', *Neighborhood Decentralization*, January 1974, pp. 6–8.

348 Notes and references to pages 210–22

Mudd, J., 'District Cabinets in New York City', *Neighborhood Decentralization*, January–February 1976, pp. 1–4.
State Charter Revision Commission for New York City, *Information requirements for local units of government*, June 1974.

Dayton

1 Commissioners receive a small annual allowance in the region of $6000. The mayor receives $9000. These figures can be compared with the salaries of department heads which range from $24 000 to $31 500.
2 City of Dayton, *Administrative councils, Progress Report*, August to December 1975, Introduction.
3 Hallman, H. W., 'Neighborhood priority boards in Dayton', *Neighborhood Decentralization*, March 1974, p. 3.

Other sources

The primary source material for this profile is a series of interviews conducted with staff of the city of Dayton in July 1976 including: City Manager, Director of the Office of Management and Budget, assistant to the city manager, various staff of the Office of Management and Budget, City Commission, and Department of Housing and Neighborhood Affairs.

Published documents

Alloway, J. A., *The success of neighborhood programs in Dayton, Ohio*. Paper to community workshop on neighbourhood participation in Fort Wayne, Indiana, September 1975.
Sterzer, E. E., 'Neighborhood grant program lets citizens decide', *Public Management*, January 1971.

City Hall documents

Program strategies document, 1975/6.
Program strategies issues document, 1975/76.
Administrative councils, progress report, Aug–Dec 1975.
Community development task force recommendations 1976.
Community involvement task force evidence, July 1976.
Job descriptions of neighborhood affairs staff, 1975.

Stockport

1   Booz-Allen and Hamilton, *Organisation recommendations for the County Borough of Stockport*, London, April 1971, p. 38. See also Brooke, R. G., 'Corporate management at the operational level', *Local Government Chronicle*, 22 June 1973, pp. 648 and 650.

2   Stockport was one of the few local authorities to pioneer the development of urban community councils. Others were the London Borough of Lambeth and Liverpool. See Harrison, P., 'The Neighbourhood Council, *New Society*, 12 April 1973, pp. 73–75.

3   Metropolitan Borough of Stockport, *Management structure*, report of the joint committee to the new council, May 1973.

4   Ibid., p. 5.

5   Ibid., pp. 13–14, 33–35, 67–72 and from a discussion paper presented to the first meetings of the area committees in March 1974.

6   Bains Committee, *The new local authorities: management and structure*, HMSO, London, 1972, pp. 32–34.

7   Further details are provided in 'Publicity and consultation on planning applications', *Report to Development Services Committee*, 30 January 1974.

8   More detail is provided by Hember, R. J., 'An approach to planning and budgeting,' *Public Finance and Accountancy*, September 1974.

9   Area digests for North, East and West available from the Chief Executive's Department, Metropolitan Borough of Stockport.

10 Hambleton, R., 'Preferences for policies', *Municipal Journal*, 25 July 1975, pp. 979–983.

11 In this and the following sections an attempt is made to assess the strengths and weaknesses of Stockport's approach. Much of my evidence is based on what sociologists would call 'participant observation' for I worked as a corporate planner with Stockport for two years.

12 Association of Neighbourhood Councils, *Neighbourhood councils in England*, published by The Neighbourhood Trust, Halstead, Essex, p. 9.

13 *Housing Policies Report,* May 1974. *Elderly Report*, March 1976, Appendix.

Other sources

The primary source material for this profile is my period of work as a corporate planner with Stockport from January 1974 to January 1976. *Inter alia*, this job involved considerable contact with the area co-ordinators, area committees, area staff and officers of all divisions. Every effort has been made to provide a detached commentary but the reader may still wish to guard against possible author bias.

Other published documents

Hambleton, R., 'Corporate and responsive', *Municipal Journal*, 6 September 1974, pp. 1063–1066.
Paine, R. E., 'Position statements – the Stockport experience', *Corporate Planning*, Vol. 2 No. 1, February 1975.
Simkins, A., 'A structure for participation', *Municipal Journal*, 30 March, 1973, pp. 465–468.

Liverpool

1   McKinsey and Co. Inc., *A new management system for the Liverpool Corporation*, 1969. See also Eddison, T., *Local government: management and corporate planning*, Leonard Hill Books, London, 1975, pp. 147–151.
2   A perceptive commentary informed by first-hand experience is provided in Shelter Neighbourhood Action Project, *Another chance for cities*, Shelter, London, 1972, pp. 87–91.
3   See Midwinter, E., *Priority education*, Penguin, Harmondsworth, 1972.
4   Shelter Neighbourhood Action Project, op. cit. See particularly pp. 149–157, 201–204, 206–207.
5   Ibid., p. 157.
6   Statement by Secretary of State for the Environment, House of Commons, 26 July 1972.
7   The consultants were Hugh Wilson and Lewis Womersley (chartered architects and town planners) in association with Roger Tym and Associates (urban and land economists).
8   Department of the Environment, *Liverpool Inner Area Study – proposals for area management*, IAS/LI/3, 1973, p. 2.
9   Ibid., p. 3.
10 Ibid., p. 4.

11 This is not to suggest that there is a high level of agreement between service districts in Liverpool. The contrary is vividly illustrated in the SNAP Report – Shelter Neighbourhood Action Project, op. cit., pp. 139–141.

12 Department of the Environment, *Liverpool Inner Area Study – area management progress report*, IAS/LI/8, 1975, p. 8.

13 In 1968 Liverpool City Planning Department conducted an analysis of census and other data in an attempt to reveal the geographical distribution of needs within the city. The results were published in 1970 as *Social malaise in Liverpool*. This study led the way for a number of similar analyses by other local authorities, often associated with their attempts to wrestle with the social aspects of structure planning. A review of a more recent social area study of Liverpool, which builds on the earlier work and also points to the limitations of the social indicator approach, is provided by Webber, R. J., *Liverpool social area study. 1971 data: final report*, PRAG Technical Paper 14, Centre for Environmental Studies, London, December 1975.

14 Department of the Environment, *Liverpool Inner Area Study – area resource analysis: methodology*, IAS/LI/5, 1974.

15 Department of the Environment, *Liverpool Inner Area Study – area resource analysis: District 'D' tables 1973–74*, IAS/LI/9, 1976.

16 Department of the Environment, *Liverpool Inner Area Study – fourth study review*, IAS/LI/12, 1976.

Other sources

Discussions were held with the Area Executive and his staff as well as staff from other departments and from the consultants to the inner area study. However, a high reliance has been placed on the published literature cited and on internal reports.

Chapter 9   Comparative analysis of Area Management

1 Yin, R. K. and Yates, D., *Street-level governments*, Lexington Books, Lexington, Mass. 1975, p. 190.

2 Dunn, E. S., *Economic and social development. A process of social learning*, Johns Hopkins University Press, Baltimore and London, 1971, p. 133.

3 Metropolitan Borough of Stockport, *Area organisation. Report*

of the Management Board to Policy and Resources Committee, February, 1977.

4   The overlapping meanings of decentralization, delegation and devolution are discussed in Chapter 3.

5   Barton, A. *et al, Decentralizing city government. An evaluation of the New York City district manager experiment*, Lexington Books, Lexington, Mass. 1977.

6   Hambleton, R., 'Local planning and area management', *The Planner*, September 1976, pp. 176–179.

7   In my own experience it takes three man-months to compile a small area gazetteer for a city population of 280 000. In this example all addresses were coded to 1971 enumeration districts which numbered 580.

8   Yin and Yates, op. cit., p. 32. In my view these authors tend to overstate the differences between services and give insufficient attention to the opportunities for inter-departmental co-operation at the local level.

9   See, for example, Skitt, J. (ed.), *Practical corporate planning in local government*, Leonard Hill, London, 1975, pp. 172–188.

10   The idea of broadening officers' opportunities is discussed briefly in Department of the Environment, *The Sunderland Study*, Vol. 2, HMSO, London, 1973, pp. 93–106.

11   See Drucker, P. F., *The practice of management*, Pan Books, London, 1972, Chapter 11. First published 1955.

12   An enthusiastic review is provided by Eddison, T., *Local government: management and corporate planning*, Leonard Hill, London, 1973, Chapter 10. A more stolid account is provided by Glendinning, J. W. and Bullock, R. E. H., *Management by objectives in local government*, Charles Knight, London, 1973.

13   Nordlinger, E. A., *Decentralizing the city: a study of Boston's little city halls*, MIT Press, Cambridge, Mass., 1972, p. 263.

14   Yin and Yates, op. cit., Chapter 1.

15   Ibid., p. 189.

16   Department of the Environment, *Final report of the working party on housing co-operatives*, 1975, and Department of the Environment, *Housing co-operatives*, Circular 8/76, 1976, both HMSO, London.

17   Richardson, A., 'Power to the co-opted', *Municipal Journal*, 23 July 1976, pp. 849–850.

18   There are also many other channels which are more spontaneous

but equally exciting. Examples are charrettes and other design experiments discussed in Chapter 6.

19 Yin, R. K. and Lucas, W. A., 'Decentralization and alienation', *Policy Sciences*, Vol. 4, 1973, pp. 327–336.

20 Ibid., p. 336.

21 Ibid., pp. 330–331.

22 As discussed in Chapter 5 deprivations are not as spatially concentrated as many have assumed but, even so, there is a degree of concentration usually in areas of older housing or in certain council estates.

23 It has been argued that labelling reinforces inequality. See Townsend, P., 'Area deprivation policies', *New Statesman*, 6 August 1976, p. 170.

Chapter 10   Towards theories of public learning

1 Faludi, A., *Planning theory*, Pergamon, Oxford, 1973, Chapter 1.

2 Lasswell, H. D., *A pre-view of policy sciences*, Elsevier, New York, 1971, pp. 1–2,

3 Dror, Y., *Public policymaking re-examined*, Chandler, Pennsylvania, 1968, pp. 7–9.

4 Ibid., Chapter 14.

5 Ibid., Chapter 12.

6 Ibid., pp. 132–141. See also Faludi, A., op. cit., Chapter 8.

7 See Lindblom, C. E., *The intelligence of democracy*, Free Press, New York, 1965. There are those who argue that these criticisms mistakenly transmute conclusions about intellectual capacity to organizational capacity and that comprehensive planning is not necessarily more difficult than other forms of planning. See Self, P., 'Is comprehensive planning possible and rational?', *Policy and politics*, Vol. 2 No. 3, 1974, pp. 193–203.

8 For the way the rational planning process has taken insufficient account of values see Chapter 2.

9 Lindblom, C. E., 'The science of "muddling through"', *Public Administration Review*, Spring 1959, reprinted in Faludi, A. (ed.), *A reader in planning theory*, Pergamon, Oxford, 1973, pp. 151–169; Hirschman, A. O. and Lindblom, C. E., 'Economic development, research and development, policymaking: some converging views', *Behavioural Science*,

Vol. 7, 1962, pp. 211–222, reprinted in Emery, F. E., *Systems thinking*, Penguin, Harmondsworth 1969, pp. 351–371; Braybrooke, and D. Lindblom, C., *A strategy of decision*, Free Press, New York, 1963.

10   Dror, op. cit., p. 146.

11   Eddison, T., *Local government: management and corporate planning*, Leonard Hill, London, 1975, p. 21.

12   Etzioni, A., 'Mixed-scanning: a "third" approach to decision-making', *Public Administration Review*, December 1967, reprinted in Faludi (ed.), *A reader in planning theory*, op. cit. pp. 217–229.

13   Ibid.

14   Drake, M., McLoughlin, B., Thompson, R. and Thornley, J., *Aspects of structure planning in Britain*, CES RP20, Centre for Environmental Studies, London, 1975, p. 194.

15   Webber, M. M., 'Planning in an environment of change', *Town Planning Review*, January 1969, pp. 291–292.

16   See, for example, Faludi, *Planning theory*, op. cit., p. 103 and Benveniste, G., *The politics of expertise*, Croom Helm, London, 1972.

17   Rittel, H. W. J. and Webber, M. M., 'Dilemmas in a general theory of planning', *Policy Sciences*, No. 4, 1973, pp. 155–169.

18   See, for example, Wilson, R. L., 'Livability in the city: attitudes and urban development' in Chapin, F. S. and Weiss, S. F. (eds.), *Urban growth dynamics*, John Wiley, New York, 1962, Chapter 11; Michelson, W., 'An empirical analysis of urban environmental preferences', *American Institute of Planners Journal*, November 1966, pp. 355–360; Hoinville, G., 'Multidimensional trade offs, An appraisal of the priority evaluator approach,' *Social and Community Planning Research*, London, 1975.

19   Pressman, J. L. and Wildavsky, A. B., *Implementation*, University of California Press, Berkeley, 1973, preface.

20   A working group at the centre for Environmental Studies, 'Education for planning' in Diamond, D. and McLoughlin, J. (eds.), *Progress in planning*, Vol. 1, Part 1, Pergamon, Oxford, 1973.

21   Friedmann, J. *Retracking America. A theory of transactive planning*, Anchor Press/Doubleday, New York, 1973, pp. 59–60. Author's emphasis.

22   Friedmann, J., *Innovation, flexible response and social learning:*

a problem in the theory of meta-planning, Internal paper, Centre for Environmental Studies, London, 1976, pp. 5–6. Author's emphasis.

23 Ibid., p. 7.

24 Dunn, E. S., *Economic and social development. A process of social learning*, Johns Hopkins University Press, Baltimore and London, 1971, Chapter 4. See also Michael, D. N., *On learning to plan and planning to learn*, Jossey-Bass, San Francisco, 1973, Chapters 1 and 2.

25 Dunn, op. cit., p. 133.

26 Heclo, H., 'Review article – policy analysis', *British Journal of Political Science*, No. 2, 1972, p. 84.

27 See Lasswell, H. D., 'The policy orientation' in Lerner, D. and Lasswell, H. D. (eds.), *The policy sciences: recent developments in scope and method*, Stanford University Press, Stanford, 1951. For a more recent statement see Lasswell, *A pre-view of policy sciences*, op. cit.

28 See Dror, op. cit. For a short volume devoted entirely to the idea of policy sciences see Dror, Y., *Design for policy sciences*, Elsevier, New York, 1971. For a view on the relevance of these ideas to local government see Dror, Y., 'Policy analysis for local government', *Local Government Studies*, January 1976, pp. 33–46.

29 Dror, *Design for policy sciences*, op. cit., preface.

30 Heclo, op. cit.,

31 Ibid., p. 106.

32 Ibid., p. 106.

33 Dror, *Public policymaking re-examined*, op. cit., pp. 274–275.

34 Ibid., p. 275.

35 Wildavsky, A., *Evaluation as an organisational problem*, University Working Paper 13, Centre for Environmental Studies, 1972, p. 51. Stafford Beer has even suggested that planning is homologous with organization. See Beer, S., *Platform for change*, John Wiley, London, 1975, p. 315.

36 Schon, D. A., *Beyond the stable state*, Temple Smith, London, 1971, Chapter 2.

37 Bennis, W. G., 'Organisational developments and the fate of bureaucracy', *Industrial Management Review*, No. 7, 1966, pp. 41–55.

38 Baker, R. J. S., *Administrative theory and public administration*, Hutchinson, London, 1972, Chapters 1, 2 and 3.

39   Burns, T. and Stalker, G. M., *The management of innovation*, Tavistock, London, 1961.

40   Lawrence, P. R. and Lorsch, J. W., *Organization and environment: managing differentiation and integration*, Harvard University, Boston, 1967.

41   Galbraith, J., *Designing complex organizations*, Addison-Wesley, London, 1973, p. 4. Author's emphasis.

42   Ibid., Chapter 2.

43   Ibid., p. 12.

44   Daniel, W. W., 'Changing hierarchies at work', *The Listener*, 7 September 1972, pp. 300–302.

45   An attempt to quantify the effect of winnowing is provided by Tullock's model of hierarchical distortion. See Downs, A., *Inside bureaucracy*, Little Brown, Boston, 1967, pp. 116–18.

46   Ibid., pp. 118–127.

47   Galbraith, op. cit., pp. 17–18.

48   Ibid., p. 51.

49   See Bains Report, *The new local authorities – management and structure*, HMSO, London, 1972, p. 61.

50   See Ludwig, S., 'Should any man have two bosses?', *International Management*, April 1970, pp. 32–34; Galbraith, J., 'Matrix organization designs', *Business Horizons*, February 1971, pp. 29–40; Galbraith, *Designing complex organizations*, op. cit., Chapters 7 and 8; Ashton, D., 'Project based management development', *Personnel Management*, July 1974, pp. 26–28 and 36; Hendry, W. D., 'A general guide to matrix management', *Personnel Review*, Vol. 4 No. 2, 1975, pp. 33–39.

51   See, for example, McLoughlin, J. B., *Urban and regional planning. A systems approach*, Faber, London, 1969; Forrester, J. W., *Urban dynamics*, MIT Press, Cambridge, Mass., 1969.

52   See, for example, Bateson, G., *Steps to an ecology of mind*, Paladin, London, 1973; Vickers, Sir Geoffrey, *Freedom in a rocking boat*, Pelican, Harmondsworth, 1972. Bateson and Vickers are writers of profound and diverse wisdom who cannot be contained within one school of thought but both acknowledge a substantial debt to systems theory.

53   Beer, S., *Decision and control*, John Wiley, London, 1966, p. 92.

54   Ibid., pp. 253–254.

55   Espejo, R., *Local government: is it a viable system?*, Working Paper N14, Manchester Business School, 1975.

56 Ashby, W. R., *Introduction to cybernetics*, John Wiley, London, 1956, Chapter 11. This may seem obvious but this is often true of great natural laws – with hindsight. See Beer, op. cit., pp. 275–282.

57 Beer, S., *Brain of the firm*, Allen Lane, London, 1972.

58 For a classic study see Beer, *Decision and control*, op. cit. For a racy and more provocative presentation see Beer, S., *Platform for change*, John Wiley, London, 1975.

59 Beer, *Decision and control*, op. cit., Chapter 14.

60 Ibid., p. 361.

61 Wildavsky, op. cit., p. 30.

62 Borger, R. and Seaborne, A. E. M., *The psychology of learning*, Penguin, Harmondsworth, 1976, p. 149. First published 1966.

63 This point is difficult to grasp partly because of the limits of language. See Beer, *Platform for change*, op. cit., pp. 255–262.

64 Pateman, C., *Participation and democratic theory*, Cambridge University Press, Cambridge, 1970, p. 1.

65 Ibid., p. 11.

66 Ibid., p. 42.

67 Hill, D. M., *Democratic theory and local government*, George Allen and Unwin, London, 1974, pp. 37–38.

68 Friedmann, *Retracking America*, op. cit., particularly Chapters 7 and 8.

69 Hunter, F., *Community power structure*, University of North Carolina Press, 1953. Republished by Anchor, New York, 1963.

70 Newton, K., 'Community politics and decision-making: the American experience and its lessons' in Young, K. (ed.), *Essays on the study of urban politics*, Macmillan, London, 1975.

71 See, for example, Dahl, R. A., *Who governs?*, Yale University Press, New Haven, Conn., 1961.

72 Bachrach, P. and Baratz, M., *Power and poverty*, Oxford University Press, London, 1970, Part One.

73 Newton, op. cit., p. 8.

74 Harvey, D., *Social justice and the city*, Edward Arnold, London, 1973, p. 93.

75 There is a fairly extensive academic literature on distributive aspects of policy. For sociological perspectives see Pahl, R. E., *Whose city?*, Penguin, Harmondsworth, 1975, and Simmie, J. M., *Citizens in conflict*, Hutchinson, London, 1974, particularly Chapter 5. For a geographer's analysis see Harvey,

op. cit., particularly Chapters 2 and 3. However, little of the literature offers practical guidance on what to do. An important exception is the following book which outlines a distributive approach to urban policy planning: Levy, F., Meltsner, A. J. and Wildavsky, A., *Urban outcomes*, University of California Press, Berkeley, 1974, Chapter 4.

76 Gans, H. J., *People and plans,* Pelican, Harmondsworth, 1972. First published 1968.
77 Friedmann, *Retracking America*, op. cit.,
78 Faludi, *Planning theory*, op. cit.
79 Deutsch, K. W., *The nerves of government – models of political communication and control*, Macmillan, New York, 1966.
80 Etzioni, A., *The active society*, Collier-Macmillan, London, 1968.
81 McEwan, J. D., 'The cybernetics of self-organizing systems' in Benello, C. G. and Roussopoulos, D., *The case for participatory democracy*, Grossman, New York, 1971, pp. 179–194.
82 Ibid., pp. 188–189.
83 For example, doubts about the relevance of cybernetics to participatory democracy are voiced in Rose, H. and Hanmer, J., 'Community participation and social change' in Jones, D. and Mayo, M. (eds.), *Community work two*, Routledge and Kegan Paul, London, 1975.
84 Smith, R. W., 'A theoretical basis for participatory planning', *Policy Sciences*, Vol. 4, 1973, pp. 275–295.
85 Hambleton, R., 'Corporate and responsive', *Municipal Journal*, 6 September 1974, pp. 1063–1066.
86 Ibid., p. 1064.
87 Likert, R., *The human organization: its management and practice*, McGraw-Hill, New York, 1967.
88 Smith, op. cit., p. 292.
89 Schon, op. cit.
90 Ibid., p. 161.
91 Ibid., p. 177.
92 Ibid., p. 200
93 Taylor, J. L., *Instructional planning systems: a gaming simulation approach to urban problems*, Cambridge University Press, 1971.
94 Eddison, T., 'Latent (anag.) talent', *The Planner*, July–August 1976, pp. 132–134.
95 See, for example, Vroom, V. H. and Deci, E. L. (eds.), *Man-*

    agement and motivation. Selected readings, Penguin, Harmonds-
worth, 1970.
96 Vickers, op. cit., p. 127.
97 The words are again Vickers's quoted by Michael, op. cit., p. 21.
98 Eddison, 'Latent talent', op. cit., p. 132.
99 De Bono, E., *The mechanism of mind*, Pelican, Harmondsworth, 1971.
100 De Bono, E., *The use of lateral thinking*, Pelican, Harmondsworth, 1971.
101 For an introduction to these techniques see Rickards, T., *Problem solving through creative analysis*, Gower Press, Boston, Mass., 1974.
102 Quoted by Beer, *Decision and control*, op. cit., pp. 202–203.
103 Eddison, 'Latent talent', op. cit., p. 134.
104 Vickers, Sir G., *The art of judgement. A study of policy making*, Chapman and Hall, London, 1965, particularly Chapter 15.
105 Ibid., p. 188.

Index

Redcliffe-Maud Commission and
Report, *see* Royal Commission on
Local Government in England
refuse collection, 130
Regional Economic Planning
Councils and Boards, 42, 130
regional policy, 115, 116
regional reports, 29
Rein, Martin, 140, 146, 148
Republican party, 145, 157–9
research, 42, 111, 112, 129, 162, 163,
170, 171, 177, 269; social, 175,
287, 288; *see also* action-research;
public learning
resources: distribution of, 25, 40, 61,
64, 76, 84, 101, 104, 116, 122, 123,
125, 128, 137, 143, 147, 163, 169,
170, 195; trends in, 9, 21–3, 60, 61;
see also budgeting
reticulists, 63, 263; *see also* network
roles
revenue sharing, *see* Federal aid
reward systems, 236, 265, 271, 277,
300, 312
Rittel, Horst, 286
Royal Commission on Local
Government in England, 40, 41,
53, 103

St Louis, 156
Salford, 41
San Francisco, 146
Schattschneider, E., 109
Schon, Donald, 10, 47, 67, 68, 293,
310, 311
School for Advanced Urban Studies,
15, 39
schools, *see* education
Schumacher, Dr E. F., 178
Scotland, 24, 25, 29, 57, 118, 129
secondment, 39, 64, 299
Seebohm Committee and Report, 52,
122, 123, 133
Senate Banking Committee, 156, 164
service delivery, 75–80, 259, 269–72;
in Boston, 193, 194; in Dayton,
217, 218, 220, 221; in Liverpool,
251, 252; in New York City, 207,
208; in Stockport, 235, 236
share holding, 25, 65
Sharpe, L. J., 90, 102, 105, 109
Shelter, 128, 241, 244
Shetlands, 25

Shore, Peter, 133, 216, 316
Skeffington Committee, 118
slum clearance, *see* urban renewal
Smith, Richard Warren, 309, 310
smoke control areas, 117, 175
social research, *see* research
social services, 21, 22, 36, 45, 46, 64,
77, 83, 122–5, 134; planning, 28,
31, 34, 116, 316
special districts, 90, 95
Springfield, Illinois, 142
Stalker, G. M., 283
State and Local Fiscal Assistance
Act 1972, 99
Stewart, John, 53, 64, 66, 183
Stockport, 12, 93, 95, 183, 254, 256,
261; area committees, 223, 226–39;
area co-ordinators, 225–30, 234,
236, 263, 270, 299; area digsets, 58,
232, 238; area management in, 58,
112, 130–3, 223–39, 256, 259, 263,
265–9, 272; corporate planning in,
51, 56, 60, 64, 232–5
Sto-Rox Neighborhood Corporation,
154
streets, 20, 130, 163
strong-mayor, *see* mayor–council
structure planning, *see* planning
Sunderland, 57
swimming baths, 25, 34
systems analysis, 291, 301
systems and systems theory, 46, 49,
300, 301

Tameside, 26
Taylor Committee, 122
tenant participation, 82, 128, 178
Town and Country Planning Act
1947, 21
Town and Country Planning Act
1968, 52, 118
Town and Country Planning Act
1971, 29, 78
Town and Country Planning
(General Development Order)
1973, 230
Town and Country Planning
(Structure and Local Plans
Regulations) 1974, 29, 316
Townsend, Peter, 138
trade unions, 65
traffic controls, 117
training, 64, 270, 296, 311